T0319550

Islamic Finance and the New Financial System

The Wiley Finance series contains books written specifically for finance and investment professionals as well as sophisticated individual investors and their financial advisors. Book topics range from portfolio management to e-commerce, risk management, financial engineering, valuation and financial instrument analysis, as well as much more. For a list of available titles, visit our Web site at www.WileyFinance.com.

Founded in 1807, John Wiley & Sons is the oldest independent publishing company in the United States. With offices in North America, Europe, Australia and Asia, Wiley is globally committed to developing and marketing print and electronic products and services for our customers' professional and personal knowledge and understanding.

Islamic Finance and the New Financial System

An Ethical Approach to Preventing Future Financial Crises

TARIQ ALRIFAI

WILEY

Cover image: ©iStock.com/dblight, ©iStock.com/tunart
Cover design: Wiley

Copyright © 2015 by John Wiley & Sons Singapore Pte. Ltd.

Published by John Wiley & Sons Singapore Pte. Ltd.

1 Fusionopolis Walk, #07-01, Solaris South Tower, Singapore 138628

All rights reserved.

No part of this publication may be reproduced, stored in a retrieval system, or transmitted in any form or
by any means, electronic, mechanical, photocopying, recording, scanning, or otherwise, except as expressly
permitted by law, without either the prior written permission of the Publisher, or authorization through
payment of the appropriate photocopy fee to the Copyright Clearance Center. Requests for permission
should be addressed to the Publisher, John Wiley & Sons Singapore Pte. Ltd., 1 Fusionopolis Walk, #07-01,
Solaris South Tower, Singapore 138628, tel: 65-6643-8000, fax: 65-6643-8008, e-mail: enquiry@wiley.com.

Limit of Liability/Disclaimer of Warranty: While the publisher and author have used their best efforts in
preparing this book, they make no representations or warranties with respect to the accuracy or
completeness of the contents of this book and specifically disclaim any implied warranties of
merchantability or fitness for a particular purpose. No warranty may be created or extended by sales
representatives or written sales materials. The advice and strategies contained herein may not be suitable
for your situation. You should consult with a professional where appropriate. Neither the publisher nor the
author shall be liable for any damages arising herefrom.

Other Wiley Editorial Offices
John Wiley & Sons, 111 River Street, Hoboken, NJ 07030, USA
John Wiley & Sons, The Atrium, Southern Gate, Chichester, West Sussex, P019 8SQ, United Kingdom
John Wiley & Sons (Canada) Ltd., 5353 Dundas Street West, Suite 400, Toronto, Ontario, M9B 6HB,
Canada
John Wiley & Sons Australia Ltd., 42 McDougall Street, Milton, Queensland 4064, Australia
Wiley-VCH, Boschstrasse 12, D-69469 Weinheim, Germany

Library of Congress Cataloging-in-Publication Data is Available

ISBN 9781118990636 (Hardback)
ISBN 9781118990698 (ePDF)
ISBN 9781118990681 (ePub)

Typeset in 10/12pt, SabonLTStd by Laserwords Private Limited, Chennai, India

Printed in Singapore by C.O.S. Printers Pte Ltd

10 9 8 7 6 5 4 3 2 1

I dedicate this book to my wife, Andrea, for her support and encouragement. Without her efforts, this book would have not been finished on time!

Contents

About the Author

Tariq Alrifai has been involved in Islamic finance for more than 18 years. He is an active public speaker on Islamic finance around the world and a leading authority on Islamic funds and investment products. He has written for prestigious publications such Euromoney Books and the Harvard University Forum on Islamic Finance, and was a contributing author of *Contemporary Islamic Finance: Innovations, Applications and Best Practices,* published in 2013. He is often quoted in print and electronic media, including the *Financial Times,* Bloomberg, Reuters, and CNBC Arabia.

Tariq was previously the Global Director of Islamic Indices at S&P Dow Jones Indices. He also served as vice president of UIB Capital, a U.S.-based private equity firm. Prior to this, he was vice president and manager of HSBC Bank's Islamic Finance Program in the United States. In 1996 Tariq founded Failaka Advisors, which was the first-ever organization to monitor and publish research on Islamic funds.

Tariq holds an MBA from DePaul University in Chicago and a bachelor's degree in international business from St. Cloud State University in Minnesota.

Acknowledgments

A lot of time and effort was spent researching this topic and gathering data. This would not have been possible without the support of the following people and organizations:

- Advisor Perspectives, Inc.
- Elliott Wave International
- Federal Reserve Bank of St. Louis Research Division
- KFH Research Ltd.
- Merk Investments LLC
- Professor Emmanuel Saez, Department of Economics, University of California, Berkeley
- Professor J. Lawrence Broz, Department of Political Science, University of California, San Diego
- Zerohedge.com/ABC Media Ltd.

Islamic Finance and the New Financial System

Introduction

Monday morning, September 15, 2008, I was sitting in my office settling into my daily routine when I heard a lively discussion among my colleagues who were gathered in our reception area. It was not uncommon for them to gather there and chat, since it was the only open space other than the meeting room where we could all talk. It was also where we had a flat-screen TV mounted on the wall blaring CNBC all day. I never paid much attention to it.

That morning, the chatter was different. I got up from my office to see what the day's topic was. What I saw was my colleagues staring at the TV in disbelief. "Tariq, get over here and check this out," said one of them. "We're screwed," said another.

In 2004, I had left my vice president's job at HSBC Bank in New York to join a start-up private equity shop in Chicago. The new firm was to be the U.S. investment arm of a Bahrain-based Islamic investment bank. The bank was also new, having been set up less than a year earlier. I was hired early on to help set up the U.S. operation and build the investment team. Management and shareholders of the bank believed that to be a world-class bank, as they strived to be, they must build up an investment capability in the United States. It was determined that private equity (PE) was the expertise they needed to develop, as they already had a good amount of expertise in real estate, which is a traditional favorite asset class among Middle East investors.

Since the dot-com bust in 2000, private equity had become one of the hottest asset classes on Wall Street, later spreading to Europe, but the Middle East was still way behind in developing a PE industry. Middle East financial institutions were envious of the high returns PE firms in the United States were generating. Middle East investors were successfully courted by these firms and invested heavily in some of the largest shops in the business, such as Carlyle Group and Thomas H. Lee Partners. All the big Wall Street firms also had PE arms and were generating high returns for their investors.

The Bahrain-based bank decided that launching a U.S. private equity office would be the best way to develop expertise in PE and eventually bring it to the Middle East. For the time being, the U.S. office would hire professionals from the PE industry and invest in U.S. companies using equity from the Middle East and leverage/debt from the United States. Thus, not only were we reliant on our parent bank for equity, we needed to source leverage locally through banks and specialized lenders that catered to the PE industry. In addition, since we had to follow Islamic finance guidelines in all of our investments, the leverage we secured from the United States had to comply with Shariah guidelines. This attracted both curiosity and interest on the part of U.S. lenders; some of them liked the concept and were interested in working with us, while others felt it was too strange and foreign and had no interest in our enterprise. I'll explain more about the differences between Islamic finance and conventional finance in Part II of this book. Needless to say, without equity from Bahrain, and without leverage from U.S. firms, we could not invest.

By 2008, we had built a team of eight people and invested in five companies worth more than $300 million, in both equity and leverage financing. For the most part, our parent bank was pleased with our achievements but, at the same time, was under increasing pressure from shareholders to use more of the bank's capital for investments in the Middle East. We were asked to start reducing our reliance on equity from Bahrain and consider sourcing both equity and leverage financing from the United States. This made the events of September 15, 2008, particularly worrisome for us.

The news on CNBC was grim. The Dow Jones Industrial Average had already lost more than 700 points in early trading, and all other markets were sinking fast. The news driving this was the announcement that Lehman Brothers, one of Wall Street's oldest and largest banks, had filed for bankruptcy protection. This seemed to come out of nowhere. When I went home the previous Friday evening, all was well. By Monday morning, all of a sudden Lehman was going out of business. How could this be happening?

I remembered that in March 2008, Bear Stearns, another one of Wall Street's oldest and largest firms, collapsed and was forced to merge with JPMorgan in a Federal Reserve brokerage bailout deal. Back then, the bank's failure didn't cause such ripples through the market. What had changed now?

In the days following September 15, global credit markets froze and major financial institutions around the world were on the brink of failure. The United States, along with regulators and governments from around the world, agreed to pump trillions of dollars into the global financial industry to save it from the worst financial crisis in recent history.

The global financial crisis of 2008 shocked everyone. Much of the world was caught off guard because of its severity and reach. Now, nearly six years since the crisis began, the world is still reeling from its effects. Global growth has not returned to the level it had reached before the crisis, developed countries are saddled with debt, and unemployment rates have yet to recover to what they were at precrisis levels. Much of Europe, as an example, has been seesawing in and out of recession, just as Japan has for the past two decades.

Never in our lifetime have we experienced such a severe recession. Governments and central bankers around the world have not been able to cure the economy of its ills, even after unprecedented government bailouts and central bank money printing.

The events of 2008 caught me and my colleagues off guard as well. We had worked in finance and banking for our entire careers, yet we failed to see this crisis coming. It hit all of us very hard—especially me. In 2006, I got caught up in the housing market. The pressure was on to buy a house before prices rose to an unaffordable level. At that time, the thought of paying rent was crazy because home prices were rising steadily, so owning a home became the best tool for building wealth. The housing market in Chicago was one of the hottest markets in the country. Quality single-family homes in Chicago were hard to find and not cheap. I decided to bite the bullet and "invest" in a new development. To avoid a big mortgage, I decided to make a large down payment (25 percent), since I wanted to build equity fast. I went with a conventional jumbo mortgage. To most financial experts, this was considered to be an excellent and conservative financial move. By the summer of 2009, I had lost my job at the firm and my 25 percent equity in the house went to zero.

So, yes, I was hit especially hard by the financial crisis. The bulk of my savings that was my home equity simply disappeared. The shock of losing my savings as well as my job led me to start asking myself questions, beginning with: How could I let this happen to me and my family? How could I not see this coming? Why didn't the experts in the field, along with all the economists and analysts, tell us about this? I spent the next five years reading, researching, and learning in order to figure out what had happened and how I could protect myself from future financial crises.

Much of what I learned I will share with you in this book. The book is divided into three parts. Part I talks about the financial system and financial crises. It also discusses the financial crisis of 2008 and the solutions that were applied. Part I ends with a discussion of the root causes of financial crises and why the next one will be worse than the last one. Part II is an introduction to Islamic finance. For those of you who are familiar with this industry, it will be nothing new. For those of you who are not familiar with Islamic finance, this will give you a good overview of its principles and practices. You will also see that some of the key principles of Islamic finance are based on sound financial and economic principles. We can all learn from this regardless of our differing faiths. This is not a religious book by any means; it's a book on financial crises and how to prevent them from happening again, for everyone's benefit. Part III outlines some practical solutions the finance industry can take from Islamic finance and apply to building a better system.

As we shall see, identifying the core problem is easy, but the solution is painful. Governments and central bankers do not have the will to take the necessary steps to fix the core of the problem, which is simply the ever-increasing mountain of debt in the world. The cure, therefore, is to reduce the level of debt, which then creates an entirely new set of problems and challenges.

We are now at the stage where the next financial crisis will put too much stress on our current system. As such, governments, economists, and central bankers will need to develop a new system to address the issues of the current one.

Islamic finance might seem like an odd place to look for ideas for a new global financial system, but, as we shall see, many of its key elements are based on sound economic principles. Global leaders may not know they are adopting Islamic financial principles when designing the new system, because they will be looking to build a system that will help protect us from the ills of the current one. Islamic finance has some of the answers to this problem.

Financial Crises and the Current Financial System

CHAPTER 1

A Brief History of Financial Systems and the Birth of Money

M ost of us know very little about our financial system and its history. Even though I had worked in the banking and finance industry for close to two decades, I knew very little about the financial system's history until I started doing my research. I was surprised to learn that our current financial system is only about 43 years old. I knew that the world had been using paper currencies for hundreds of years and that, before this, coins were used, mainly gold and silver. However, the circumstances for the shift from coin to paper as well as the shift to fiat currency were all new to me.

What I came to realize was that our financial system moves in cycles much like an economy does. It goes through periods of growth and expansion and then decline. There have always been crises in financial systems. No financial system has ever been perfect and free of flaws. Crises can be sparked by many factors—wars, speculation (bubbles), runaway government borrowing and spending, and government mismanagement of the economy or its currency.

To understand where we are and where we are heading, we must first understand where we have been, beginning with the history of money and financial systems. Literally hundreds of books have been written on early currencies and financial systems. This topic alone deserves time to explain in detail. However, to keep focused on the topic of this book, I will attempt to summarize the evolution of currencies and financial systems in this chapter.

EARLY FINANCIAL SYSTEMS AND CURRENCIES

Financial systems existed long before gold and silver were used as a medium of exchange. One of the earliest forms of money was cattle and other animals, which were used as a medium of exchange and a store of value as early as 9000 BCE.[1] Animals were used as payment under Roman law, whereby

7

fines were paid in oxen and sheep.[2] Sacks of grain, salt, and even seashells have been used as a form of currency for trade at one point in time.[3] Thus, trade, taxation, and payment of fines existed before metal coins and money as we know them today were used.

There is even some research supporting the idea that debt and credit existed before coins and other money came into existence.[4] According to David Graber's research and his book, *Debt: The First 5,000 Years,* the first recorded credit and debt systems developed more than 5,000 years ago as means of accounting. Credit and debt existed in the Sumerian civilization around 3500 BCE. In this system of credit, farmers would often become so indebted that their children would be forced into slavery as a means to repay the debt. These debt slaves were periodically released by kings, who canceled all debts and granted them amnesty under what came to be known as the Law of Jubilee in ancient Israel. One of the conclusions of this research was that indebtedness throughout history often led to unrest, insurrections, and revolts.

Though barter was also used throughout ancient societies, it was never a complete system or means of account, as other social factors came into play. Social currencies (i.e., interaction among the community and mutual expectations and responsibilities among individuals) completed early financial systems. Social bonds were also created through gifts, marriages, and general sociability. This type of economy stood in contrast to the moral foundations of exchange, based on formal equality, reciprocity, and hierarchy. This system established the customs in a society, which also led to the development of caste systems (the "haves" and the "have nots").[5]

One of the first written codes of law mentioning money and debt was the Code of Hammurabi, enacted by the Babylonian king Hammurabi, who ruled from 1792 BCE to 1750 BCE.[6] The code consisted of 282 laws dealing with a wide range of matters, from trade to family relationships. Nearly half of the code dealt with laws for contracts, the establishment of wages, interest rates on debt, inheritance, and property rights.[7]

The first mention of the use of money within the Bible is in the book of Genesis,[8] which refers to the criteria of the circumcision of a bought slave. There are other early references to money going back as far as the twentieth century BCE, such as Abraham's reference to the purchase of the Cave of the Patriarchs.[9]

An example of an ancient currency is the shekel. It was an ancient unit of account used in Mesopotamia around 3000 BCE[10] to define both a specific weight of barley and equivalent amounts of materials such as silver, bronze, and copper.

The use of coins later developed primarily as a means to pay soldiers in ever-expanding empires around the world. The rise of great empires in

China, India, and the Mediterranean was marked by extreme violence as these empires grew and required more and more resources to pay for their expansion. In this way, coins developed to pay soldiers in far-off lands as well as to enforce the payment of taxes by the state's subjects to subsidize its growing armies. Around 1000 BCE, money in the shape of small knives and spades made of bronze were in use in China. The first manufactured coins appeared in India, China, and cities around the Aegean Sea between 700 and 500 BCE.[11]

GOLD AND SILVER

Throughout history, gold and silver have been the most common form of money. In many languages, such as Spanish, French, and Italian, the word for silver is still directly related to the word for money. Although gold and silver were commonly used to mint coins, other metals were used, such as iron and copper.

The earliest known records of gold and silver being used for monetary exchange date back as far as the third millennium BCE, when gold, specifically, was used in Mesopotamia and ancient Egypt.[12] The first gold coins were minted in Lydia (modern-day Turkey) during the Grecian age around the year 700 BCE.[13] By the fourth century BCE, coins had become widely used in Greek cities. The coins were supported by the city-state authorities (the issuing authorities), who strived to ensure they retained their value regardless of fluctuations in the availability of whatever base precious metals they were made from.

Once well-established in Greece, the use of coins spread slowly westward throughout Europe and eastward to India. By the second century BCE, coin usage in India had become central to commercial transactions. Monetary systems that were developed in India were so successful that they spread through parts of Asia well into the Middle Ages. During the fourteenth century, much of Europe had converted from use of silver in currency to minting of gold.[14]

Metal-based coins had the advantage of carrying their value within the coins themselves. One disadvantage, however, was that they could be manipulated. The clipping of coins was a fairly frequent practice. The clippings were then traded and recycled. Governments, over time, also had the habit of diluting the precious metal content in coins, such as blending copper with gold or copper with silver. This, of course, caused inflation and, in some cases, loss of faith in the issuing authority. Governments did so because they were short on precious metals and had bills to pay.

A bigger problem was the use of coins made of different metals—copper, gold, and silver in Europe. Gold coins, for example, were valued more than silver coins, and silver coins were valued more than copper coins. In England in the 1670s and 1680s, the gold-based guinea coin began to rise against the English silver-based crown. The huge amounts of gold coming into Europe from discoveries in the New World shifted trade away from silver and into gold. In Asia, the situation was the opposite: Gold was leaving for Europe in favor of silver. Some prominent Europeans such as Isaac Newton, Master of the Royal Mint, were uneasy about these movements, as they created instability and made it difficult to value one metal over another.[15]

Soon thereafter, national banks were set up to bring stability to the system by guaranteeing to change money into gold at a promised rate. This, however, did not come without its own challenges. The Bank of England came close to a major financial crisis in the 1730s when customers demanded their money be changed into gold at a moment of crisis. The crisis was avoided only when London's merchants saved the national bank with financial guarantees.[16]

What's important to note about this period is that money evolved from being a unit of weight to being a unit of value. A distinction could be made between its *commodity value* (i.e., its weight in gold) and its *specie value* (its value in the market).[17]

PAPER MONEY, PROMISSORY NOTES (*SUKUK*), AND BILLS OF EXCHANGE

Once money became a unit of value, it no longer needed to be held in commodity form. Paper money began to appear in China in the seventh century, under the Tang Dynasty.[18] The development of banknotes (paper currency) was rooted in merchants' desire to avoid the weight and bulk of transporting coins to settle large commercial transactions. They developed a system whereby they would issue credit notes, which were for a limited duration and at a discount to the promised amount. This new paper currency did not replace coins until later, in the Song Dynasty, in the eleventh century. The banknotes were used alongside the coins until the central government noticed the economic advantages of printing banknotes and holding a monopoly right over their issuance.

It was not until the thirteenth century that paper money reached Europe through the accounts of travelers, such as Marco Polo.[19] In medieval Italy and Flanders, money traders started using promissory notes due to the high risk and impracticality of transporting large sums of money over long distances. These notes are considered to be the predecessor of the regular banknotes we know today. In 1661, the first European banknotes were issued by Stockholms Banco, later known as the Bank of Sweden.[20]

At the same time banknotes started to appear in China, another form of paper currency began to appear in the Islamic world, the *sakk,* more commonly known as the promissory note. These notes were seen during the rise of the Islamic Umayyad Caliphate from the year 661 to 750 CE.[21, 22] Each note individually was called a *sakk,* and in the plural, *sukuk,* which is cognate with the European root *cheque.* A *sakk* meant any document representing a contract or conveyance of rights, obligations, or monies done in conformity with the Shariah.[23] *Sukuk* were used extensively during the medieval period in Islamic society for the transfer of financial obligations originating from trade and other commercial activities. The essence of *sukuk,* in the modern Islamic perspective, lies in the concept of asset monetization, also known as securitization. *Sukuk* are discussed in detail in Part II.

Europe during the Middle Ages witnessed a lot of financial innovations, not only with the development of banknotes but also with the development of trade bills of exchange. Their development was directly the result of the rapidly increasing trade throughout the region. A thriving trade business is heavily dependent on credit for expansion. Bills of exchange worked by allowing the buyer to receive the goods in return for the buyer delivering to the seller a bill of exchange, which constituted the buyer's promise to make payment at a specified date in the future. The seller could then present the bill to a merchant banker and redeem it in money at a discount to its value before it actually became due. The seller would get paid sooner and remove the risk of repaying in return for accepting a lower price against the bill's value. This transferred the risk to the merchant banker, who would accept the bill and make a profit in return for taking on the repayment risk.

As you can imagine, merchant bankers would need to ensure that the buyer is reputable and that the bill was endorsed by a credible guarantor. This evolved into a regional credit system whereby a bill of exchange could be issued in one town and redeemed in another town through a network of merchant bankers. In England, bills of exchange became an important form of credit and money during the late eighteenth century up to the early part of the nineteenth century before banknotes, checks, and credit lines were widely available.[24]

Another innovation during this period came from England in the twelfth century. The English monarchy introduced a notched piece of wood known as a *tally stick* to record the various amounts of taxes to be payable to the crown. The reason for using tallies was mainly because paper was rare and costly at that time. However, tallies were so popular that they continued to be used until the early nineteenth century, even after paper forms of money had become prevalent.

Initially, tallies were simply used as a form of receipt to the taxpayer indicating that the dues had been paid. As tallies became successful for collecting taxes, the revenue department found new uses for them and began issuing tallies to denote a promise by the tax assessee to make future tax payments at specified times during the year. Each tally consisted of a matching pair: One stick was given to the assessee, representing the amount of taxes to be paid by which date, and the other was held by the revenue department, representing the amount of taxes to be collected by which date.

It was soon discovered that these tallies could also be used to create money. When the government was short on money it would use tally receipts, which represented future tax payments due, as a form of payment to its own creditors. These creditors would be able to collect the tax revenue directly from the assessees or use the same tally to pay their own taxes to the government. This led to the development of a thriving market for trading tallies, which would be traded at a discount reflecting the length of time remaining until the tax was due for payment. The longer the time remaining on the tally, the larger the discount. Thus, the tallies became an accepted medium of exchange for some types of transactions and an accepted medium for storage of value. Once the market for tallies took off, the government realized that it could issue tallies that were not backed by any specific assessment of taxes. By doing so, the government was able to create new money that was backed by public trust and confidence in the monarchy rather than by specific revenue receipts.[25]

GOLDSMITH DEPOSITS AND THE ESTABLISHMENT OF BANKS

As trade flourished in Europe, merchants grew to be very wealthy, and many of them amassed huge hoards of gold. The safest place to store this wealth at the time was to entrust it to the Royal Mint. However, in 1640, King Charles I of England seized the private gold stored in the mint, calling it a loan, which was to be paid back over time.[26] This caused merchants to remove their gold from the mints and place it instead with goldsmiths. Goldsmiths in England had been craftsmen, bullion merchants, money changers, and money lenders since the sixteenth century, but did not actively get involved in gold storage until this event. They also possessed private vaults.

Merchants began storing their gold in goldsmiths' vaults for a fee. In exchange for each deposit of precious metals—namely, gold and silver—the goldsmiths issued receipts certifying the quantity and purity of the metal they held in trust. These receipts could not be assigned to another party. Only the original depositor could collect the stored precious metals. With all the precious metals stored in vaults sitting idle, goldsmiths soon began lending out the metals on behalf of depositors and issuing promissory notes for money deposited. These deposits were treated as loans from the depositor to the goldsmith. The depositors allowed the goldsmith to use the money for any purpose, including advances to his customers. Goldsmiths did not charge a fee for accepting these deposits and, in many cases, paid interest on them. This was the beginning of the fractional reserve banking system, as these promissory notes were payable on demand and the loans to the goldsmith's customers were repayable over a longer time period. Gold deposits were relatively stable, often remaining in the goldsmith's vault for years, so there was little risk of default so long as the goldsmith maintained public trust and was financially sound.

The promissory notes developed into an assignable instrument, which could circulate as a safe and convenient form of money backed by the gold-smith's promise to pay. Goldsmiths were able to advance loans, issue promissory notes, and offer checking accounts allowing depositors to draw down their balances held by issuing checks.[27] This is how the London goldsmiths became the issuers of money and credit, and went on to give birth to the banking system.

This led to the establishment of banks, which issued paper notes called *banknotes*. These notes circulated in the same way that government-issued currency circulates today. In essence, each bank would have the ability to issue its own currency. This practice continued until 1694, when England decided to monopolize the right to issue banknotes and established the Bank of England (central bank).

In the United States, this practice continued through the nineteenth century until the Federal Reserve Bank was established in 1913. At one time there were more than 5,000 different types of banknotes issued by various commercial banks in the United States, some reputable and some not so reputable. The notes issued by the largest, most creditworthy banks were widely accepted. The banknotes of the smaller and less reputable banks circulated locally. Farther from home banknotes were accepted only at a discounted rate, if they were accepted at all. The proliferation of types of money went hand in hand with a multiplication in the number of financial institutions.

These banknotes were a form of representative money, which could be converted into gold or silver by application at the bank. Since banks issued notes far in excess of the gold and silver they kept on deposit, sudden loss of public confidence in a bank could cause mass redemption of banknotes and result in bankruptcy.

The use of banknotes issued by private commercial banks as legal tender has gradually been replaced by the issuance of banknotes authorized and controlled by national governments. Until recently, these government-authorized currencies were forms of representative money, since they were partially backed by gold or silver and were theoretically convertible into gold or silver. This has since changed, as convertibility and linking currency to any tangible asset was dropped in favor of being backed by simply the trust in the issuing authority and its creditworthiness, otherwise known as *fiat currency*.

It is important to understand why nations switched from representative money to fiat money, as this is where the story begins to explain why we are in a financial mess today.

FINANCIAL GLOBALIZATION AND THE GOLD STANDARD (1821–1913)

Before financial globalization there were regional powers, which dominated trade; hence, their currencies were most commonly used and accepted. Before the Roman Empire reached its height of power, the Persian Empire was the dominant force and its currency, the *daric*, was the most widely used currency. This was succeeded by the Roman currency, the *denarius*, and then the gold *dinar* of the Islamic empire. During the age of Imperialism (sixteenth to twentieth centuries), the currencies of European colonial powers dominated foreign trade, beginning with the Spanish dollar, followed by the Dutch guilder, then the French franc, and ending with the British pound in the late nineteenth century. With Europe in ruins following World War I, the U.S. dollar became the dominant trading currency and is the basis for the current international monetary system.

Until the nineteenth century, the global monetary system was not very well integrated. The system was regional in focus, with colonial powers wielding influence over their former colonies in Africa, Asia, the Middle East, and South America. The influence of the former Spanish empire led to the integration of American and European economies and monetary systems. European influence in Asia led to the dominance of European currencies, most notably the British pound.

In the eighteenth century, much of the world was on a bimetallic standard, meaning more than one precious metal was legal tender. The main metals used were gold and silver, and copper to some extent. This created problems, as mentioned earlier. During the Napoleonic Wars (1803 to 1815), the United Kingdom suffered a silver shortage and was forced drop this standard and go on a fiat standard. The main change to this system began in 1821 when the United Kingdom returned to a convertibility system and established the classical gold standard.[28] This new system allowed banknotes to be redeemed for gold bullion at the Bank of England. The redemption rate was set at 4.24 pounds for one ounce of gold. So anyone holding pounds at the time could go to the Bank of England and redeem their pounds for gold at this fixed rate. The main objective of this was to bring trust and stability to the system. Over the next decades, more and more countries embraced this new standard and dropped silver. By 1880, most of the countries around the world were on some form of gold standard.[29]

With currencies stabilized, world trade began to grow at a faster pace than it had in prior decades. World leaders began to promote free trade, which led to a huge expansion in communications, railway transportation, and transatlantic shipping. This period also witnessed record levels of migration.

Once the globalization wave started to take hold, protectionism began to rise, beginning in Germany in 1879. German Chancellor Otto von Bismarck introduced tariffs on agricultural and manufacturing goods, making Germany the first country to institute protectionist trade policies. France and the United States followed shortly with their own protectionist policies. Despite these measures, global trade continued to flourish, leading to an increase in foreign investment and capital flows.

As a result of the rise in capital flows between Europe and the Americas, new financial centers developed. Before 1870, London and Paris were the main financial centers. However, Berlin and New York soon began to compete on par with London and Paris. Other financial centers grew in importance as well, such as Amsterdam, Brussels, Geneva, and Zurich. London remained the leading international financial center in the four decades leading up to World War I.[30]

At the end of this period, another major event occurred. The U.S. Congress passed the Federal Reserve Act on December 23, 1913, giving rise to the Federal Reserve System, which acts as the country's central bank. The authority of the Federal Reserve System is derived from statutes enacted by the U.S. Congress and is subject to congressional oversight. There is, however, some controversy surrounding the establishment of this system, as it removed the right of Congress to issue and control the currency, as stated in Article 1, Section 8, of the U.S. Constitution.[31]

The Federal Reserve Bank (the Fed), contrary to popular belief, is not a government entity. It is independent from the government and owned by member banks. The specific shareholding of the bank is not disclosed, but the bank's website states that more than one-third of U.S. commercial banks are members.[32] Member banks receive an annual statutory dividend of 6 percent of their capital investment in the Fed, and the U.S. government receives the remaining profits.[33]

The main objective of the Fed was to become the sole lender of last resort and to resolve the inelasticity of the money supply in times of crisis. However, this liberated banks from the need to maintain their own reserves, and they began taking on greater risks. The system that was set up to safeguard the country from financial crises actually made the economy more prone to crises, as we shall see in the following chapters.

THE TWO WORLD WARS AND THE GREAT DEPRESSION (1914–1945)

On June 28, 1914, Austrian Archduke Franz Ferdinand was assassinated while on a visit to the Bosnian capital, Sarajevo. This event led to Austria's invasion of Serbia one month later. Germany sided with its Austro-Hungarian ally, and Russia sided with its allies in the Balkans. Soon, Belgium, Luxembourg, and France were invaded by Germany, and the United Kingdom declared war, sparking the first world war of the century.[34]

Over the next four years, there would be 16 million deaths and 20 million wounded, making it among the deadliest conflicts in human history.[35] Economically speaking, Europe was in shambles, with the exception of four allies—Britain, Canada, Italy, and the United States, which saw their gross domestic product (GDP) increase during the war. The decline in the GDP in Austria, France, Russia, and the Ottoman Empire reached 30 to 40 percent. In Germany, the GDP declined by 27 percent.[36]

In addition to the cost of war, high inflation and food shortages can be blamed for sparking the Russian Revolution in 1917. The tsar was overthrown, and a civil war began, bringing the Communist Party to power. The Union of Soviet Socialist Republics (U.S.S.R.) was established in 1922.

The war officially ended in November 1918, but the Treaty of Versailles was not signed until six months later, in June 1919. The treaty forced Germany to disarm and imposed harsh reparations to pay for war damages. Notable economist of the time John Maynard Keynes voiced his concerns about excessive reparations, saying it was too hard a punishment and counterproductive.[37] Most of Germany's reparations payments were funded by loans from U.S. banks. Between 1919 and 1932, Germany paid out 19 billion gold marks in reparations and received 27 billion gold marks in loans from New York bankers and others. These loans were later paid back by West Germany after World War II.[38]

During the war, countries enacted trade embargoes on gold exports, leading many countries to abandon gold redemptions, thus dropping the gold standard altogether. This allowed their currency exchange rates to float freely. After the war, some countries deliberately weakened their currencies, hoping to boost exports and help their economies. In the 1920s, Austria, Hungary, Germany, Russia, and Poland began experiencing hyperinflation. Seeing the negative effects of this, the United States tried to persuade countries to go back to the gold standard and was fairly successful. By 1927, many countries had returned to the gold standard,[39] but this wouldn't last long, as the world was again headed toward protectionist policies, which eventually made their way to the United States.

The Stock Market Crash of 1929 and the onset of the Great Depression raised protectionist fears in the United States, leading President Herbert Hoover to sign the Smoot–Hawley Tariff Act in 1930. The act raised import tariffs on thousands of goods. U.S. trading partners responded by introducing tariffs on U.S. goods.[40] Exports from the United States dropped 60 percent from 1930 to 1933.[41] Worldwide international trade virtually ground to a halt. The international ramifications of the Smoot–Hawley Act—the spread of trade policies and the rise of economic nationalism—are credited by economists with prolonging the Great Depression.[42]

The Great Depression brought about bank runs in Austria, Germany, and the United States, which put pressure on gold reserves in the United Kingdom to such a degree that the gold standard became unsustainable. Germany became the first country to formally abandon the post–World War I gold standard in July 1931. In September 1931, the United Kingdom allowed the pound to float freely. By the end of 1931, several other countries, including Austria, Canada, Japan, and Sweden, abandoned gold.[43]

Some historians believe that the effects of the Great Depression, which lasted nearly a decade, were also the result of high interest rates and a contraction of the money supply.[44] The Fed could not increase the money supply without more gold, putting pressure on the ability of the United States to maintain its gold standard. In 1934, Congress passed the Gold Reserve Act, nationalizing all gold by ordering the Fed to turn over its supply to the U.S. Treasury. In return, the banks received gold certificates to be used as reserves against deposits and Federal Reserve notes. The act also authorized the president to devalue the dollar gold redemption rate from $20.67 per ounce to $35 per ounce, effectively devaluing the dollar by more than 40 percent.

The Allied Powers thought to avoid history repeating itself and saw financial cooperation as a way to encourage mutual cooperation among the countries affected by the war. In 1930, during the early days of the Great Depression, the Bank for International Settlements (BIS) was established. The main purposes of the BIS were to manage Germany's reparations payments imposed by the Treaty of Versailles as well as to function as a bank for central banks around the world. Countries can hold a portion of their reserves as deposits with the BIS. The BIS also operates as a trustee and facilitator of financial settlements between countries.[45]

These efforts, however, did not stop the rise of nationalism, which was further fueled by the economic depression and protectionist trade policies. The crippling effects of the Treaty of Versailles on the German economy gave way to the rise of Hitler in the 1930s. In 1939, another world war was started, which would last six years and claim 61 million lives.[46]

THE BRETTON WOODS AGREEMENT (1945–1971)

In the aftermath of World War II, world powers again looked for ways to prevent future conflicts and bring about peace, stability, and prosperity. There were three major developments during this period: the birth of the United Nations, establishment of the Marshall Plan, and the negotiation of the Bretton Woods Agreement.

The United Nations (UN) was born on October 24, 1945, as an intergovernmental organization established to promote international cooperation, replacing the League of Nations, which had been deemed ineffective.

In 1948, the United States launched the Marshall Plan. The initiative was aimed at helping Europe rebuild after the war in order to prevent the spread of Soviet communism. The plan was in operation for four years, beginning in April 1948. Other objectives of the plan included removing trade barriers, modernizing industry, and making Europe prosperous again.[47]

In 1944, delegates from the soon-to-be-created United Nations held a conference at a hotel in Bretton Woods, New Hampshire, called the United Nations Monetary and Financial Conference, which is now commonly referred to as the Bretton Woods Conference. With the effects of the Great Depression and two world wars still fresh in their minds, delegates devised a new system that would relieve them of the challenges of maintaining a gold standard while also reducing currency volatility and instability.

Delegates at Bretton Woods favored pegged exchange rates for their flexibility over the previous fixed exchange rates. This arrangement would come to be known as the Bretton Woods System. Under this system, countries would peg their exchange rates to the U.S. dollar and the U.S. dollar would be convertible to gold at $35 per ounce.[48] Countries pegging their currencies to the U.S. dollar would allow their exchange rates to fluctuate within a 1 percent band of the agreed-upon exchange rate. To achieve this, central banks would buy or sell their currency against the dollar to maintain the peg.[49]

This effectively made the U.S. dollar, rather than gold, the world's reserve currency. The U.S. dollar would still be redeemable for gold; however, other countries would no longer be required to hold large gold reserves or ship gold back and forth to adjust any payment imbalances, since the dollar would now serve that purpose. A country wishing to receive gold would first need to convert its currency to U.S. dollars and then present them to the Fed for gold.

Another important development following the Bretton Woods Agreement was the creation of two new institutions: the International Monetary Fund (IMF) in 1947 and the International Bank for Reconstruction and Development (IBRD) in 1946, which later became the World Bank. The IMF was established to support the Bretton Woods monetary system with the mission of facilitating multilateral cooperation on international monetary issues, providing assistance to member states, and offering emergency lending to countries experiencing crises and help in restoring their balance of payments.[50]

Under the agreement, members were authorized and encouraged to employ capital controls as necessary to help manage payment imbalances and meet pegging targets, but were prohibited from relying on IMF financing to cover particularly short-term capital hemorrhages.

The IBRD was established to serve as a financial intermediary for channeling global capital toward long-term investment opportunities and postwar reconstruction projects.[51] The creation of these two organizations was a crucial milestone in the evolution of the international financial architecture, and some economists consider it the most significant achievement of multilateral cooperation following World War II.

POST–BRETTON WOODS—FIAT CURRENCIES (1971–TODAY)

Under the Bretton Woods system, international trade grew, but this success masked an underlying flaw in the system's design. There was no mechanism for increasing the supply of international reserves to support continued growth in trade. In the late 1950s and early 1960s[52] central banks worldwide needed more dollars to hold as reserves but were unable to expand their money supplies, as that meant exceeding their dollar reserves and threatening their exchange rate pegs. For the system to be successful, the United States needed to run dollar deficits. As a consequence, the value of the dollar began exceeding its gold backing.

During the early 1960s, investors could sell gold at a higher price in London than the stated rate of $35 per ounce in the United States, indicating that the dollar was overvalued. In 1960, Belgian-American economist Robert Triffin defined this problem, which came to be known as the Triffin dilemma, whereby a country's economic interests conflict with its international objectives as the custodian of the world's reserve currency.[53] This means that the United States couldn't provide the world with a reserve currency while at the same time doing what is best for the country's economy; it had to choose one policy to follow at the expense of the other.

France voiced concerns over the artificially low price of gold in 1968 and even called for a return to the former gold standard. Around this same time, excess dollars flowed into international markets as the United States expanded its money supply to accommodate the costs of its military campaign in the Vietnam War. Speculators began attacking the dollar to exploit this weakness.

In August 1971, President Richard Nixon suspended the exchange of dollars for gold. The suspension of convertibility effectively shifted the adjustment burdens of a devalued dollar to the rest of the world. Speculators moved on to attacking other currencies and began selling dollars in anticipation of these currencies being revalued against the dollar. Central banks were faced with choosing between inflating money supplies, imposing capital controls, or floating exchange rates.[54]

In response to these developments, the Group of 10 member countries, also known as the G-10, which represented the 10 largest economic powers of the IMF at the time, met in Washington in December 1971 to sign what is known as the Smithsonian Agreement. The agreement called for the dollar price of gold to be raised to $38 per ounce, effectively depreciating the dollar by a further 8.5 percent. In addition, the Bretton Woods System was modified to allow fluctuations within an expanded band of 2.25 percent instead of 1 percent. The agreement was not very effective and merely delayed the system's collapse. Market forces continued to put pressure on the dollar/gold price, which devalued the dollar by another 10 percent over the next two years. In February 1973, Japan and European Economic Community (EEC) members decided to let their currencies float freely in the market. Within a decade all industrialized nations had done so, creating the fiat system we have today.[55]

OTHER RELEVANT EVENTS IN OUR CURRENT MONETARY SYSTEM

There have been a few small adjustments to this system over the years, but it remains largely unchanged. Due to increasing volatility in foreign exchange markets under the new fiat system in the 1980s, two additional agreements were reached: the Plaza Accord in 1985 and the Louvre Accord in 1987. These accords created the managed float system by which central banks jointly intervene to resolve under- and overvaluations in the foreign exchange market to stabilize otherwise freely floating currencies.[56]

In the 1990s, foreign exchange markets were relatively calm. Volatility did not come back to the market until the dot-com bubble burst in 2000 and became even more volatile since the most recent financial crisis in 2008.

There is now increasing pressure on world leaders to find alternatives to the dollar-based fiat system, as the cracks are appearing ever more frequently.

Some suggested alternatives have been to go on a multicurrency system, which would consist of a basket of currencies, such as U.S. dollars, euros, and yen. Another alternative would be to use the IMF's special drawing rights (SDRs) to back currencies. Developed in 1969, SDRs are another type of reserve instrument that consist of a basket of 16 major currencies.[57] (I discuss SDRs in more detail in Chapter 11.) Other alternatives include moving away from the dollar to another reserve currency, such as the euro or Chinese yuan. Some politicians and economists in the United States have even suggested going back to the gold standard. No one knows for sure what the next system will look like, but one thing is for sure: The current system needs to change, and this will happen only once another crisis hits and breaks it beyond repair.

Now we can see how our current monetary system was born, in 1971. There have been a few modifications over the years, but in essence the system remains the same. The world is on a fiat system using currencies based on trust and faith in the issuing authorities. Though there are benefits to this system, the negatives tend to outweigh the positives. The primary advantage of this system is that money supply can expand (without limit) and contract more easily than on a gold standard. This gives central banks comfort in knowing they can try to balance out market forces. The primary drawback of such a system is that governments eventually abuse it, as solving their budgetary problems by turning on the money printing press is too tempting to forgo. History does not favor fiat currencies, as they have all disappeared, either by default or as a result of hyperinflation.

To see why the fiat currency system is not sustainable, we need to look at the reasons such a system leads to instability and recklessness among governments and financial institutions. In the following chapters we look at past financial crises and see what caused them. We then turn to our current situation to see if we can spot a new crisis forming.

SUMMARY

- Early financial systems existed before the invention of money, dating back as far as 9000 BCE, and were based on social interactions, customs, barter, mutual reciprocity, and hierarchy in the community.
- Some of the first forms of currency were animals, grains, salt, and seashells.
- Later, precious metals emerged and became the preferred medium of exchange as empires grew and the need to pay soldiers and collect taxes also grew.

- With the expansion of trade during the Middle Ages, the need for better and safer alternatives to transporting large quantities of metals led to the development of promissory notes (*sukuk*) and bills of exchange.
- Since precious metals were still the main store of value, the need for storage vaults to house these metals grew in line with the expansion in trade.
- Merchants and kings stored their wealth in royal mints until attempts at confiscation and abuse took place, which caused merchants to move their metals to private storage vaults at goldsmiths.
- Goldsmiths, in turn, started to find new and creative ways to make a profit out of the vast sums of wealth in their vaults and began making loans, taking deposits, and issuing promissory notes.
- As paper currency became more accepted, banks were launched off the backs of the success goldsmiths had in issuing notes. Banks issued their own notes, called banknotes, which is how our paper currency today came to be.
- Having seen the success of these banknotes and their ability to create money, governments monopolized the right to create money, and central banks were formed to handle this task, beginning with the Bank of England in 1694.
- Central banks sought to create stability in the financial system by making the paper notes redeemable for gold at a set price. In 1821, this formally became known as the gold standard.
- This system worked well until governments got into financial trouble or wars wrecked the economy, at which point governments dropped the redemption rights in order to print their way out of trouble. It never ended well, and governments switched back to the gold standard.
- The Great Depression put enormous pressure on countries to maintain currency stability and gold reserves, leading some to devalue their currencies against gold, as the United States did with the Gold Reserve Act.
- After World War II, the Bretton Woods Agreement was established, removing the requirement that other countries hold large gold reserves to support their currencies. Instead, the new system called for the U.S. dollar to become the reserve currency. The U.S. dollar, in turn, would remain redeemable for gold at a set price, thus maintaining a quasi–gold standard.
- Cracks began to appear in the Bretton Woods Agreement, and by 1971 the United States was forced to suspend the exchange of dollars for gold. Currencies are now backed by the faith in and credibility of the issuing authority, and are better known as fiat currencies.

CHAPTER 2

Past Financial Crises and Their Causes

Financial crises have been around as long as people and societies have been engaged in trade. A look back at history shows a past littered with financial crises. Some were mild and limited in their spread and duration, while others were severe and affected many other countries.

The earliest recorded financial crises occurred during the Roman and Byzantine empires. Wars and periodic droughts drained government resources, forcing the treasuries to raise taxes on the populace in order to maintain their vast empires. This not only led to a widening of the gap between rich and poor, but also led to the ultimate decline of these empires. Centuries later, with the expansion of global trade, which was facilitated by the development of financial instruments such as promissory notes and bills of exchange (as discussed in Chapter 1), financial crises started to occur more frequently. One of the earliest known crises during this period of trade expansion was the Dutch tulip mania, which began in 1634 and ended in 1637 (Figure 2.1).

The dominance of global trade at the time by the Dutch East India Company brought new and exotic goods to Holland. One such exotic item was the tulip brought over from Austria by way of the Ottoman Empire. Trading in tulips took off, as they became a must-have item in Dutch society. Not long after the craze took off it ended, having lasted just over two years and resulted in great financial distress to those who got caught up in the mania. This caused an economic downturn in the country, although some historians have suggested that other factors were at play.[1]

The Dutch tulip mania was a classic speculative bubble, which eventually popped and caused a panic, or financial crisis. This bubble, however, was limited in its spread and duration. In this chapter, the focus is on financial crises beginning with the Great Depression up to the dot-com bubble in 2000. Table 2.1 lists the top 10 financial crises during this period. What they

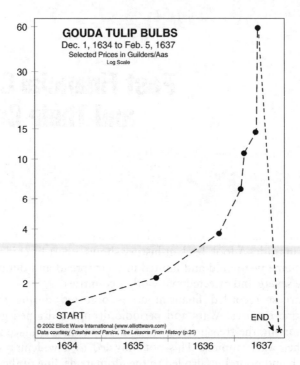

FIGURE 2.1   Tulip bulb price in guilders from 1634 to 1637
Source: Elliott Wave International

TABLE 2.1   Top 10 Financial Crises, 1929–2001

	Year Crisis Began	Crisis Name	Crisis Trigger
1	1929	Wall Street Crash of 1929 and Great Depression	Stock market crash
2	1973	Oil crisis	Oil price shock
3	1982	Latin American debt crisis	Debt default
4	1987	Black Monday	Stock market crash
5	1989	U.S. savings & loan crisis	S&L failures
6	1990	Japanese asset bubble	Real estate bubble
7	1994	Mexican peso crisis	Currency crisis
8	1997	Asian financial crisis	Currency crisis
9	1998	Russian financial crisis	Currency crisis
10	2000	Dot-com bubble	Stock market bubble

all have in common is that they had a contagion effect, spreading to other countries as well.

During this same period there were many other financial crises, such as Kuwait's Souk Al-Manakh crash in 1982, the Israeli Bank Stock crisis in 1983, the Argentinian economic crisis in 1998, and the Turkish economic crisis in 2001, as well as a host of stock market crashes, currency devaluations, and runaway inflation stretching from Brazil to Zimbabwe. The key difference between these events and the ones listed in Table 2.1 is that these crises were contained, for the most part, in the country where they began. Let us instead begin with the Great Depression, since it was such a significant global event, and then jump to the major financial crises since the world switched to a fiat currency system in 1971. As you can also see from Table 2.1, each crisis had its own trigger event. This does not mean that this is what caused the crisis; it simply means that this is the event that set off the crisis. In all of these cases there were other factors at work that led to the crisis, as we shall see beginning with the stock market crash in 1929.

THE WALL STREET CRASH OF 1929 AND THE GREAT DEPRESSION

A runaway bull market boom and eventual burst of speculative bubbles was nothing new to Wall Street in the fall of 1929. The 1800s had been plagued by protracted recessions and depressions. Walter Bagehot, editor of *The Economist* from 1860 to 1877, famously argued that all financial panics occur "when the blind capital of the public floods into unwise speculative investments."[2] This theme would be repeated over and over again throughout modern financial history.

The financial crisis, which started in the United States in 1929, was not formally given the name Great Depression until 1934, after British economist Lionel Robbins published his book, *The Great Depression*.[3] It wasn't the first depression the world had seen, nor was it the last. More than 10 depressions affected Europe and the United States since 1800, two of which were very severe—one in 1837, and one in 1873.[4] There have also been depressions in recent times. Latin America suffered a depression in the 1980s, which included Argentina, Brazil, Chile, and Mexico. Argentina suffered another depression from 1998 to 2002. The breakup of the Soviet Union in the 1990s caused a depression and hyperinflation across the breakaway countries, which was even more severe than the Great Depression.[5] Greece today is going through a depression, which shows no sign of ending soon. The most discussed and debated depression, however, remains the Great Depression, which was an asset bubble inflated by easy credit in the 1920s and exacerbated by the government's response to it in the 1930s.

After World War I, war-torn countries began rebuilding and modernizing their economies once again and transitioning from wartime to peacetime economies. With this came unprecedented industrial growth. It also ushered in a new era of technology. Homes were connected to electricity for the first time. Consumer tastes and demands were changing as automobiles, telephones, and motion pictures gained wide acceptance and use. These lifestyle changes were also fueled by the rise of woman suffrage in much of Europe and the United States.[6] The economic and cultural advances in this decade became known as the Roaring Twenties.

The euphoria sweeping across the industrialized world brought with it a rise in entrepreneurship and an appetite for risk. Some thought the best way to become rich and enjoy what modern society had to offer was to take a shortcut by playing the stock market. Banks and stockbrokers were eager to lend up to 90 percent of a stock's value, leaving investors to come up with only 10 percent. This, of course, led to a rapid rise in stock prices, and, with it, even more investors jumped into the market with even more banks eager to lend to them. From 1921 to just before the market crash in 1929, the Dow Jones Industrial Average (DJIA) had gone up almost 500 percent, as shown in Figure 2.2.

FIGURE 2.2   Dow Jones Industrial Average from 1921 to 1932
Adapted from: Bloomberg

On October 28, 1929, the DJIA dropped 13 percent, forcing brokers to call in their margin loans, which, of course, could not be paid back. The next day the market fell another 12 percent, causing widespread market panic.[7] As debtors defaulted on their loans, banks and brokers began to fail. Depositors rushed to their banks in an attempt to withdraw their money, triggering multiple bank runs. Government guarantees and banking regulations designed to prevent such panics were ineffective or not used. Bank failures led to the loss of billions of dollars in assets. After the panic, and during the first 10 months of 1930, 744 U.S. banks failed. By 1933, $140 billion in depositors' money would be lost through bank failures. During the 1930s, a total of 9,000 banks would fail.[8]

The stock market crash was merely the trigger that snowballed into panics and bank runs, causing the massive failures. The economy in 1929, however, was already showing signs of weakness. A good harvest of wheat that year led to oversupply in the market, wiping out farmers' profits and threatening their survival. To make matters worse, severe drought in the following season, not only in the United States, but in Canada and South America, caused gaps in the world supply of wheat, not to mention the effects this had on an already struggling farming industry.[9]

With a weak economic outlook, capital investment and construction slowed or completely ceased. Banks that survived became even more conservative in their lending, spending slowed, unemployment and bankruptcies shot up, and a vicious deflationary cycle developed, accelerating the downward spiral. This deflationary cycle affected all industrialized countries. Government policies at the time only made matters worse—namely, the protectionist trade policies that sprang up to try to stem the slide in GDP. In 1930, President Herbert Hoover signed the Smoot–Hawley Tariff Act, raising tariffs on imported goods to protect U.S. jobs and companies. Europe quickly followed with its own tariffs, leading to a trade war. From 1930 to 1933, U.S. exports dropped 60 percent.[10] One of the positive government actions at that time was the enactment of the Glass–Steagall Act of 1933, which separated commercial and investment banking activities. The goal of this was to separate riskier banking and investment activities from deposit-taking banks to avoid a repeat of 1929.

The Great Depression in most countries technically lasted until 1933, but the economies did not fully recover until the late 1930s, just as World War II was brewing. From 1929 to 1932, industrial production dropped 46 percent in the United States, 41 percent in Germany, 24 percent in France, and 34 percent in the United Kingdom.[11] By 1932, U.S. GDP had fallen 31 percent, unemployment topped out at 24.9 percent, and the stock market lost 89 percent of its value. U.S. GDP did not reach the 1929 level until 11 years later, in 1940.[12]

THE OIL CRISIS (1973)

In a post–Bretton Woods world, the U.S. dollar, as well as other major currencies, was able to freely float. The U.S. dollar, unable to hold its value once the gold redemption window closed, immediately depreciated against the major currencies, upsetting the United States' main trading partners. It also upset the Organization of Petroleum Exporting Countries (OPEC), since oil was priced in dollars. OPEC was slow to readjust prices to reflect this depreciation. During the previous two decades, the price of oil in U.S. dollars remained very stable, rising at an annual rate of 2 percent. This stability made OPEC members unprepared for the rise in price volatility once currencies began to float. As a result, the income of OPEC members lagged for several years until they were able to affect the price of oil[13] (Figure 2.3).

OPEC's chance came on October 6, 1973, at the start of the Yom Kippur War in the Middle East between Israel, Egypt, and Syria. Arab OPEC members decided to retaliate against the United States for choosing to resupply Israel with arms. Their retaliation came in the form of an oil embargo against Canada, Japan, the Netherlands, the United Kingdom, and the United States. The price of oil quickly quadrupled, from $3 per barrel to $12 per barrel. The world financial system, which was already under pressure from the breakdown of the Bretton Woods Agreement, was headed for recession and high inflation that continued into the early 1980s.[14]

By 1974, developed countries were in recession. Unemployment in the United States reached 9.1 percent, and industrial production was down by 15 percent. In the United Kingdom, the spike in oil prices has been blamed

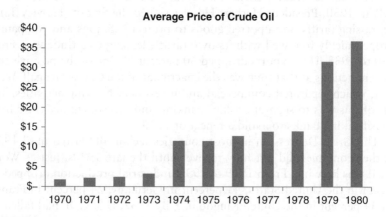

FIGURE 2.3 Average oil prices from 1970 to 1980
Source: BP Statistical Review of World Energy 2014

for the downturn in the housing market. At the time, the Bank of England was in the midst of raising interest rates to combat the easy lending policies in place since the 1960s that led to a housing bubble. When it popped in 1973, the United Kingdom found itself in the middle of a banking crisis. The Bank of England ended up bailing out around 30 banks and provided support for some 30 others.[15]

In the two years of 1973 and 1974, stock markets around the world crashed (Figure 2.4). The Dow Jones Industrial Average lost 45 percent of its value, Hong Kong's Hang Seng Index lost more than 83 percent of its value, and the London Stock Exchange's FT30 Index lost more than 73 percent during this two-year period. When the economies did start growing again in 1975, they also brought along high inflation and high unemployment, which were not supposed to happen. This era became known as the era of stagflation. The stock market during this time was a terrible place to invest. The FT30 did not recover from the crash until 1987, just before Black Monday on Wall Street. The DJIA, on the other hand, did not recover until 1993, some 20 years later.[16]

The crisis had a huge impact not only on the economies of developed countries, but also on international relations. Relations were strained

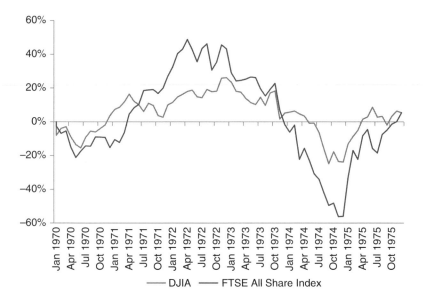

FIGURE 2.4 Stock market crash—Dow Jones Industrial Average and FTSE All Share Indices from 1970 to 1975
Adapted from: Bloomberg

between the United States and OPEC members as well as between the United States and Europe. Some European countries, along with Japan, tried to distance themselves from U.S. foreign policy in the Middle East. In addition, Arab oil producers demanded that an end to the embargo needed to be linked to efforts to create peace in the Middle East, which further complicated matters.

Although the United States was able to negotiate an agreement to end the embargo in March 1974, the damage to world economies was already done. Stagflation took hold of the economy for the remainder of the decade. By 1980, unemployment hovered above 10 percent and inflation had been averaging more than 11 percent over the previous few years. The situation did not improve until Paul Volcker, the Fed chairman at the time, took drastic measures to combat inflation and get the economy on track again by raising interest rates as high as 20 percent. His strategy worked. By 1983, inflation had dropped to 3.2 percent.[17] This, combined with President Ronald Reagan's lower taxes and economic policies, got the economy back on track.

LATIN AMERICAN DEBT CRISIS (1980s)

In the 1960s and 1970s, Latin American countries had ambitious plans for industrializing. They were off to a good start, as their economies were growing fast and spending fast on large infrastructure projects. The money for these projects had to come from somewhere, and it did. U.S. banks were eager to lend to them at higher rates than they could get at home. In the aftermath of the 1973 oil crisis, U.S. banks had more money than they could invest, thanks to the recycling of petrodollars—which were U.S. dollars paid to OPEC countries for their oil and deposited in U.S. banks for safekeeping and spending later.

Argentina, Brazil, and Mexico, among others, borrowed heavily from U.S. banks. From 1970 to 1982, Latin America's debt increased by more than 1,000 percent. In 1970, the region had a total outstanding debt of $29 billion. By 1982, this number had skyrocketed to $327 billion.[18] With higher debt came higher debt service. Debt service grew to $66 billion in 1982, up from $12 billion in 1975.[19]

Paul Volcker's plan to combat inflation in the United States by raising interest rates rippled through Latin America. Debt service skyrocketed, and indebted countries faced enormous challenges in keeping up their rising payments. In August 1982, Mexico declared that it would no longer be able to service its $80 billion in debt to foreign creditors, effectively defaulting. By October 1982, 27 countries, owing over $239 billion, defaulted and were in discussions to reschedule their debts. As a result, several of the world's largest banks, including Citibank, faced collapse.[20]

The banks had to somehow restructure the debts to avoid financial collapse. The IMF, and later the World Bank, stepped in to restructure the payments and reduce consumption in debtor countries. For the banks, this involved new loans with very strict conditions. For the debtor countries, this involved imposing harsh austerity plans that prevented them from further spending. As a result, living standards fell alongside the growth rate, which caused much anger and hatred from the people toward the IMF. The citizens of Latin America did not like the fact that their government was being controlled by "outsiders," and they blamed the international organizations for the fall of their standard of living.[21] In the late 1980s, Brazilian officials planned a debt negotiation meeting, where they decided to "never again sign agreements with the IMF."[22]

With the IMF and World Bank plans not working out as the United States had hoped, in 1989 U.S. Treasury Secretary Nicholas Brady proposed a new plan to solve Latin America's debt crisis and, more important, save U.S. banks. The Brady Plan, as it was known, established Brady Bonds to buy the defaulted debt and issue new debt with guarantees, along with permanent reductions in loan principal and existing debt-servicing obligations. It also called for some debt forgiveness in return for getting payments back on schedule. The plan was a success. Eighteen countries signed on to the Brady plan agreed to domestic economic reforms that would enable them to service their remaining debt, and lenders forgave $61 billion in loans, about one-third of the total outstanding debt. However, it would take many years for the memories and effects of this crisis to fade.[23]

BLACK MONDAY (1987)

The term *Black Monday* most commonly refers to Monday, October 19, 1987, when stock markets around the world crashed. October 28, 1929, was also called a Black Monday followed by a Black Tuesday the next day, when the stock market crash kicked off the Great Depression. In 1987, however, times were different. Markets were interconnected, and computers were taking over trading. Many people think that Black Monday was a U.S. event, but, in fact, it was worldwide. It began in Hong Kong and spread west to Europe before hitting the United States like a tsunami and shaving off 22 percent of the Dow's value in one afternoon[24] (Figures 2.5 and 2.6).

Stock markets around the world kicked off 1987 with a bang. The DJIA gained 44 percent in the first seven months of the year. Other markets were on a similar trajectory. By October, market momentum began to fizzle, with a number of markets starting to incur large daily losses. On October 19, stock

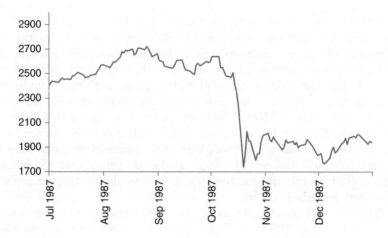

FIGURE 2.5   Black Monday—Dow Jones Industrial Average from July to
December 1987
Adapted from: Bloomberg

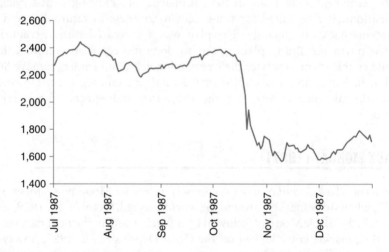

FIGURE 2.6   Black Monday—FTSE 100 Index from July to December 1987
Adapted from: Bloomberg

markets around the world crashed, beginning in Hong Kong and spreading
to Europe, then the United States, as markets opened that day. The DJIA
incurred its largest ever daily loss of 508 points, or a loss of roughly
22.6 percent.[25] By the end of October, the stock market in Hong Kong
had lost 45.5 percent, Australia 41.8 percent, Spain 31 percent, the
United Kingdom 26.5 percent, the United States 22.7 percent, and Canada
22.5 percent.[26]

Was this a sudden crash, or were there factors leading up to it? Some market watchers have blamed Black Monday on computerized trading, but a closer look at the events leading up to Black Monday tells a different story.

The mid-1980s was a great time to be on Wall Street. It was a time of greed, excess, and Andy Warhol–style pop culture. This period was glorified in the 1987 movie, *Wall Street*. Junk bonds were in vogue as well as stocks trading on the market. In 1986 total corporate bond issuance reached $200 billion, more than double the amount of the bonds issued in the previous year, and issuance showed no sign of slowing down. However, what was more in vogue than junk bonds was insider trading.

In 1987, insider trading and securities fraud were rampant on Wall Street. Popular firms at the time, such as Drexel Burnham Lambert, Kidder Peabody, PaineWebber, Shearson Lehman, Salomon Brothers, and E.F. Hutton & Co., which now no longer exist, were behind much of the greed on Wall Street. They were also being investigated and were indicted by the Securities and Exchange Commission (SEC) and other agencies. These firms were being hit with fines, and some of their traders were being sent to jail. Some of the biggest names on Wall Street involved in insider trading and fraud were Michael Milken, Ivan Boesky, Robert Wilkis, Carl Icahn, Randall Cecola, Robert Freeman, Martin Siegel, Lyndon LaRouche, and Gilbert Schulman, and the list goes on. The bottom line was that the game was rigged, and more and more people started to realize this and lose confidence in the markets. There was even the crazy story of the Wall Street law firm Davis, Polk & Wardwell operating a cocaine ring in its office.[27] These were definitely crazy times. It didn't help that the dollar was weakening at the same time and bond yields were shooting up. They went from 7.28 percent to 10.22 percent in nine months.[28] So I would strongly disagree with anyone who says the crash of 1987 was the result of computerized trading.

In the midst of the turmoil, the Fed offered liquidity to the market and encouraged banks to continue to lend to one another on their usual terms. Even though the banks lost money at this, they continued to do so at the Fed's request in order to preserve the financial system. Some experts suggest that the Fed's response to the crash returned confidence to the market, helping the DJIA recover the losses of Black Monday within the following two years.

After Black Monday, regulators overhauled trade-clearing protocols and developed circuit breakers, allowing exchanges to halt trading temporarily in instances of large price declines, to avoid panic selling.

U.S. SAVINGS AND LOAN CRISIS (1989–1991)

The savings and loan (S&L) crisis started in the early 1980s, but it was incremental and did not balloon until the late 1980s. Regulators had initially turned a blind eye to the growing problem, hoping it would resolve itself, but they were forced to act in 1989, when the problem started to get out of control. The seeds of this crisis were sown in 1980, when the Fed declared war on inflation. As interest rates rose, profits at S&Ls went negative. The cumulative losses for S&Ls in 1981 and 1982 were over $9 billion.[29] Some S&Ls began to fail, but regulators did not see this as a growing problem.

At the time, S&Ls faced two main problems. First, the interest rates that they could pay on deposits were fixed by the government and were set well below what depositors could earn elsewhere. This gave them a competitive disadvantage, as they were losing depositors to banks paying higher interest rates. Second, S&Ls primarily made long-term fixed-rate mortgage loans. When interest rates shot up, these mortgages lost their value, which essentially wiped out the S&L industry's net worth.[30]

Regulators responded by passing the Depository Institutions Deregulation and Monetary Control Act of 1980, hoping that deregulation and increased competition were what the industry needed to survive. Regulators, however, did not have sufficient resources to handle the challenges these S&Ls were facing. As a result, one of their responses was to offer insolvent institutions forbearance—they allowed zombie S&Ls to remain open, covering up their accounting and hoping that they would work out their problems. They also reduced capital standards by relaxed legislation. Federally chartered S&Ls were allowed to make riskier loans other than residential mortgages; the regulators' thinking was that letting them chase higher returns would help them in the end.

As a result of these changes, the S&L industry experienced rapid growth. From 1982 to 1985, S&L industry assets grew 56 percent, more than twice the rate for banks during the same period. This growth was fueled by an influx of deposits, as zombie S&Ls offered exceptionally high interest rates to attract deposits. These institutions began investing in riskier and riskier projects, hoping they would pay off in higher returns and also be able to pay bank depositors their high interest rates. Keep in mind that many of these institutions were already insolvent, so engaging in these types of activities was reckless.

Much like Black Monday, there was also a lot of fraud occurring that involved some of the same players. Rather than admit to insolvency, lax regulatory oversight allowed some CEOs of S&Ls to operate Ponzi schemes using creative accounting strategies. In one case, Charles Keating, one of the poster boys for the S&L crisis, paid $51 million from Michael Milken's junk bond operation for Lincoln Savings and Loan, which at the time had a negative net worth exceeding $100 million.[31] In another case, the Federal Savings and Loan Insurance Corporation (FSLIC), the institution set up to provide deposit insurance to S&Ls, decided it was cheaper to burn down unfinished condos that a bankrupt Texas S&L had financed rather than try to sell them.[32]

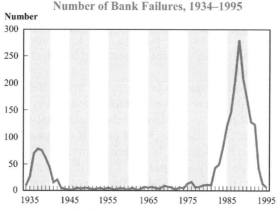

FIGURE 2.7 U.S. bank failures 1934 to 1995
Source: FDIC

The delayed closure of insolvent S&Ls made the crisis escalate. Regulators could have avoided such a large crisis by closing down zombie institutions in 1983. Instead, Congress chose to keep them on life support and look the other way, compounding the problem and putting off dealing with it for another day.

By the late 1980s, Congress had finally decided to address the industry's problems. In 1989, it passed the Financial Institutions Reform, Recovery and Enforcement Act, which instituted several reforms. The Federal Home Loan Bank Board, the main S&L regulator, was abolished, and the FSLIC was bankrupt. To replace them, Congress created the Office of Thrift Supervision and placed S&L deposit insurance under the Federal Deposit Insurance Corporation (FDIC), which already insured banks. In addition, the Resolution Trust Corporation (RTC) was established and funded to resolve the remaining troubled S&Ls. The crisis came to its end when the RTC was officially closed down on December 31, 1995. During its tenure, the RTC closed 747 S&Ls with assets of over $407 billion, as you can see in Figure 2.7. This crisis cost taxpayers more than $124 billion.[33]

JAPANESE ASSET BUBBLE COLLAPSE (1990s)

Within two decades following the end of World War II, Japan's economy had been rebuilt and transformed into an industrial powerhouse. In the 1970s and 1980s, Japan had one of the fastest-growing economies and its per capita income had risen to become one of the highest in the world. The formula for Japan's economic miracle had been admired and studied, and even emulated by other countries. The main reasons for its success were government's hand-in-hand support for manufacturing, high technology, and other export-driven industries.

This success created demand for industrial and commercial real estate, not to mention residential real estate, which Japan had in limited supply. By the late 1980s, real estate prices had reached catastrophic levels. By 1991, commercial land prices had risen 302.9 percent compared to 1985, while residential land and industrial land prices jumped 180.5 percent and 162.0 percent, respectively, compared to 1985.[34] In 1989, the total value of Japanese real estate reached $24 trillion, or four times the value of all the real estate in the United States, in a country smaller than the state of California[35] (Figure 2.8).

Japanese companies were also generating large amounts of cash due to the success of their exports. This cash needed to be invested, not only in Japan but elsewhere around the world. The United States was a major recipient of Japanese investments—so much so that there was some political paranoia going around at the time suggesting that Japan was out to crush U.S. industries and buy up the country. Some of this money, however, stayed in Japan and was pumped into local real estate, banks, and the stock market. A bubble quickly formed in the stock market. From 1984 to the end of 1989, the Nikkei 225 Index had risen nearly 400 percent (Figure 2.9).

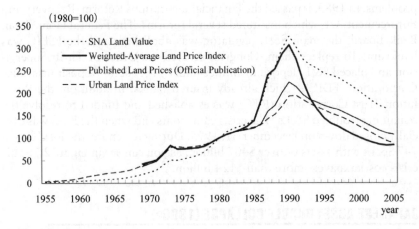

FIGURE 2.8 Real estate bubble in Japan
Source: The Bank of Japan

FIGURE 2.9 Japan's stock market bubble—Nikkei 225 from 1970 to 2014
Adapted from: Bloomberg

Not recognizing that this bubble was unsustainable until it was too late, the Bank of Japan (BoJ) sharply raised interest rates in late 1989. Not only did this expedite the bursting of the real estate bubble, it also led to a stock market crash. As you can see from Figures 2.8 and 2.9, Japanese real estate and stock market prices are nowhere near the prices they were at in the late 1980s and show no signs of getting close to those levels.

Immediately following the collapse in real estate and stock market prices, a debt crisis ensued, taking down with it the highly indebted Japanese banks and insurance companies. The financial institutions were bailed out through capital infusions from the government and loans from the Bank of Japan. To make it easier on the banks, the Bank of Japan also allowed these struggling institutions to postpone the recognition of losses. This only made matters worse, since real estate prices never recovered, and it ultimately turned these financial institutions into zombie banks. Hoping for a quick recovery, the Bank of Japan kept injecting more money into unprofitable zombie firms to keep them afloat, arguing that they were too big to fail. However, most of these institutions had such high bad-debt levels that they could barely survive on the bailout funds, much less return to growth. Some economists believe that this was one of the reasons Japan's economy stagnated for such a long time after.[36]

Eventually, many of these failing firms became unsustainable, and a wave of consolidation took place, resulting in four national banks in Japan.

This period of Japan's economic stagnation, in the 1990s and, some suggest, even up to now, has been labeled the "lost decade(s)."

There were other factors on the global scene that would make matters worse not only for Japan but for the rest of the world. In 1990, the United States was in the middle of tackling the S&L crisis, which also had an effect on its main trading partners—Europe, Canada, and Japan. On August 2, 1990, however, the weakness in the global economy finally hit a wall after Saddam Hussein drove his army into Kuwait. Oil prices quickly doubled, causing severe strain on the global economy, which led to recessions in many countries of the industrialized world, including the United States and Japan.

The United States–led coalition drove Saddam out of Kuwait in February 1991, liberating Kuwait and calming oil markets. Saddam, however, left behind 700 burning oil wells, resulting in one of the worst deliberate environmental disasters in history.[37]

The effects of high oil prices also helped pop other fragile bubbles, in Sweden and Finland. Both countries had banking crises in 1990, which were caused by easy lending practices. Once these bubbles popped, regulators stepped in to nationalize some banks, while others were bailed out.

MEXICAN PESO CRISIS (1994)

Mexico had its "lost decade" in the 1980s during the Latin American debt crisis. In the early 1990s, the Mexican economy seemed healthy. The economy was growing, and inflation had been falling from the highs of the 1980s. The country regained the confidence of foreign investors, and they were once again investing in the country. On top of these positive developments, Mexico, the United States, and Canada signed the North American Free Trade Agreement (NAFTA), which took effect at the beginning of 1994. The agreement was set to reduce trade barriers, boosting trade and investment among the countries. The hard times of the 1980s seemed to be history. However, less than 12 months after NAFTA took effect, Mexico faced another financial crisis. On December 20, 1994, the Mexican government devalued the peso, cutting its value in half, sparking inflation, and sending the country into a severe recession[38] (Figure 2.10).

Fearing a repeat of the 1980s Latin American debt crisis and to stop any possible contagion, the U.S. government stepped in to bail out Mexico. The United States' assistance was provided via the U.S. Treasury's Exchange Stabilization Fund (ESF). The total size of the bailout was set at $50 billion, which included assistance from the IMF and the BIS. This was slightly controversial, as President Bill Clinton tried and failed to pass the Mexican Stabilization Act through Congress. However, the ESF had a provision allowing disbursement of funds without the approval of Congress.

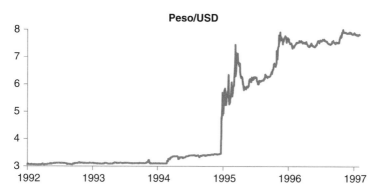

FIGURE 2.10 Mexican peso crisis—Peso/U.S. dollar exchange rate from 1992 to 1997
Adapted from: Bloomberg

The Mexican bailout attracted criticism not only in the U.S. Congress but also from the media for the role of U.S. Treasury Secretary Robert Rubin, a former cochairman of Goldman Sachs. Rubin used a Treasury Department account under his personal control to buy $20 billion in Mexican bonds as part of the ESF. Goldman Sachs played a key role in facilitating these bond purchases.[39]

The quick action of the bailout was successful at stopping any contagion and actually lessened the severity of the recession. By 1996, the economy was growing, reaching 7 percent growth in 1999. In 1997, Mexico repaid all U.S. Treasury loans ahead of schedule. By the end of the crisis, the United States had made a $500 million profit on the loans.[40]

ASIAN FINANCIAL CRISIS (1997)

The Asian financial crisis of 1997 was one of the worst financial crises to hit Southeast Asia in recent memory. It quickly raised fears of a worldwide economic meltdown due to the speed of the contagion. The crisis affected all Southeast Asian countries along with some developing countries.

Just before the crisis hit, Asia had been attracting almost half of the total capital inflow into developing countries, or roughly $93 billion per year.[41] The economies of Southeast Asia in particular received most of these capital flows, as they had a policy of maintaining high interest rates, which attracted foreign investors looking for higher returns. Many of these countries also maintained fixed exchange rates pegged to the dollar or a basket of major currencies, which was also attractive to foreign investors. Thailand, Malaysia, Indonesia, Singapore, and South Korea experienced high growth rates ranging from 8 to 12 percent of GDP in the late 1980s and early 1990s. Thus, it was no surprise to see a dramatic run-up in asset prices, particularly in real estate and stock markets. The IMF and the World Bank celebrated this success, calling it the "Asian economic miracle."

Asset bubbles were forming across the region, but economists and regulators were blinded by the rapid growth in GDP, even though by the mid-1990s GDP growth had started to slow. At the time, Thailand, Indonesia, and South Korea developed large private current account deficits and put pressure on the fixed exchange rates system, which encouraged more and more foreign borrowing. This created excessive exposure to foreign exchange risk as well as an over-indebted financial system. From 1993 to 1996, debt-to-GDP ratios rose from 100 percent to 167 percent in the four large ASEAN* economies and continued to rise beyond 180 percent during the height of the crisis.[42]

The crisis struck in July 1997 after a speculative attack on the Thai baht followed by attacks on other regional currencies. The foreign ministers of the 10 ASEAN countries believed that the coordinated manipulation of their currencies was a deliberate attempt to destabilize the ASEAN economies.

From 1985 to 1996, Thailand's economy grew at an average rate of more than 9 percent per year, the highest economic growth rate of any country at the time. Inflation remained relatively low given the pace of the growth, staying within the range of 3.4 to 5.7 percent,[43] and the baht was pegged at 25 to the U.S. dollar. In June 1997, the Thai government pledged not to devalue the baht as a result of these speculative attacks. However, the government failed to defend the currency, which was pegged to the basket of currencies in which the U.S. dollar was the main component.

Without foreign reserves to support the currency peg, the Thai government was forced to float the baht, which quickly lost more than half its value against the U.S. dollar. Thailand's booming economy came to a halt amid massive layoffs in banking, real estate, and construction. In addition to the currency depreciation, the Thai stock market lost 75 percent of its value during the crisis and the country's largest financial institution, Finance One, collapsed.[44]

The crisis quickly spread to neighboring countries. Indonesia, South Korea, and Thailand were affected the most. However, Hong Kong, Malaysia, Laos, and the Philippines were also affected by the crisis.

---

*Association of Southeast Asian Nations (ASEAN) members include Brunei, Burma, Cambodia, Indonesia, Laos, Malaysia, the Philippines, Singapore, Thailand, and Vietnam.

All these countries saw their currencies depreciate to varying degrees and likewise saw their stock markets and real estate values drop. Other countries in the region, such as China, Taiwan, Singapore, Brunei, and Vietnam, were affected less but suffered from a loss of demand and confidence along with their neighbors. All told, the $93 billion that was once coming into the region quickly became $12 billion flowing out of the region in 1998.[45]

Malaysia, however, reacted differently to the crisis than its neighbors did. It was the only country to refuse IMF bailout money. Before the crisis, Malaysia had a large current account deficit of 5 percent of its GDP and was one of the more popular investment destinations for foreign investors. By the end of 1997, the crisis had already spread to Malaysia. Both the country's stock market and its currency, the ringgit, had lost 50 percent of their value. The ringgit, once stable at 2.50 to the dollar, fell to 4.57 in January 1998.

The prime minister at the time, Mahathir Mohammad, imposed strict capital controls, introduced a 3.80 peg against the U.S. dollar, stopped the overseas trade in the ringgit, and imposed a minimum one-year "stay period" for foreign portfolio funds to discourage hot money from coming into the country.[46]

In 1998, the output of the real economy declined, plunging the country into its first recession in years. The construction sector contracted 23.5 percent, manufacturing shrunk 9 percent, and the agriculture sector declined by 5.9 percent. Overall, the country's GDP dropped 6.2 percent in 1998. Various task force agencies were formed and bad debts were restructured. Growth then settled at a slower but more sustainable pace. The once high current account deficit developed into a $14 billion surplus by 2005.[47]

Large banks were better capitalized, and smaller banks were bought out or merged with stronger ones. Asset values, however, have not returned to their precrisis highs. In 2005, the ringgit was taken off the fixed exchange rate system and put on a managed float system, like the Singapore dollar. This was the last of the remaining crisis measures.

As for the rest of the countries in the region, they opted for an IMF bailout. The IMF came up with a $40 billion program to stabilize the currencies of South Korea, Thailand, and Indonesia. The efforts to stem the spread of the crisis did little to stabilize the domestic situation in Indonesia. In May 1998, the collapse of the rupiah led to sharp price increases, which caused widespread rioting across the country. After 30 years in power, President Suharto was forced to step down.

Afterward, the IMF created a series of bailouts for the most-affected economies to enable affected nations to avoid default, tying the packages to currency, banking, and financial system reforms. The IMF asked that crisis-struck nations reduce government spending and deficits, allow insolvent banks and financial institutions to fail, and aggressively raise interest rates. The reasoning was that these steps would restore confidence in the nations' fiscal solvency, penalize insolvent companies, and protect currency values.

The dynamics of the situation were similar to those of the Latin American debt crisis. The effects of the bailouts were mixed and their impact controversial. Some critics, however, questioned the contractionary nature of these policies, arguing that, in a recession, the traditional Keynesian response was to increase government spending, prop up major companies, and lower interest rates.

The "Asian flu" had also put pressure on the United States and Japan. Their markets did not collapse, but they were hit nonetheless. After the Asian crisis, international investors were reluctant to lend to developing countries, leading to an economic slowdown across emerging markets. The crisis also led to a significant drop in the price of oil, which reached a low of about $11 per barrel toward the end of 1998. This caused a financial pinch in OPEC members and other oil exporters. More important, the reduction in oil revenue contributed to the 1998 Russian financial crisis, which is discussed next.

By 2001, most countries recovered from the crisis and were growing again. Their current account balances were adjusted, currencies were stabilized, and company finances were in good shape. Some countries, such as Thailand, were able to repay their debts to the IMF four years ahead of schedule. Foreign investors once again began returning to the region, albeit more cautiously.

The crisis, however, hit Asia hard, and the effects would not be forgotten anytime soon. In nominal terms, at the height of the crisis, U.S. dollar GDP per capita fell a staggering 42.3 percent in Indonesia, 21.2 percent in Thailand, 19 percent in Malaysia, 18.5 percent in South Korea, and 12.5 percent in the Philippines.[48]

RUSSIAN RUBLE CRISIS (1998)

The Asian financial crisis spread across Southeast Asia like wildfire. It also spread to a lesser degree to other countries, as mentioned earlier. Some of these effects were instant, such as a drop in stock prices around the world; some effects developed over time, one of which was the drop in oil prices. The effect of the drop in oil prices wasn't immediately felt in oil-producing countries. A prolonged rise or fall in oil prices takes months to make its way into the economy. Short dips or spikes, on the other hand, typically do not have any effects on oil producers or the world economy.

However, as a result of the dramatic slowdown in Asian economies, the price of oil dropped by more than 50 percent, from a high of $22 per barrel

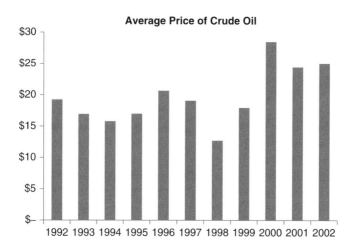

FIGURE 2.11   Average price of crude oil from 1992 to 2002
Source: BP Statistical Review of World Energy 2014

in October 1997 to a low of $10.9 per barrel in December 1998. The average price of oil in 1997 was $20.6 per barrel compared with an average price of $14.4 per barrel in 1999, as shown in Figure 2.11.

Oil-producing countries were affected by this two-year slump in oil price. Not only did it reduce their income, but it also led to a financial crisis, as was the case for Russia.

In 1998, Russia was facing several challenges internally. It was busy fighting a war in Chechnya, there was a political crisis brewing sparked by Russian president Boris Yeltsin's sudden dismissal of Prime Minister Viktor Chernomyrdin, and the country had dwindling foreign currency reserves. On top of this, there was also a coal miners' strike, which exacerbated the growing political crisis. The miners were on strike because of unpaid wages.

At the time, Russia's ruble was on a "floating peg," which meant that the Central Bank set the floating range but could change it at any time. The ruble was allowed to fluctuate within a set band against the U.S. dollar. If there was any threat that the ruble might drop out of the band, the Central Bank would intervene by spending foreign reserves to buy rubles. Before the crisis, the band was set at 5.3 to 7.1 RUR/USD, meaning that it would buy rubles if the market exchange rate threatened to exceed 7.1 rubles per dollar. Similarly, it would sell rubles if the market exchange rate threatened to drop below 5.3.

In August 1998, a financial crisis hit Russia. It was later revealed that between October 1997 and August 1998, the Central Bank had spent close

FIGURE 2.12 Russian stock market from 1996 to 2001
Adapted from: Bloomberg

to $27 billion of its U.S. dollar reserves to maintain the floating peg. The drop in reserves as well as the drop in income the country was getting from oil exports made foreign investors nervous, especially since the Asian financial crisis was still going on. Fearing a ruble devaluation, foreign investors fled, causing the stock, bond, and currency markets to collapse. Annual yields on the ruble-denominated bonds shot up to more than 200 percent. From January to August 1998, the stock market had lost more than 75 percent of its value, 39 percent in the month of May alone (Figure 2.12).

In September 1998, the Central Bank decided to abandon the "floating peg" policy and float the ruble freely. By the end of September, the exchange rate had reached 21 rubles for 1 U.S. dollar, meaning it had lost two-thirds of its value in less than a month (Figure 2.13). Inflation took off, welfare costs shot up, and several banks were closed down, including Inkombank, Oneximbank, and Tokobank. Russia would also default on its bonds.

Russia, however, bounced back from the financial crisis with surprising speed. Much of the reason for the recovery is that world oil prices rapidly rose during the period from 1999 to 2000. Another reason is that domestic industries, such as food processing, had benefited from the devaluation, which caused a steep increase in the prices of imported goods.[49]

The Russian ruble crisis resulted in some contagion. The Dow Jones Industrial Average fell 984 points, or 11.5 percent, in three days at the end of August 1998. The U.S. stock market remained depressed until October, when a series of interest rate reductions by the Federal Reserve propelled it

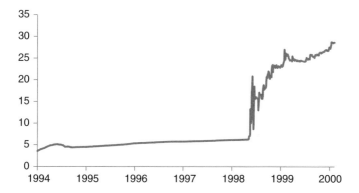

FIGURE 2.13   Ruble/U.S. dollar exchange rate 1995 to 2000
Adapted from: Bloomberg

back upward.[50] However, the most notable victim of the crisis outside of Russia was a U.S. hedge fund called Long-Term Capital Management L.P. (LTCM).

LTCM was a hedge fund management firm based in Greenwich, Connecticut, founded in 1994 by John W. Meriwether, the former head of bond trading at Salomon Brothers. His board of directors included not one but two Nobel Prize–winning economists: Myron S. Scholes and Robert C. Merton. They were awarded the prize in 1997 for their new method of determining the value of derivatives.[51] They applied this method in the firm, which utilized absolute-return trading strategies combined with high financial leverage. The firm had been very successful since its launch. The firm's flagship fund, Long-Term Capital Portfolio L.P., reported an annual return of more than 21 percent in 1995, 41 percent in 1996, and 43 percent in 1997.

In 1998, the fund lost $4.6 billion in less than four months, blaming it on the Asian financial crisis and the Russian ruble crisis. The fund collapsed, sparking fears of a financial crisis in the United States. As a result, 14 financial institutions agreed to a $3.6 billion recapitalization (bailout) under the supervision of the Federal Reserve[52] in order to contain the fallout. Both Wall Street and the Fed feared the spread of this crisis, since many of the leading Wall Street firms had exposure to LTCM, either through investing in one of the firm's funds or, more likely, providing the high leverage needed for the fund to carry out its strategy.

The crisis was contained, and LTCM was ultimately closed down. However, this did not stop Meriwether from trying his strategy again. He launched a new firm called JWM Partners, which would continue many of LTCM's strategies, but this time would use less leverage. From

September 2007 to February 2009, the firm's fund lost 44 percent, prompting redemptions and, ultimately, the firm's closure in July 2009. This time, the global financial crisis was blamed for the strategy's failure.[53]

THE DOT-COM BUBBLE OF 2000

The dot-com bubble was a historic speculative bubble, which I consider to be the tulip mania of our time. The words of Walter Bagehot were as true here as they were back in the 1800s. This time, however, the mania began in the mid-1990s with the rise of the Internet and climaxed in March 2000.

The boom started after the launch of the Mosaic web browser in 1993, which allowed the masses to access the World Wide Web. This created seemingly endless opportunities for entrepreneurs, "techies," and venture capitalists to turn them into customers. The potential to commercialize the Internet further accelerated investment in Internet-based companies. By the late 1990s, venture capitalists were investing heavily in this new industry and taking these companies public by way of initial public offerings (IPOs) as fast as they could. Once public, these companies experienced meteoric rises in their stock prices, which only encouraged more companies to follow suit.

The low interest rates in 1998 and 1999 helped encourage investors to seek higher returns in riskier asset classes. As the amount of available start-up capital swelled, fundamental business principles went out the window and were replaced with a new "dot-com" business model, which relied on operating at a sustained net loss and the drive to build market share. This, after all, was the "new economy," and new rules were being applied. These companies offered their products or services for free with the expectation that they could build enough brand awareness to charge profitable rates for their services later. Common terms that were used at the time included *eyeballs* and *clicks,* referring to numbers of potential customers exposed to a product or service via a website, which were used to value a dot-com company and justify its business model.

At the height of the boom, it was normal for a dot-com company to make an IPO of its stock and raise millions of dollars even though it had never made a profit or, in some cases, had any revenue. Under this new business model, a company's life span was measured by its burn rate—the rate at which an unprofitable company lacking a viable business model spent its capital. At one point, the key factor for a successful IPO seemed to be having an "e" at the beginning of the company's name or a ".com" at the end.

Not surprisingly, the "growth over profits" mentality and the aura of "new economy" invincibility led some companies to spend lavishly—for example, on elaborate business facilities and luxury vacations for employees. Each new dot-com company would try to outspend the next in outrageous public relations stunts aimed at getting more eyeballs and clicks on their websites. Executives and employees who were paid with stock options instead of cash became instant millionaires when the company made its IPO; many invested their new wealth into yet more dot-coms.

This phenomenon was not limited to Silicon Valley. It spread to other cities around the world that attempted to create the "next Silicon Valley." In Europe, capital was being invested in dot-coms, network operators, broadband operators, and technology parks from London to Helsinki. The same phenomenon caught on in Asia. In Malaysia, for example, the government spent heavily on building what it called the "Multimedia Super Corridor," which was its answer to Silicon Valley.

In 1999, the Fed began to raise interest rates. From 1999 to 2000, the Fed raised rates six times, and the economy began to lose momentum.[54] On March 10, 2000, the technology-heavy NASDAQ Composite Index peaked at 5,048.62, more than double its value just a year before. From then on, the NASDAQ began to lose value. The bubble had effectively popped, as you can see in Figure 2.14.

As the economy slowed and interest rates rose, the pile of money waiting to be invested in dot-com companies began to shrink. Over the next 12 months, scores of highflying start-ups used up all their cash and were unable to raise more to continue their burn rate. By 2001, the bubble

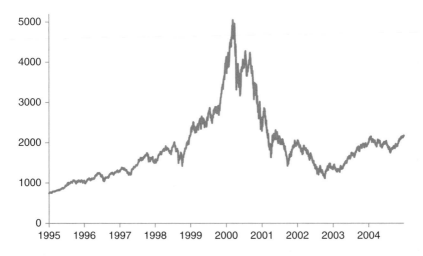

FIGURE 2.14 The NASDAQ Composite Index from 1995 to 2004
Adapted from: Bloomberg

was deflating at full speed. Once these companies ran out of cash to burn, many ceased trading on the exchange and went out of business. Some of the highflying names at the time that went bust are Pets.com, Boo.com, theGlobe.com, and Excite@Home. Other profitable companies lost large percentages, such as Cisco Systems, which lost 86 percent of its value, once the dust settled. Stock markets and technology companies around the world suffered. The NASDAQ alone lost 78 percent of its value from March 2000 to October 2002, wiping out over $5 trillion in market capitalization.[55] Fourteen years later, the NASDAQ has yet to reach the high of March 2000.

What was different about the dot-com bust, however, was that it was primarily equity based, meaning that there was little debt involved. Banks were not lending to start-ups; they were being funded by equity from venture capital companies and eventually from people buying their shares on the stock market. As a result, the bust was severe but contained to the technology industry. It also meant that there was little contagion to other sectors of the economy, helping the economy recover quickly. The recession that ensued lasted eight months, and peak unemployment reached only 6.3 percent. By 2003, the economy was back on track again.

SOME OBSERVATIONS ON PAST FINANCIAL CRISES

After looking at some of the major financial crises of our time, it is easy to see patterns in how bubbles are formed and crises are sparked. The economies of the world are more interconnected than they have ever been in human history. A characteristic of financial crises in our current financial system is that bubbles created in one market pop and move on to create bubbles in other markets. Take, for example, the oil crisis in the 1970s. High oil prices caused high inflation and stagnation in the United States, but the huge amounts of dollars OPEC countries received were being sent back to the United States for safekeeping at U.S. banks. These banks, in turn, needed to find places to invest this money. Latin America seemed like a wise choice at the time due to the higher rates they could earn there.

Low interest rates in the United States in the 1990s made investing in emerging markets more attractive for U.S. investors, helping to develop the bubble in Asia, which then led to the Asian financial crisis. The drop in oil prices from this crisis helped spark the Russian ruble crisis and the collapse of one of the highflying hedge funds in the United States. These same low interest rates helped pour money into dot-com companies in the late 1990s as the boom in the Internet just started to take off. The mania that ensued led many investors to throw their investment fundamentals out the window in order to participate in it.

If we look at the cycle we are in, we can see that we are going from boom to bust in a shorter amount of time than we think. Counting only the aforementioned nine crises from 1973 to 2000, we have had a major financial crisis in the world every three years on average!

Another characteristic of popping bubbles is that once they pop, all kinds of criminal activities are revealed. In each and every speculative bubble, there have been cases of fraud, theft, and misleading of investors. Take, for example, Black Monday in 1987; it didn't take the market crash to bring to light all the insider trading, fraud investigations, and criminal activities. They were rampant well before the crash. However, during the euphoria of all the money being made, it's easy to overlook a few shady deals.

The S&L crisis revealed similar fraudulent activities, which affected the economy more than the market crash just a couple of years earlier. During the dot-com bust, even greater fraudulent activities were revealed. The names of three firms became synonymous with fraud in the post-dot-com world: Enron, WorldCom, and Arthur Andersen. The trend of bigger booms and bigger busts coupled with bigger frauds continues, as we shall see.

SUMMARY

- The Great Depression was the worst financial crisis the world has seen in the past 100 years.
- Easy credit may have helped form the bubble, but the government's inaction before the crisis combined with the government's poor policies after the crisis made the problem much bigger than it needed to be.
- Financial crises since the world went on a fiat currency have been more frequent than we imagine, averaging one major crisis every three years.
- The oil crisis of the 1970s helped fuel the next crisis, which was the Latin American debt crisis in the early 1980s.
- Easy credit, lax oversight, and rampant fraud helped create Black Monday, the global stock market crash, followed by the savings and loan crisis in the United States.
- Similar easy credit and low interest rates not only created the massive asset bubble in Japan in the 1990s, which later led to two decades of stagnation in the country, but also led to hot money rushing to Southeast Asia, leading up to the Asian financial crisis.
- All of the crises so far have involved banks and debt to varying degrees except for the dot-com bubble in 2000, which was primarily equity

based, helping to stop contagion and limiting the length of time needed to recover.

■ The boom-and-bust cycle is one of the characteristics of our financial system; the bursting of one bubble sets the stage for the next bubble.

■ Fraud, insider trading, and other criminal activities, which seem hidden under the euphoric atmosphere of a bubble, become exposed once the bubble pops.

CHAPTER 3

The Global Financial Crisis of 2008

Back in my office in Chicago, the week of September 15, 2008, was a week filled with headlines and disbelief. Our business froze overnight, and all private equity transactions in the market were put in a permanent holding pattern until someone could figure out what was going on. All we could do at that point was watch the news and see how the rest of the events played out.

Not long after we heard that Lehman Brothers had filed for bankruptcy news surfaced that AIG, one of the oldest and largest insurance companies in the United States, was on the verge of collapse. Markets around the world were in turmoil. U.S. Treasury Secretary Henry Paulson was urged to submit a plan to rescue financial markets to avoid an all-out meltdown. On September 20, Paulson submitted a three-page proposal calling for the Treasury to purchase up to $700 billion in toxic mortgages and calm markets. The plan was rejected by the U.S. House of Representatives, which called it too short on details and told the Treasury to come up with a real plan to save the financial markets.[1] Fed President Ben Bernanke stressed to Congress the urgency of rescuing financial institutions, saying that "if we don't do this, we may not have an economy on Monday."[2]

Paulson went back to draw up a more detailed plan, while at the same time U.S. lawmakers started working on the Emergency Economic Stabilization Act, a comprehensive bill to bail out financial institutions and, it was hoped, save the economy. That same week, the FBI announced it was investigating Freddie Mac and Fannie Mae, the two quasi-governmental organizations set up to help Americans buy homes, for fraud, along with 26 other financial institutions.[3] AIG and Lehman were among the institutions under investigation.

On September 25, Washington Mutual was seized by the Federal Deposit Insurance Corporation (FDIC), making it the largest bank to fail in U.S. history. Its banking assets were sold to JPMorgan Chase for just $1.9 billion.[4] Contagion began to spread fast. On September 29, the Emergency Economic Stabilization Act was defeated in the House of Representatives, causing panic across world stock markets. The Dow Jones Industrial Average lost 777 points on that day.[5]

More than two weeks after the Lehman failure, on October 1, the House of Representatives passed an amended Emergency Economic Stabilization Act—all 451 pages of it. President Bush then signed it into law.[6] Though politicians may have felt relieved that they were able to pass the bill, world markets were not pleased. Stock markets continued their fall, and contagion was spreading to Europe even as bailout money was being handed out left and right. Paulson, who championed the purchase of toxic mortgages, quickly switched strategies and decided that Treasury money would be better spent recapitalizing banks instead of buying mortgages.

One month after the crisis began, it was already raging all over the world. I watched in amazement as trillions of dollars were handed out by governments and central banks hoping to save the global economy. The main question on my mind was how did we get to this point?

THE BUILDUP TO THE CRISIS

As I mentioned in Chapter 2, one of the characteristics of our current financial system is that as one bubble pops, it sets the wheels in motion for the next crisis. So, based on this, what was the bubble that popped and created this new financial crisis? For this, let's go back to the dot-com bust.

In December 1998, the Fed began to raise interest rates in an attempt to try to cool overheating stock markets in what the Fed chairman at the time, Alan Greenspan, referred to as "irrational exuberance"—to put it lightly. The Fed raised its discount rate from 4.75 percent in December 1998 to 6.5 percent by June 2000, shortly after the dot-com bubble popped. Some economists blamed this for killing the tech mania, but in reality we saw how caught up investors and the public were in the Internet boom. Nevertheless, the Fed put the brakes on further interest rate hikes for the rest of 2000 to see if markets would recover. However, markets didn't recover, and the economy began to slow. It was clear that the economy was headed for a recession, so in 2001 the Fed began lowering its discount rate, first to 6.5 percent, in January 2001. But then it quickly dropped the rate all the way down to a historic low at the time of 1.75 percent by December 2001 as the recession was in full swing, as shown in Figure 3.1.

The tragic events of September 11, 2001, were another factor in the Fed's further lowering of the rates because it feared a protracted recession resulting from the terrorist attacks. By the end of 2001, however, the economy was

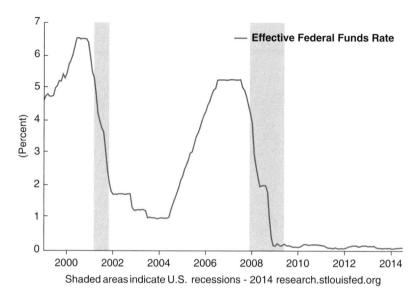

FIGURE 3.1   Fed discount rate from December 1998 to April 2014
Source: Federal Reserve Bank of St. Louis

officially out of recession, yet the Fed decided to maintain lower interest rates until the economy picked up speed. The United States was also at war in Afghanistan and was preparing to go to war with Iraq in March 2003. Not only did the Fed lower rates further before the U.S. invasion of Iraq, it also kept lowering rates until they reached a new record of just 1 percent in July 2003. The reasoning behind this drastic move was twofold. First, the economy had just started recovering from the tech bust and the Fed needed to keep rates low to energize the economy. Second, it wanted to preempt any negative effects the wars would have on the economy.

The Fed felt that the best way to get the economy moving again was to support the housing market. After all, one of the goals of President Bill Clinton in the 1990s was to help as many Americans as possible realize the American dream of home ownership. Various programs from the U.S. Department of Housing and Urban Development (HUD) were already in place. Incentives, subsidies, and other tax credits were established to help lower-income families buy homes. This included the mandates set for Freddie Mac and Fannie Mae, which were aimed at providing liquidity to mortgage lenders by way of buying the mortgages they issued, thus freeing up their balance sheets to lend more money for home purchases.

Through these programs and the Fed's record low interest rates, the housing market took off beyond what anyone had expected. The wealth

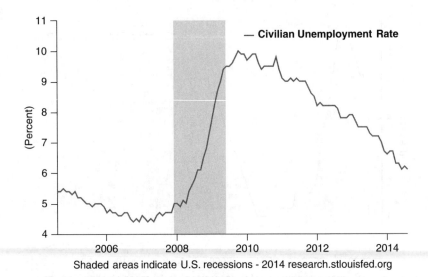

Shaded areas indicate U.S. recessions - 2014 research.stlouisfed.org

FIGURE 3.2   Unemployment rate from 2004 to 2014
Source: Federal Reserve Bank of St. Louis

effect was significant. The economy was on a steady growth trajectory, and the unemployment rate was dropping, eventually reaching a low of 4.4 percent in October 2006, as shown in Figure 3.2.

What was even more impressive was the nationwide rise in home values. As the country fell out of love with tech companies, it fell in love with housing and home ownership. Everybody wanted to own a home—in many cases, people wanted to own several homes. By 2006, housing seemed to be a sure bet. "You can never lose in this market" was the saying, and "home values never go down" was the thinking.

The Fed again felt the market mania take off and started to raise interest rates yet again beginning in July 2004. Rates peaked in July 2006, just after the housing market peaked in April 2006, as shown in Figure 3.3. Even though the housing market peaked, the mania and shady deals behind the scenes were just getting started.

The signs of a crisis, however, were already in plain view. In 2007, there were multiple signs of trouble ahead. Here are some of the major ones:[7]

- February: Freddie Mac announced that it would stop buying subprime mortgages.
- April: Subprime mortgage lender New Century Financial filed for bankruptcy.

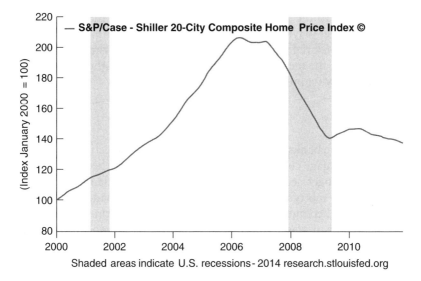

FIGURE 3.3   S&P/Case Shiller Home Price Index from 2000 to 2012
Source: Federal Reserve Bank of St. Louis, S&P Dow Jones Indices and CoreLogic

- July: Bear Stearns liquidated two hedge funds that had invested heavily in subprime mortgage loans.
- August: American Home Mortgage Investment, which specialized in adjustable-rate mortgages (ARMs), filed for bankruptcy.

By the time we entered 2008, it was too late. Once Bear Stearns collapsed that March, the crisis snowballed out of control. Few outside the banking industry saw the crisis coming. For those who did see it, ignoring the facts seemed to be the best strategy at the time.

ANATOMY OF A BUBBLE

In 2006, developers in some of the hottest housing markets were in full swing. From Miami to Las Vegas, developers were busy building thousands of new condos and single-family homes. There was no shortage of buyers. Many buyers jumped into the market simply to "flip" the property (i.e., resell it), in some cases even before it was finished being built. As prices kept rising, flipping became a good investment strategy. The purchasers no longer had any interest in living at the property; they were merely "investors" looking to sell the place as soon as they could get a higher price.

In addition to the property developers and buyers, there were at least three other parties playing along to ensure the mania continued: the lenders, government-sponsored enterprises, and Wall Street. All three played major roles in creating the mess, and all three took part in another major characteristic of a growing bubble: fraud.

The Lenders

It wasn't only the banks that were eager to lend to prospective home buyers; specialized mortgage companies were flourishing simply because a financial institution no longer needed to have its own capital or balance sheet in order to lend. Once a mortgage was issued, it would be offloaded to one of the government-backed agencies or sold to a Wall Street firm. Thus, for these mortgage issuers, it was a volume game; all they had to do was generate as many new mortgages as possible.

The period from 2002 to 2007 redefined the term *easy credit*. Banks and mortgage companies started to develop ever more creative ways to generate new business. The standard mortgage application and credit procedures, such as credit scores and income verification, went out the door. They were replaced with new mortgage products designed to lure buyers who normally would not qualify for a mortgage or, in many cases, would not be able to afford such an expensive home. The lenders' response to criticism that they were becoming predatory was brushed off; they contended that they were merely trying to help people realize their American dream.

One of the more popular mortgage products at the time was adjustable-rate mortgages (ARMs). These mortgages would offer low teaser rates, which were fixed for one year up to seven years and then would rise to the prevailing market rate once the fixed period expired. The attraction of these mortgages was the low rates that could be offered compared to a standard fixed-rate 15-year or 30-year loan. A lower interest rate meant that the borrower could afford to buy a more expensive house, since the payments would be lower.

Other mortgage products that were popular include low-doc and no-doc loans, which were commonly referred to as "subprime mortgages" due to their riskier nature. These loans do not require borrowers to provide proof of their income to lenders. Actually, they required very little documentation at all. They were designed for borrowers who do not qualify for normal loan products because of fluctuating or hard-to-verify incomes, such as the self-employed or those with little or no credit history, many of whom are immigrants.[8] In exchange, applicants are often required to provide higher down payments, and the loans carry higher interest rates. Nevertheless, at the peak of the housing bubble, subprime loans accounted for roughly 40

Subprime Mortgage Originations

In 2006, $600 billion in subprime loans were originated, most of which were securitized. That year, subprime lending accounted for 23.5% of all mortgage originations.

IN BILLIONS OF DOLLARS

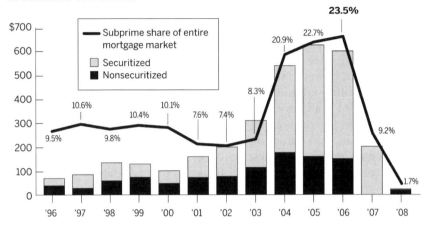

NOTE: Percent securitized is defined as subprime securities issued divided by originations in a given year. In 2007, securities issued exceeded originations.

FIGURE 3.4   Subprime mortgage issuance from 1996 to 2008
Source: The Financial Crisis Enquiry Report (http://www.gpo.gov/fdsys/pkg/GPO -FCIC/pdf/GPO-FCIC.pdf)

percent of newly issued mortgages in the United States.[9] In total, they represented 23.5 percent of all outstanding mortgages during the height of the boom, as shown in Figure 3.4.

It's easy to see here how the incentive for the lender was to issue as many mortgages as possible regardless of the quality. Lenders did this well. They did this so well, in fact, that in many cases fraud became rampant. I discuss some of the instances of fraud later in this chapter.

Government-Sponsored Enterprises (Freddie and Fannie)

The two leading government-sponsored enterprises (GSEs) are the Federal National Mortgage Association (FNMA), commonly known as Fannie Mae, and the Federal Home Loan Mortgage Corporation (FHLMC), known as Freddie Mac. Their goal was to provide liquidity to the secondary market for mortgages in the United States. Freddie and Fannie would buy mortgages on the secondary market, pool them, and sell them as a mortgage-backed security (MBS) to investors on the open market. This secondary mortgage market increases the supply of money available for mortgage lending and increases the money available for new home purchases. To make these pools for mortgages attractive for investors, Freddie and Fannie guaranteed that the principal and interest on the underlying loan would be paid back regardless of whether the borrower actually repays. They would also charge fees for these guarantees. By assuming the credit risk, these MBSs became very attractive to investors on Wall Street.[10]

The GSEs, however, were allowed to buy only conforming loans, which were loans with established criteria and credit standards. They also had a size limit of $417,000 for each mortgage. There were some exceptions to this limit, depending on the housing market. In more expensive housing markets, such as Hawaii, the conforming limit could rise as high as 50 percent above the national amount. With these established standards, the secondary market for nonconforming loans—that is, for loans that fell outside these criteria (aka subprime)—was very limited, with fewer buyers/investors.

The shift toward riskier mortgages and MBSs occurred as financial institutions sought to maintain earnings levels that had been elevated due to the historically low interest rates. Earnings depended on volume, so maintaining elevated earnings levels meant expanding the borrower pool using lower underwriting standards and new products that the GSEs could not, at that time, securitize. Thus, there was a huge shift toward private-label MBSs that did not carry the Freddie and Fannie guarantee. This led to a sharp deterioration in mortgage underwriting standards.[11] Freddie and Fannie were also in the volume game and didn't like seeing their earnings growth slow down, so they, in turn, lowered their underwriting standards in an attempt to reclaim lost market share.[12]

By 2006, the growth of private-label securitization and lack of regulation resulted in the oversupply of housing finance that led to an increasing number of borrowers who were unable to pay their mortgages, particularly those with ARMs. This caused an escalation in home foreclosures, leading to home price declines. This drop in home prices led to growing losses for the GSEs, which in 2008 had owned or guaranteed about half of the $12 trillion mortgage market in the United States.[13]

In July 2008, with mounting losses at both GSEs, the government attempted to ease market fears by reiterating its view that "Fannie Mae and Freddie Mac play a central role in the U.S. housing finance system." The U.S. Treasury Department and the Fed tried to bolster confidence in the GSEs by both granting access to Federal Reserve low-interest loans and removing the prohibition on the Treasury from purchasing GSE shares. Despite these efforts, by August 2008, shares of both Fannie and Freddie had tumbled more than 90 percent from their one-year-prior levels.[14] On September 7, the government took over the GSEs, effectively nationalizing them. This event alone should have sparked the panic, but it wasn't until a week later, with the Lehman failure, that the market's full-blown panic and eventual collapse were triggered.

Wall Street

Much like the other manias of our time, it's no surprise to see that Wall Street played a major role in this crisis. I would even argue that Wall Street played the leading role in this crisis. Wall Street investment banks were raking in millions from securitizing pools of mortgages. The motto at the time was that if it had a cash flow, it could be securitized. Not only mortgages were being securitized; the door had been pushed wide open for a variety of revenue streams to be securitized. Here are some of the more interesting ones:[15]

- David Bowie Bonds: securitization of David Bowie's music royalties.
- Bond Bonds: securitization of the revenue streams from James Bond movies.
- Calvin Klein: securitization of perfume trademark royalties.
- Guess? Inc.: securitization of trademark licensing agreements.
- Drug royalty securitization.
- Life settlement contracts: securitization of a pool of life settlement contracts.

So it wasn't a stretch of the imagination to see what Wall Street did next with mortgage-backed securities. It wasn't until the crisis had hit that I heard of CDOs and CDSs. These two terms would become synonymous with the mess Wall Street had created in the name of making money.

A collateralized debt obligation, or CDO, is a form of asset-backed security similar to an MBS (Figure 3.5). CDOs were created to solve one of the pressing problems for the Wall Street banks: how to sell the poor-quality mortgages to investors. By solving this problem they would be able to sell billions of junk mortgages to investors. Investors at the time preferred the safer MBSs guaranteed by Freddie and Fannie. The solution was to create the CDO. A CDO would lump together high-quality loans with lower-quality loans of varying degrees. The pool of high-quality loans would be lumped together and rated AAA, and the lower-quality loans pooled together would be rated junk, BB or less. Investment banks would take higher-rated pools and lump them together with lower-rated pools and still be able to keep a high rating.

Collateralized Debt Obligations

Collateralized debt obligations (CDOs) are structured financial instruments that purchase and pool financial assets such as the riskier tranches of various mortgage-backed securities.

3. CDO tranches

Similar to mortgage-backed securities, the CDO issues securities in tranches that vary based on their place in the cash flow waterfall.

1. Purchase

The CDO manager and securities firm select and purchase assets, such as some of the lower-rated tranches of mortgage-backed securities.

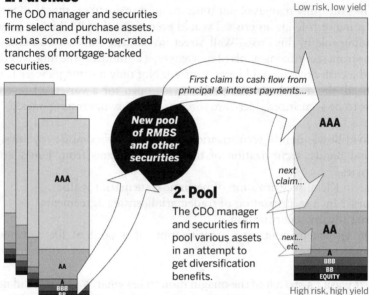

FIGURE 3.5   Collateralized debt obligations (CDOs) diagram
Source: The Financial Crisis Enquiry Report

A typical CDO would consist of approximately 80 percent AAA-rated loans, and the remainder would be sliced up into various other rated loans, as shown in Figure 3.5. CDO securities would be sold using a waterfall mechanism, another Wall Street innovation, whereby AAA investors would get paid first, followed by AA, and so on. If the riskier loans defaulted, the bottom pool of investors would be hit first, since they got paid last. In return, investors in the bottom-rated pools would get paid the highest interest rates, since they were taking on the riskiest loans. This worked out well for a while, as long as the markets were humming along and property values were still rising. The banks played out different scenarios to show how the CDOs would behave given certain delinquency and default ratios, none of which assumed an extreme case, such as a nationwide housing slump. As such, the rating agencies played along and gave their highest AAA ratings to the securities at the top.[16] Then investors bought these CDOs by the truckload.

To make these investments even more attractive, Wall Street came up with another innovation, the credit default swap (CDS). This turned out to be an even more lucrative moneymaker for Wall Street than CDOs.

Created in 1994,[17] a CDS is a financial derivative product designed to provide insurance to the buyer against default or loss from an investment. It is essentially a financial swap agreement that the seller of the CDS will compensate the buyer in the event of a loan default or other credit event. The buyer of the CDS makes a series of payments to the seller. In the event of default, the buyer receives a payoff, such as the face value of the loan, and the seller of the CDS takes possession of the defaulted loan.

On the face of it, CDSs seem like a good instrument to have—after all, they provide investors with protection in case their investments don't pan out. However, here's where Wall Street got creative: Anyone can purchase a CDS, even buyers who do not hold the loan instrument and who have no direct insurable interest in the loan.[18] These are called *naked CDSs*. So a bank or investor with no interest in your mortgage can buy a CDS, which gives them a payout if you default. Why would anyone with no interest in a particular loan or investment want to hold insurance against loss unless they are hoping it loses?

Another feature of the CDS is that it can be sold or assigned to another investor, thus creating a secondary tradable market for these instruments. CDSs can be traded and packaged into CDS pools and carved out and repackaged into other derivative products.

It didn't take long before CDSs were being used to encourage investors to jump into riskier markets such as Latin America and Russia by insuring their debt. Later, after corporate scandals and the busts of Enron and WorldCom, it became clear there was a big need for protection against company implosions. Wall Street came to the rescue with CDSs to protect against such defaults. CDSs exploded on the market, dwarfing the size of the U.S. stock market. In 2000, the total size of the CDS market was roughly $100 billion. By 2004, the market had grown to $6.4 trillion, and, by 2007, the total size of the CDS market reached a dizzying $45.5 trillion, as shown in Figure 3.6. By this time, investors and hedge funds were buying and selling CDSs on every type of investment, regardless of whether they had an interest in the underlying performance of the loan or asset. The best way to describe this scenario is to say that it was the largest casino in the world.

Taking both the CDO and CDS markets into account, the picture of how Wall Street blew up once the housing market dropped becomes clearer.

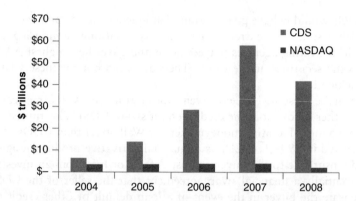

FIGURE 3.6 Growth of CDS market compared with the growth in market capitalization of the NASDAQ exchange
Source: Bank for International Settlements and World Federation of Exchanges

As delinquency rates in these CDOs rose above what the bank had modeled in its scenarios, the entire CDO with its waterfall blew up. Cashing in the CDSs became a nightmare, since tracking down which CDS belonged to which CDO was a challenge. The unwinding of these two instruments created a huge mess. This is where AIG got stuck. The $85 billion bailout of AIG was simply to help keep it from falling apart from the CDS payouts it had to make. This is where the term *systemic risk* came into the spotlight. The collapse of AIG would have brought down the entire Wall Street casino.

In actuality, the global financial crisis was not caused by the subprime mortgage problem in the United States. It was caused by an out-of-control derivatives market. Total losses from subprime mortgages amounted to less than $300 million, whereas total losses from CDOs, CDSs, and other derivatives reached more than $6 trillion.[19] The magnitude of derivatives losses dwarfed losses in mortgages. The lack of transparency in the derivatives market combined with the lack of regulation are the main reasons regulators did not see the crisis coming, nor did they understand the size of the problem. This is also why the bailouts switched from helping out Main Street to helping out Wall Street.

FRAUD

Another characteristic of a mania is that fraud becomes rampant. In this mania there was a lot of fraud going on and all parties were involved. It's easy to see how home buyers were lying about their income and the source of their down payment. Some of these down payments were actually other loans shown to banks as savings in order to qualify for the mortgage. However, it's even more interesting to see how the three players played their roles in the fraud.

The Lenders

These easy credit policies—or more like no credit policies—opened the door to all kinds of fraud. I've had firsthand experience with what went on back then during my time working at HSBC Bank in New York from 2001 to 2004. In addition to having its own mortgage department, which primarily handled conforming mortgages, the bank also handled a lot of adjustable-rate mortgages. Overall, the bank had pretty decent underwriting procedures, unlike some of its competitors. The underwriting and credit process to qualify for a confirming mortgage was straightforward. These loans offered the lowest rates other than the ARMs. To qualify, borrowers needed to have high credit scores and provide three years of tax returns. A similar process was in place for the ARMs. The key attraction of the ARM, however, was that the borrower would qualify for a larger and more expensive home, since the monthly payments would be lower.

The potential for fraud here would come from three different sources: the buyer, the lender, and the appraiser. In many cases, the prospective home buyer would not qualify for a mortgage, so the bank salesperson would encourage the buyer to lie on the application. In some cases, the salesperson would get in touch with a tax preparer and rewrite the buyer's tax returns to show the required amount of income. If the value of the home was not in line with what it needed to be, the appraiser was told what value to place on the property. In the end, everybody was happy: The home buyer got the house, the salesperson got the commission, the tax preparer got a fee, the appraiser got a fee, and the bank got the mortgage, which it could sell to Wall Street. For the shadier mortgage banks and mortgage brokers, this was the business model.

Government-Sponsored Enterprises (Freddie Mac and Fannie Mae)

Freddie Mac and Fannie Mae were familiar with the way Washington worked. Both GSEs gave contributions to lawmakers sitting on committees that primarily regulate their industry: the House Financial Services Committee; the Senate Banking, Housing and Urban Affairs Committee; and the Senate Finance Committee. This, however, did not protect them in the end when it came to fraud.

In 2003, Freddie understated earnings by almost $5 billion, one of the largest corporate accounting restatements in U.S. history. It was fined $125 million for this incident.[20] In 2004, Fannie was under investigation for its accounting practices. The Office of Federal Housing Enterprise Oversight released a report in September 2004 alleging widespread accounting errors.[21]

In 2006, Freddie was fined $3.8 million for illegal campaign contributions. The illegal fund-raising benefited members of the House Financial Services Committee, a panel whose decisions could affect Freddie Mac.[22]

In December 2006, regulators filed 101 civil charges against Fannie's CEO, Franklin Raines; CFO, J. Timothy Howard; and controller, Leanne Spencer. The three were accused of manipulating earnings to maximize their bonuses. The lawsuit sought to recoup more than $115 million in bonus payments, collectively accrued by the trio from 1998 to 2004, and about $100 million in penalties for their involvement in the accounting scandal. Eight years later, however, in 2012, a summary judgment cleared the trio, citing the government's insufficient evidence.[23]

In December 2011, six Fannie Mae and Freddie Mac executives, including Daniel Mudd, were charged by the Securities and Exchange Commission with securities fraud. "The SEC alleges they 'knew and approved of' misleading statements claiming the companies had minimal exposure to subprime loans at the height of home mortgage bubble."[24]

In June 2008, the *Wall Street Journal* reported that two former CEOs of Fannie Mae, James A. Johnson and Franklin Raines, had received loans below market rate from Countrywide Financial Corporation. Fannie was the biggest buyer of Countrywide's mortgages. The "Friends of Angelo" VIP Countrywide loan program involved many people from Fannie, including lawyers and executives.[25]

Countrywide's CEO, Angelo Mozilo, was not spared the fallout. In June 2009, the SEC charged him with insider trading and securities fraud. He settled a year later, agreeing to pay $67.5 million in fines and accepted a lifetime ban from serving as an officer or director of any public company. To date, it is the largest settlement by an individual connected to the 2008 housing collapse.[26]

Wall Street

Many books have been written on the Wall Street fraud in this financial crisis. One such book is *Bailout: An Inside Account of How Washington Abandoned Main Street While Rescuing Wall Street* (Free Press, 2012), written by Neil Barofsky, the inspector general in charge of overseeing administration of the bailout money. His book details his experience overseeing the bailout of Wall Street. Suffice it to say that this financial crisis was no different from those in the past. For the best read on what happened, the *Financial Crisis Enquiry Report* prepared by the Financial Crisis Enquiry Commission gives the most detailed account of what was happening on Wall Street and Main Street that led to the crisis.

It's not easy to summarize all the fraud that went on leading up to the crisis. Instead, I will highlight only a couple of actions taken by one investment bank, which will give you a picture of what was going on. During the real estate boom, Goldman Sachs was a big issuer of CDOs. From July 2004 through April 2007, Goldman created 23 CDO products worth over $7.8 billion, which it offloaded onto investors.[27] Goldman would short these securities, betting that they would lose money. Altogether, Goldman packaged, sold, and shorted a total of 47 synthetic CDOs, with an aggregate face value of $66 billion between July 1, 2004, and May 31, 2007.[28] As a result, Goldman was able to profit from the collapse in subprime mortgage bonds in the summer of 2007 by short-selling subprime mortgage-backed securities—the same securities it was selling to its investors.[29]

In May 2009, the firm agreed to pay up to $60 million to end an investigation by the Massachusetts attorney general's office into whether the firm helped promote unfair home loans in the state.[30]

In 2010, the SEC filed a fraud suit against Goldman alleging that the firm misled investors with its CDO products. In the end, however, the SEC suit did not go to court, as a financial settlement was reached. The firm agreed to pay $550 million—$300 million to the U.S. government and $250 million to investors—one of the largest penalties ever paid by a Wall Street firm.[31] Goldman did not admit or deny wrongdoing, but it did admit that its marketing materials for the investment "contained incomplete information" and agreed to change some of its business practices regarding mortgage investments.[32] These types of activities were not unique to Goldman Sachs; other Wall Street firms were involved in similar activities.

AFTERMATH

One year after the Lehman Brothers bankruptcy, millions of workers were losing their jobs, thousands of families were losing their homes every month, property values were falling, and financial markets were in shambles. The unemployment rate kept rising until it reached 10 percent on a nationwide level (see Figure 3.2), and it remained stubbornly high for years after. Property values fell hard in the most speculative markets, such as Miami and Las Vegas, and foreclosure rates skyrocketed.

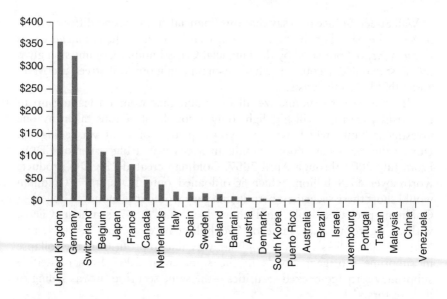

FIGURE 3.7   Peak amount of debt owed to the Federal Reserve by foreign banks during the crisis (billions, USD)
Source: American Political Science Association

By March 2009, the Dow Jones Industrial Average had lost 54 percent of its value. Financial institutions lined up for government bailouts, and hundreds more lined up to take advantage of the Fed's emergency funding lines, many of which were foreign banks (see Figure 3.7).

The U.S. Treasury's Capital Purchase Program was also hugely popular among the banks. The program, which was initially sold to lawmakers as a plan to help those hurt by the mortgage crisis, was quickly changed to recapitalizing banks, as mentioned earlier in this chapter. Table 3.1 shows the top 10 banks that received bailout capital from the Treasury. In total, the Treasury pumped more than $200 billion into 734 financial institutions.[33]

Not all banks were bailed out. Many failed. From January 2008 to April 2014, 495 commercial banks failed in the United States.[34] The largest two were Washington Mutual and IndyMac. Table 3.2 lists the top 10 bank failures during the crisis.

Investment banks for the most part were spared from failure, largely due to their being classified as "too big to fail" (which we will get to in Chapter 4). Bear Stearns and Lehman Brothers, however, were not spared and were allowed to fail. In the case of Bear Stearns, the Fed helped negotiate a fire sale to JPMorgan Chase in March 2008 for $10 per share, a far cry

TABLE 3.1 Top 10 Financial Institutions Receiving Capital Support from the Treasury Department

Date	Financial Institution	Amount
10/28/2008	Wells Fargo & Co.	$25,000,000,000
10/28/2008	JPMorgan Chase & Co.	$25,000,000,000
10/28/2008	Citigroup Inc.	$25,000,000,000
10/28/2008	Bank of America/Merrill Lynch	$15,000,000,000
10/28/2008	Morgan Stanley	$10,000,000,000
10/28/2008	Goldman Sachs Group Inc.	$10,000,000,000
1/9/2009	Bank of America	$10,000,000,000
12/31/2008	PNC Financial	$7,579,200,000
11/17/2008	U.S. Bancorp	$6,599,000,000
11/17/2008	Capital One Financial	$3,555,199,000

Source: CNN (http://money.cnn.com/news/specials/storysupplement/bankbailout/)

TABLE 3.2 Top 10 Bank Failures During the Financial Crisis by Assets Size at Time of Failure

Financial Institution	State	Year	Assets at Time of Failure
Washington Mutual	Washington	2008	$307 billion
IndyMac	California	2008	$32 billion
Colonial Bank	Alabama	2009	$25 billion
FBOP Corp. banking subsidiaries	Illinois	2009	$18.4 billion
Guaranty Bank	Texas	2009	$13.0 billion
Downey Savings and Loan	California	2008	$12.8 billion
BankUnited FSB	Florida	2009	$12.8 billion
AmTrust Bank	Ohio	2009	$12.0 billion
Western Bank	Puerto Rico	2010	$11.9 billion
United Commercial Bank	California	2009	$11.2 billion

from its 52-week high of $133 per share. At the time, Bear Stearns was the seventh-largest securities firm in the United States, with assets of $395 billion.[35] It's also important to note that Bear Stearns had $13.40 trillion in derivative exposure,[36] which was almost equal in size to the entire GDP of the United States.

Derivatives, a Wall Street financial innovation that gained widespread acceptance among the financial community in the 1990s, had mushroomed into an out-of-control financial monster by 2007. What were designed to offer investors better protection against financial loss, as well as bring stability to financial markets, instead had the opposite effect. Not only have derivatives destabilized financial markets, they have become so complex and intertwined that few people truly understand how they work. Banks and other issuers of derivatives such as AIG brought to light what we now refer to as *counterparty risk*. A problem in one derivative could quickly bring down its issuer, which in turn could spread to all other parties connected to AIG in some way. This is exactly what we saw in 2008. Lehman Brothers, for example, had assets worth $639 billion at the time of its failure. Compared with Bearn Stearns, Lehman had *only* $729 billion in derivative exposure.[37] The firm failed as a result of its high exposure to those toxic low-rated CDOs, the same ones Goldman was dumping on investors. In the aftermath of the financial crisis, it was expected that regulators would finally step in and bring accountability and transparency to the derivatives market. This, however, has not been the case. Instead, the derivatives market has continued to grow and is now much larger than any stock or bond market. We will get into more details on the derivatives market in Chapter 10 as well as discuss a commonsense solution to this problem.

HSBC Bank, although luckier than Bear or Lehman, ran into trouble, too, but not due to derivatives exposure or exposure to toxic assets. It ran into trouble as a result of its acquisition of a toxic company. Back in 2003, when I was working there, the bank decided to expand its presence in the United States by acquiring Household International for $15 billion. Household was a subprime lender with a large, yet shady mortgage and credit card business. I knew people who had worked at Household and heard their stories of predatory lending. The acquisition was a bad idea, and it should never have happened. Just a year earlier, Household had paid $486 million to settle predatory lending charges by attorneys general in 46 U.S. states.[38] HSBC Bank, at the time, had a presence primarily in New York, with a handful of branches in Florida. Executives at HSBC saw the Household acquisition as good value for the money and the best way to gain a nationwide presence. In 2009, Stephen Green, HSBC's chairman at the time, publicly stated his regrets for the Household acquisition, saying, "It's an acquisition we wish we hadn't done with the benefit of hindsight, and there are lessons to be learned."[39] In 2011, banking regulators required the bank to set aside more than $65 billion for bad loans in addition to billions of dollars in write-offs in the credit card division.[40]

CONTAGION

What had started off as a subprime mortgage problem quickly became a global financial crisis. It was not because the rest of the world had a stake in the success or failure of the U.S. housing market but, rather, the financialization and repackaging of mortgages into derivative instruments that led to the spread of the crisis. Not only were CDOs and CDSs popular among U.S. financial institutions; banks, pension funds, and insurance companies all over the world were buying U.S. mortgage-backed securities, CDOs, and other toxic instruments coming out of Wall Street. The returns were too attractive to ignore. Much of what was developed on Wall Street was also exported to other developed markets.

In the United Kingdom, for example, a subprime mortgage crisis was brewing at the same time as the crisis in the United States. One of the early victims of the global financial crisis was Northern Rock, a United Kingdom–based building society with more than £113 billion in assets and a big subprime lender.[41] In 2007, the bank faced a liquidity crunch due to slowing demand for subprime mortgage-backed securities. The bank's partner in securitization was Lehman Brothers. In September 2007, the bank had to seek emergency funding from the Bank of England. What began as a £2 billion loan in September quickly grew to £26 billion by January 2008. A month later the bank was taken over by the government, sparking a run on the bank by depositors.[42]

Once the housing market collapsed, so, too, did mortgage-backed securities and the derivatives on which they were based. A pension fund in Europe all of a sudden realized how exposed it was to the U.S. housing market as well as the financial health of U.S. financial institutions. This interconnectedness brought down all holders of these instruments regardless of where they were based. Regulators were caught unaware of how exposed global financial institutions were to the U.S. housing market and were unprepared for the fallout from the counterparty risk. As such, the Fed opened its doors wide to all financial instructions affected by the crisis and allowed them to tap into its lending facilities. Foreign institutions took advantage of the Fed's offer and borrowed by the billions. This, however, came too late to stem the fall of some financial institutions as well as to halt the global economy from the pain that it would soon experience.

By 2009, the entire developed world was in recession (Figure 3.8). Iceland saw its banking system collapse and a near collapse of its entire economy. Dubai witnessed its most severe economic downturn in the Emirate's history. Portugal, Ireland, Italy, Greece, and Spain, known as the PIIGS, not only had a property crisis but also moved into a sovereign debt crisis in 2010, which was sparked by the severe recession of 2009. These countries to this day have not recovered, and some are in full-blown depressions, as is the case for Greece.

The financialization of the global economy created what we now refer to as systemic risk in the financial system. A severe shock in one country can easily spread to other countries. With this crisis came solutions that would only make matters worse in the next crisis.

Countries with Positive GDP Growth

Countries in Recession

Armenia, Austria, Belgium, Botswana, Brazil, Bulgaria, Canada, Chile, Costa Rica, Croatia, Cyprus, Czech Republic, Denmark, Dominica, El Salvador, Estonia, Finland, France, Georgia, Germany, Greece, Grenada, Honduras, Hungary, Iceland, Ireland, Italy, Jamaica, Japan, Kuwait, Latvia, Lithuania, Luxembourg, Malaysia, Mexico, Netherlands, New Zealand, Norway, Paraguay, Portugal, Romania, Russian Federation, Serbia, Singapore, Slovak Republic, Slovenia, South Africa, Spain, Sweden, Switzerland, Thailand, Turkey, Ukraine, United Arab Emirates, United Kingdom, United States, Venezuela

Afghanistan, Albania, Algeria, Angola, Argentina, **Australia**, Azerbaijan, Bahrain, Bangladesh, Belarus, Belize, Bolivia, Cambodia, Cameroon, Chad, **China**, Colombia, Cote d'Ivoire, Cuba, Djibouti, Ecuador, Egypt, Ethiopia, Ghana, Guatemala, Guyana, Haiti, India, Indonesia, Iran, Iraq, **Israel**, Jordan, Kazakhstan, Kenya, Kyrgyz Republic, Lebanon, Liberia, Libya, Malawi, Mali, Mauritius, Morocco, Mozambique, Nepal, Nigeria, Oman, Pakistan, Panama, Peru, Philippines, **Poland**, Qatar, Rwanda, Saudi Arabia, Senegal, Sierra Leone, South Korea, Sri Lanka, Sudan, Tajikistan, Tanzania, Togo, Tunisia, Turkmenistan, Uganda, Uruguay, Uzbekistan, Vietnam, Yemen, Zambia, Zimbabwe

FIGURE 3.8 Countries in recession in 2009 vs. countries showing positive GDP growth
Source: The World Bank: GDP growth (annual percentage) (http://data.worldbank
.org/indicator/NY.GDP.MKTP.KD.ZG)

SUMMARY

- The global financial crisis that began in 2008 was the most severe financial crisis the world has seen since the Great Depression.
- The stage was set for the crisis not long after the dot-com bubble burst in 2000, helped by the Federal Reserve's low interest rate policy and the government's goal of encouraging more and more Americans to buy homes.
- Early signs of the coming crisis were ignored. These signs included:
  - Lending programs aimed at getting less-qualified buyers into homes they couldn't afford.
  - Wall Street's financial innovations, which led to the development of CDOs and CDSs.
  - Lack of prudent credit and underwriting policies, which led to widespread fraud by all parties involved, including the home buyers.
- Even as the housing market began to slow and companies started to fail, regulators failed to see the severity of the crisis.

- The lack of regulation and transparency in these complex financial instruments encouraged Wall Street to go off into riskier areas, one of which was allowing naked CDSs, effectively launching a global casino for betting on gains or losses in financial assets.
- CDSs ballooned to more than twice the size of the U.S. stock market in less than a decade. The complexity of these instruments makes them even more dangerous.
- The government bailouts that followed were more about saving Wall Street than Main Street.
- Due to the interconnected nature of the U.S. financial system, the housing crisis turned into a CDO and CDS crisis, which quickly spread across the world. By 2009, all of the developed world was in recession.
- The global recession also sparked a sovereign debt crisis in Europe, which has yet to be resolved.

CHAPTER 4

Solutions Create More Problems

Look back at past financial crises and a pattern starts to emerge. The pattern of boom and bust is one of the characteristics of our financial system. In the United States, some experts like to blame the Federal Reserve for the increasing number and severity of financial crises, citing the birth of the Fed in 1913 as the date when our financial systems began experiencing more turbulence. This, however, is not true. There were financial crises before the Fed was born, and depressions back then were quite common. Other experts take the opposite view, believing that the financial system has become more stable since the birth of the Fed. This is also not true, as I have discussed in Chapters 2 and 3.

So why then are there two strongly opposing views? The two main caretakers in an economy that we trust to run it smoothly are the government (and its regulatory agencies) and the central bank, such as the Federal Reserve, Bank of England, and European Central Bank. My conclusion, after studying both sides, is that rising turbulence and financial crises in an economy are the direct result of the type of monetary system in that economy. Looking back through history, we can see that when discipline was forced upon governments and central bankers (typically, through a gold standard) the world economy was much more stable. It was not until war or other political situations forced governments to abandon the gold standard that discipline was removed from the monetary system. This traditionally led to inflation, rising debt, and financial crises down the road.

In addition to the type of monetary system in an economy, there are other factors that come into play and cause the financial system to go off balance—namely, government regulations and central bank intervention. Based on this, let's take a look at the role these two factors played after the 2008 global financial crisis to see if they were able to prevent the system from repeating the mistakes of the past.

It has been six years since the official start of the global financial crisis. This is plenty of time to assess the progress that has been made as well as determine whether the solutions that were applied have worked.

GOVERNMENTS' RESPONSE TO THE CRISIS

With global GDP rates collapsing in 2008 and 2009 (Figure 4.1), governments in North America, Europe, and Asia quickly responded to the crisis by
passing stimulus packages and offering support, including bailouts, to their
respective financial systems. There were also some coordinated efforts on
the global level to help minimize the effects of the crisis and help economies
regain their growth momentum. The Group of Twenty Finance Ministers
and Central Bank Governors (also known as the G-20) held two summits,
one in November 2008 and one in April 2009. They proposed new international financial regulations, agreed to take actions to stimulate employment,
and pledged not to resort to any protectionist measures as they did during
the Great Depression. They also committed to maintain the supply of credit
by providing more liquidity and recapitalizing the banking system.

In the United States, lawmakers passed the Emergency Economic Stabilization Act authorizing the Treasury to buy up $700 billion in troubled
mortgages. The Treasury, however, quickly changed the plan to recapitalizing banks rather than buying mortgages, as discussed in Chapter 3. The
bigger policy change came after the passage of the Dodd–Frank Wall Street
Reform and Consumer Protection Act, also known as Dodd-Frank. The
objective of this act was to promote financial stability by improving accountability and transparency in the financial system, to end "too big to fail"
financial institutions, to protect the U.S. taxpayer by ending bailouts, and to

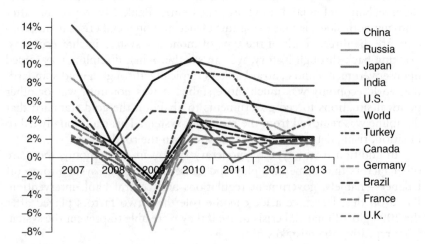

FIGURE 4.1   GDP per-capita growth rates from 2008 to 2012
Adapted from: Bloomberg

protect consumers from abusive financial services practices. This legislation, which took up more than 2,200 pages of text, has so far done little toward addressing its objectives. On the flipside, it has created a new regulatory headache for financial institutions.

What Dodd-Frank should have done is reinstate the Glass–Steagall Act separating commercial banks, investment banks, and insurance companies. This would have addressed the too-big-to-fail problem by breaking up the big banks that were deemed too valuable and too risky to let fail. The new regulatory requirements from Dodd-Frank have put pressure on smaller banks as they struggle to keep up with all the new regulatory requirements. What was meant to end "too big to fail" ended up institutionalizing it. Dodd-Frank also aimed to make derivatives more transparent by regulating them and have them traded on exchanges. This has yet to be seen, as the derivatives market continues to grow out of control.

One good thing, however, came out of Dodd-Frank: the Volcker Rule, which instituted a ban on proprietary trading by commercial banks.

The European Commission proposed a €200 billion European stimulus plan to help its member countries cope with the effects of the crisis. In the United Kingdom, the government came up with a £500 billion bank rescue plan, which had three parts. Part one included injecting £200 billion into the financial system to improve bank liquidity. Part two consisted of £50 billion to recapitalize weaker banks, also known as nationalizing the banks, similar to what was done in the United States. Part three included £250 billion to support banks in writing off bad loans.

In Asia, governments from Japan to India launched stimulus plans aimed at supporting their economies, the largest of which was in China. The Chinese program was a RMB¥ 4 trillion ($586 billion) economic stimulus package.

The overall theme these stimulus packages had in common was that they did not allow any big banks to fail. Governments supported big banks any which way they could, even if it meant nationalizing them. Belgian, Luxembourgian, and Dutch authorities, for example, partially nationalized Fortis, one of the largest financial institutions in those countries. In Germany, the government bailed out Hypo Real Estate, a real estate financing bank, to the tune of €112 billion.[1] In the Middle East, governments from Bahrain to the United Arab Emirates gave direct support to their local banks and did not allow any to fail.

CENTRAL BANKS' RESPONSE TO THE CRISIS

The trillions of dollars in support and bailouts by central banks would put the government bailouts to shame. First, central bankers around the world

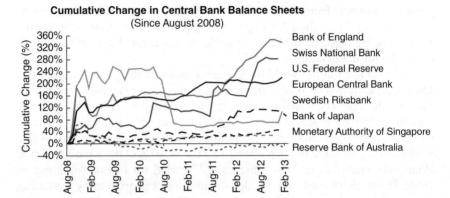

FIGURE 4.2   Central bank balance sheets
Source: Merk Investments LLC

pledged to maintain low-rate policies as long as necessary. They then agreed to inject trillions of dollars of liquidity into the market in order to kick-start credit markets. Finally, they opened up their credit lines and emergency lending facilities, offering even more trillions of dollars to financial institutions.

The Federal Reserve alone is said to have offered $29 trillion in credit lines and lending facilities (Figure 4.2). Of this amount, over $8 trillion was lent to the European Central Bank (ECB), $919 billion to the Bank of England, $466 billion to the Swiss National Bank, and $387 billion to the Bank of Japan.[2] Thus, the Fed bailout was nearly twice the U.S. annual GDP and it bailed out not only U.S. banks but also too-big-to-fail banks around the world.

As central banks lowered interest rates to near zero, their balance sheets ballooned with bonds and other debt, known as *quantitative easing* (QE). The Federal Reserve in the United States embarked on an unprecedented quantitative easing program, buying $600 billion in mortgage-backed securities,[3] which would nearly double its balance sheet of $870 billion from August 2007.[4] Four months later, in March 2009, the Fed was holding $1.75 trillion of bank debt, mortgage-backed securities, and Treasury notes (Figure 4.3). It also announced that the program would be expanded by an additional $750 billion in purchases of mortgage-backed securities and bank debt, and $300 billion in purchases of Treasury securities. This debt-buying program was halted in June 2010, but two months later the Fed decided that the economy was not growing fast enough so it embarked on another $600 billion bond-buying program, which lasted until June 2011.[5] This new program became known as QE2.

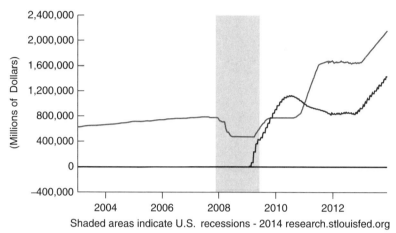

— **U.S. Treasury Securities Held by the Federal Reserve: All Maturities**
— **Mortgage-Backed Securities Held by the Federal Reserve: All Maturities**

FIGURE 4.3 U.S. Federal Reserve Treasury and mortgage-backed securities held
Source: Federal Reserve Bank of St. Louis

Three months later, in September 2011, the Fed launched Operation Twist. This plan called for the purchase of $400 billion in bonds with maturities of 6 to 30 years and the sale of bonds with maturities of less than 3 years. This would enable the Fed to keep the size of its balance sheet the same while putting pressure on long-term interest rates to remain low. The Fed was feeling pressure not to continue buying debt without end, so Operation Twist was aimed at calming the skeptics while, at the same time, maintaining low interest rates.[6] In June 2012, the program was extended by another $267 billion.

As if this wasn't enough to get the economy going again, the Fed embarked on yet another QE program, which was even more ambitious than the ones before. QE3, as it was known, called for the purchase of over $1 trillion of debt per year or $85 billion per month—$45 billion in Treasury securities and $40 billion in mortgage-backed securities[7] (Figure 4.4). Unlike the other programs, there was no end date to this program, which was given the nickname "QE Infinity." Frustrated with the lackluster improvement in the economy, the Fed decided to continue this program until it felt the economy had sufficiently improved. Additionally, the Fed announced that it would likely maintain the federal funds rate at near zero "at least through 2015," giving the economy almost seven years of near-zero interest rates.[8] This had never happened before in history.

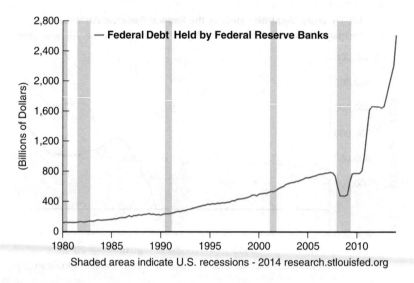

FIGURE 4.4 Federal debt held by Federal Reserve Banks
Source: Federal Reserve Bank of St. Louis

In September 2013, the Fed began discussion on slowing down this program, also known as *tapering,* but the mere talk of slowing down its trillion-dollar debt-buying program caused jitters across world stock markets. As a result, the Fed decided to hold off on tapering until December 2013, giving markets more time to digest the news. Since then, the Fed went through with slowing down its debt purchases by $10 billion per month,[9] until finally ending the program in October 2014.

Other central banks followed the Fed's lead by launching various forms of QE programs. In May 2009, the European Central Bank announced a program to buy up to €60 billion in covered bonds, a form of corporate debt.[10] In the United Kingdom, the Bank of England bought gilts (government securities) from financial institutions, along with a smaller amount of relatively high-quality debt issued by private companies. The QE program initially called for the purchase of £165 billion in debt in September 2009,[11] but it quickly became a multiple QE program, mirroring the Fed's QE programs. By July 2012, the total size of the Bank of England's QE programs amounted to £375 billion.[12]

The Bank of Japan was even more ambitious than the Bank of England. In October 2010, the Bank of Japan announced that it would purchase ¥5 trillion ($60 billion) in assets. The objective was to weaken the yen in order to stimulate export growth. It did not work.[13] In October 2011, the bank

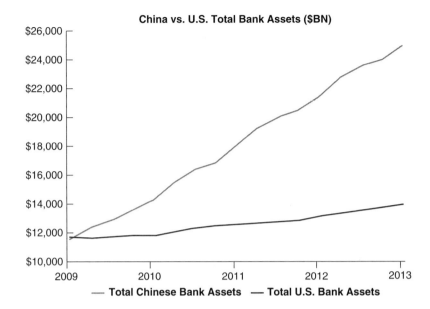

FIGURE 4.5 Increase in total Chinese banking assets vs. U.S. total assets
Source: ZeroHedge.com

expanded its asset purchase program by another ¥5 trillion to a total of ¥55 trillion ($726 billion).[14] When this didn't work, in April 2013 the bank expanded the program by $1.4 trillion over the next two years.[15]

China took a different route. It decided to directly support its banking system rather than launching QE programs. As shown in Figure 4.5, Chinese banking assets swelled to $15.4 trillion in 2013 in the hope that this would preserve its debt-driven growth model a little longer. This, however, doesn't seem to be working, as China's huge shadow banking system is opaque, with an estimated growing number of bad debts. This, coupled with a slowing economy, slowing exports, and falling house prices, is setting up China for a lot of pain in the near future. As a result, Chinese officials are now talking about implementing a QE program[16] while at the same time trying to manage a slowdown in the economy.

UNINTENDED CONSEQUENCES

The government and central bank programs and bailouts—though, I'm sure, well-intended—have not achieved their desired results. In the central bankers' defense, they were limited by only having monetary tools at their disposal. What they tried, however, was unprecedented in terms of size and scope. Governments, on the other hand, carry much of the blame for the mess we are in today. Taking the necessary pain to restructure the labor force and economy was unpopular politically, so they opted to take on more debt from the private sector and pressured central banks to pump cheap money into the economy.

It's been six years since the crisis began, and we can see the results. Not only were governments and central bankers surprised to see that their cheap money did not solve the problem, but there has also been a rise of some serious unintended consequences.

The Bailouts and "Too Big to Fail"

The single most important reason for bailing out the large banks was that they were deemed "too big to fail" and considered integral to the financial system. If one were allowed to fail, then it would cause ripples throughout the financial system, taking down others with it. We saw this in 2008 with the failure of Lehman Brothers, which quickly hit AIG and the rest of the big banks. But how do you solve the problem of letting banks fail for taking on big bets that go the wrong way? This begs another question: Why were banks allowed to take on such big bets?

Politicians at the time had a good point: The financial system was experiencing a meltdown caused by big banks making big bets on financial instruments that either were junk or could not be explained. The main issue then was to solve the problem at hand and stop the meltdown. This was the basis of the bailouts. What was supposed to be step two of this process—breaking up too-big-to-fail banks and making them less important to the financial system the next time one fails—never happened. Step three never happened, either. Not only was Dodd-Frank supposed to break up these banks, it was also supposed to increase transparency in the system and regulate the opaque derivatives that brought it down.

Instead, big banks are here to stay, and their derivatives exposure is even bigger than ever. Figure 4.6 shows that, as of June 2013, the six largest banks represent 67 percent of all banking assets in the United States. The remaining 6,934 banks in the country, combined, make up 33 percent. At this point, I think we have gone from "too big to fail" to "too big to bail," because the next time these banks run into trouble (and they will), the government will not be able to bail them out—not because of the political backlash it will cause, but because they will be in the hole for many more trillions than what they needed in 2008.

Because the U.S. government did not proceed with the next steps of breaking up the banks and regulating the derivatives market after the bailout

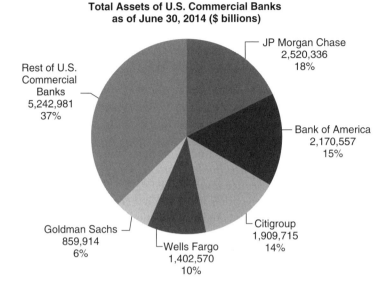

**Total Assets of U.S. Commercial Banks
as of June 30, 2014 ($ billions)**

JP Morgan Chase
2,520,336
18%

Rest of U.S.
Commercial
Banks
5,242,981
37%

Bank of America
2,170,557
15%

Goldman Sachs
859,914
6%

Wells Fargo
1,402,570
10%

Citigroup
1,909,715
14%

FIGURE 4.6 Too-big-to-fail banks
Source: FDIC and SEC 10Q filings

of 2008, a moral hazard has been created. Big banks are too confident that the next time they run into trouble they will be bailed out again. They also believe that, due to their size and importance in the market, they can get away with unethical, unlawful, and outright fraudulent behavior. They believe this because they are getting away with it at the moment.

During my research I came across some data that I am still finding hard to believe. I found some figures published by the Bank for International Settlements (BIS) based in Switzerland, which is the central bank for central banks. The BIS explains and describes the size of the global derivatives market: As of June 30, 2008, the total notional amount of the entire global over-the-counter derivatives market was $683.7 trillion![17] In 2008, the global GDP of all countries on the planet was estimated to be $61.4 trillion.[18] How can the derivatives market be more than 11 times larger than the global economy? What's even more unbelievable is that, by the end of 2013, the size of the derivatives market had grown by more than $26 trillion from 2008, reaching $710 trillion.[19]

It is clear that too-big-to-fail banks are too confident in the government's ability to bail them out. Governments and central banks, in turn, are also confident in their abilities to save the day the next time we are faced with a financial crisis, even though we have had six years to see the lackluster results and the mess that has been created. For now, the Wall Street motto seems to be working: Privatize the profits and socialize the losses.

Rising Debt = Instability in the Financial System

Unsustainable debt levels are what brought about the financial crisis, yet debt levels today show no signs of going down. Governments taking on private debts seem to be the way to go. After all, governments' creditworthiness is always good compared with that of the private sector, right? They can always raise taxes and collect revenue from other sources. Actually, this is more theory than reality. If the economy is weak, raising taxes does not raise revenue. It might actually reduce revenue even further. We have already seen this in Greece, Spain, and the other PIIGS countries. In 2010, the aftermath of the global financial crisis triggered a Eurozone debt crisis as people finally realized that countries such as Ireland, Greece, Spain, Portugal, Italy, and, really, most of the Eurozone countries, were carrying too much debt. The reality is that much of this debt will never be repaid. A fact that seems to have been erased from peoples' memories is that countries do default and debts are not always repaid. Today, in 2015, we are still dealing with the fact that many of the Eurozone countries, and the rest of the world, have too much debt and that this debt cannot and will not be repaid, yet markets are behaving as if all is well and no debt level is too high.

We also tend to forget that much of the economic growth in the developed world is based on debt: debt to buy a house, debt to go to school, debt to buy a car, even debt to pay for food, as we are seeing today. As such, debt must grow in order for the economy to grow.

As shown in Figure 4.7, the slight drop in debt in 2008 and 2009 nearly brought down the entire economy. The prudent action for both the public and the private sectors would be to reduce their debt load. However, since that requires painful choices now, it is pushed back to a later date, making the pain down the road likely to be even more severe. Governments, for political reasons, cannot pull back on spending, and consumers are tapped out and have no choice but to borrow, so the game continues and debt grows, creating more instability down the road.

The Markets Are Hooked on the Fed

Markets, not only in the United States but around the world, have become used to central bank intervention to prop them up. Stock and equity markets have been big beneficiaries since central banks began buying up debt and other financial instruments. The mere mention of central banks normalizing the situation causes markets to go into panic mode.

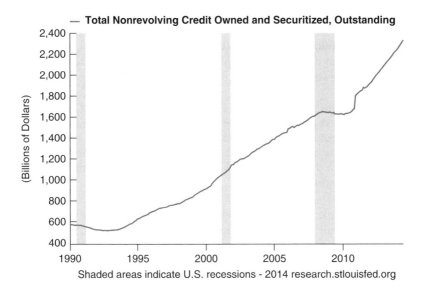

FIGURE 4.7 Total outstanding debt in the United States
Source: Federal Reserve Bank of St. Louis

During the past five years, I have watched market reaction to Fed and ECB news. An improving economy meant that they would pull back the level of stimulus, while a poor or deteriorating economy meant that the stimulus would continue. Whenever good economic news was released, markets would take a nosedive. Whenever economic news was bad, stock markets would rally, celebrating more central bank stimulus. This distortion can be seen not only in the equity market but also in the bond markets globally. The mention of the Fed tapering its QE3 program in September 2013 caused emerging markets to drop dramatically because the cheap money being pumped out of the Fed was being sent over to emerging markets in order to get higher returns. Bond investors in the United States and Europe could not make a decent return at home with zero-interest-rate policies in place, so sending their money overseas to higher-yielding markets (aka higher-risk markets) seemed like a no-brainer.

Central banks, for their part, feel that they cannot continue to prop up markets forever and are moving toward reducing their presence in the markets, thus bringing back market forces to dictate prices. It has been so long since market forces were at play in both equity and bond markets, it would be interesting to see how they would get on without central bank intervention.

Income Inequality

One of the most dire consequences of government and central bank policies globally has been the widening gap of income inequality. Here's an excerpt from a recent news article:

> Economic statistics show that incomes for the top 1 percent of U.S. households soared 31 percent from 2009 through 2012, after adjusting for inflation, yet inched up an average of 0.4 percent for those making less. Many economists are sounding alarms that the income gap, greater now than at any time since the Depression, is hurting the economy by limiting growth in consumer spending.[20]

Central bank and government policies have clearly favored the wealthy—and not just any wealthy, but the ultrawealthy, or the top 0.01 percent of households (see Figure 4.8). From 2002 to 2012, the bottom 90 percent have seen their incomes drop by almost 11 percent, while the ultrawealthy have seen their incomes rise more than 76 percent over the

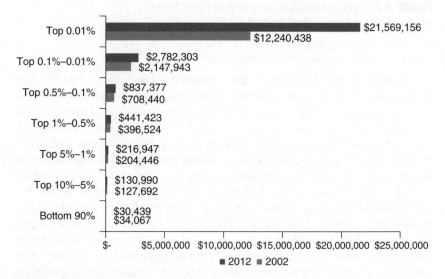

FIGURE 4.8   The rising income inequality
Source: Thomas Piketty and Emmanuel Saez, "Income Inequality in the United States, 1913–1998," *Quarterly Journal of Economics* 118(1), 2003: 1–39, series updated to 2012 in September 2013

same period. Much of this rise in wealth is attributed to the government bailouts and stock market euphoria postcrisis. Let's not forget that the Dow Jones Industrial Average, after bottoming out in March 2009, has risen more than 155 percent up to June 2014. The bottom 90 percent were the least likely to benefit from the stock market's rise.

This rise in income gap has also led to rising social tensions across the globe. The Occupy Wall Street movement in the United States, which began in September 2011, was not an anomaly. Protests, social movements, and social unrest have increased all over the world. The Arab Spring, which swept across the Middle East in 2011, has been attributed to rising food costs for the poor and working class. The Arab Spring has so far taken down the governments in Tunisia, Egypt, and Libya, sparking social unrest from Bahrain to Morocco and, in some cases, civil war, such as in Syria. The Arab Spring was not confined to the Middle East. Social movements sprang up across Europe, Asia, and South America. Their message was clear: Their voices were no longer going to be unheard.

SUMMARY

- The solutions that were applied to the global economy are setting us up for another financial crisis down the road.
- Government bailouts, which were well-intended at the time, ended up protecting the large banks and ignoring the structural problems in the economy, such as high unemployment and high levels of debt.
- The Dodd–Frank Act, which was supposed to reform the financial industry, break up large banks, and regulate the derivatives market, has done little beyond institutionalizing too-big-to-fail banks and holding back from derivatives regulation.
- Central bank balance sheets swelled into the trillions of dollars as they bought up government bonds, mortgage-backed securities, and bank debt. These quantitative easing programs became known simply as QE.
- Central banks, frustrated at the lack of effectiveness of their QE programs, were forced to launch multiple QE programs, achieving similar lackluster results.
- The results of the QE programs are a clear sign that central banks not only do not understand the problems but also do not have the tools to fix them.
- The bailouts and QE programs led to some significant unintended consequences—namely, too-big-to-fail banks were allowed to become

even bigger; debt has continued to rise, creating a more unstable financial system; markets have become addicted to central bank stimulus and have distorted free-market prices; and income inequality has risen to levels not seen since the Great Depression.

- The largest beneficiaries of the bailouts and QE have been the ultra-wealthy households.
- The decline in household wealth for a vast majority of the population has given rise to social movements such as Occupy Wall Street and has cause social unrest, revolutions, and civil wars in other parts of the world.

CHAPTER 5

The Next Financial Crisis and the New Financial System

Today we seem to have forgotten one of the characteristics of our financial system: As one bubble pops, another one is formed. There are clear bubbles in the global economy today, yet most people tend to brush them aside, citing two reasons why they should not be worried:

1. *"The global economy just went through a crisis and we are not due for another one for at least a few years."* However, if you go back to Chapter 2, you will see that we have averaged one major financial crisis every three years since 1971. It has already been six years since the global financial crisis. I consider the Eurozone debt crisis, which began in 2010, an extension of that crisis.
2. *"Governments and central banks know how to handle it and will be able to jump in to save the day if another crisis were to happen."* When I hear someone say that the Fed or the central banks can fix the problem, my response is: If they knew what the problems were and had the power to fix them, then shouldn't they have done so by now? After all, they've had six years to work on it. QE1, QE2, and QE3 are clear examples of the Fed not understanding the problem, much less being able to solve it. The European Central Bank, with all its strong words, has not fixed a single problem among its members.

I am certain that another crisis is just around the corner. This time, however, the problem will be much bigger and the effects will last much longer. To see why I believe this, let's look at the main reasons cited for the global financial crisis:

1. Easy credit and subprime borrowers.
2. Too-big-to-fail banks taking on too much risk.

3. Too much debt in the system.
4. Complex derivatives that grew out of control.

EASY CREDIT AND SUBPRIME BORROWERS

In 2008, the subprime borrowers were individuals looking to buy or flip homes they could not afford. Today, the subprime borrowers have shifted from home buyers to car buyers, college students, subprime government borrowers, and other risky emerging markets. The reason for this is simple: The Fed, the European Central Bank (ECB), and Bank of Japan (BoJ) have forced interest rates so low that they are now at or near zero. What was meant to spur lending and business activity domestically ended up pushing investors to take this cheap money and look for higher-yielding investments elsewhere. In some cases these investments were risky auto loans, and in other cases it was emerging market debt. So much money has flowed into emerging markets that the yields on debt have dropped to record lows, making it attractive to buy debt in even the riskiest parts of the world, such as Sub-Saharan Africa.

Investors' search for yield has led them to make high-risk investments, creating bubbles in these markets. The following news headlines summarize the current predicament:

> "Emerging Debt Sales Hit Surprise Record in 2013, Outlook Upbeat"
> **Reuters, December 4, 2013**[1]

> "Warning Signs Flash for Junk-Bond Investors"
> **USA Today, May 18, 2014**[2]

> "Special Report: How the Fed Fueled an Explosion in Subprime Auto Loans"
> **Reuters, April 3, 2013**[3]

> "Auto Loan Delinquencies Rise as Subprime Lending Gains Steam"
> **Fortune, August 20, 2014**[4]

> "U.S. Student Debt Reaches $1.1 Trillion, Surpasses Credit Card Debt and Auto Loans"
> **International Business Times, May 13, 2014**[5]

> "The Next Big Bailout: Student Loans"
> **Fox Business, June 3, 2014**[6]

Alarm bells and warnings aside, investors don't seem to care. Their main concern is to get a return on their money. This is the same scenario that played out from 2002 to 2007, when investors rushed to buy mortgage-backed securities. As the market became flooded with them, yields dropped and investors looked for higher-yielding securities. Higher yield meant riskier assets; however, investors didn't seem to care—until one day they did. Nobody knows when this rush into risky debt will end because rates are so low and subprime/junk debt issuance continues to break new records. One thing is for sure: When it ends, a lot of this debt will not be paid back.

TOO-BIG-TO-FAIL BANKS TAKING ON TOO MUCH RISK

The story here has taken a turn for the worse since the most recent crisis. Too-big-to-fail banks are even bigger today than they were during that crisis. What has changed for them today is that their overconfidence has increased and their behavior has gotten even worse.

Governments have created a moral hazard by bailing out the big banks. Calling them "too big to fail" has enabled them to go on gambling, because they expect governments to bail them out again if they get into trouble. They have also become reckless, unethical, and in some cases outright criminal. Take, for example, JPMorgan Chase. In January 2014, the board of directors agreed to give the bank's CEO, Jamie Dimon, an $18.5 million bonus even though the bank had just agreed to pay the U.S. Justice Department $13 billion[7] in fines to settle charges that it misled investors when it sold them junk mortgage-backed securities leading up to the global financial crisis. The justification for the bonus was that he settled the charges!

In 2012, HSBC and Standard Chartered Bank were caught laundering money to terrorist organizations and drug cartels through the U.S. banking system. HSBC was ordered to pay a $1.9 billion fine,[8] yet the U.S. Justice Department declined to file criminal charges out of fears that such action would cause systemic risk to the banking system due to the bank's size. *The Economist* termed this "too big to jail."[9] So the precedent was set: Big banks can go on breaking the law as long as they pay fines if they are caught. As a result, the big banks have taken unethical and illegal behavior to a new level. Here are three more examples.

LIBOR Scandal: In 2012, regulators around the world exposed global fixing of the London Interbank Offer Rate (LIBOR), which is an interest rate used as a benchmark to set payments on about $800 trillion worth of financial instruments, including some mortgages. More than 20 banks have been named in this scandal, including the usual suspects—Barclays, Citigroup, Deutsche Bank, HSBC, JPMorgan Chase, RBS, and UBS.[10]

Forex Scandal: In 2013, regulators in the United States, Europe, and Asia revealed that they were investigating foreign currency exchange (forex) banks for collusion on price-fixing. The global foreign currency market handles roughly $5.3 trillion per day in trading. There are hundreds of banks involved in global currency markets, but here again the usual suspects were named in the investigation—Barclays, Deutsche Bank, JPMorgan Chase, Citigroup, and UBS.[11]

Gold Manipulation Scandal: In 2014, Barclays was fined £26 million for failures in internal controls that allowed a trader to manipulate the setting of gold prices, after the bank was fined $450 million for rigging LIBOR interest rates in 2012.[12]

The big banks just can't seem to make money the honest way. Even when scandal after scandal is exposed, banks continue with business as usual, setting aside funds to pay legal fees and fines. There is no sign that this culture will change anytime soon.

TOO MUCH DEBT IN THE SYSTEM

The economy and financial system are built on debt. Every dollar, pound, and euro in existence today came about as an IOU. Money in the system today is created/issued only once a new loan is issued. Thus, every currency out there is issued on the back of new debt. For an economy to grow today, debt must also grow. If debt stalls or slows down, then the economy falls. In 2008, it was the consumer who had too much debt. Today, governments have too much debt, and it keeps growing, with no end in sight. Why? Because governments realize that to get the economies moving again, debt needs to grow. If consumers are not willing to take on more debt, then governments will. They have even assumed, backed, or guaranteed a lot of junk debt from the previous crisis as a way to please the banks and get the debt machine rolling again.

Figure 5.1 shows the unstoppable growth of government debt in some countries. Japan is the worst of these, with a debt-to-GDP ratio approaching 250 percent. This is unheard-of in modern history. History also tells us that countries with debt-to-GDP ratios above 100 percent have a high probability of defaulting. Remember back in 2010, when the Eurozone debt crisis took center stage? As the economies slowed in southern European countries, tax receipts also slowed, leading to difficulty in making their bond payments. Prior to the crisis, these countries couldn't believe their luck after joining the Eurozone and being able to borrow at record low interest rates. So they borrowed as much as they could. Then it blew up in their faces. In 2010, Greece was one of several European countries that sought a bailout or risked defaulting on its debt payments. The main reason cited for the bailout was to help Greece lower its debt-to-GDP ratio. Well, in 2010 and 2011 Greece received two bailouts totaling €240 billion, yet in 2014 it was

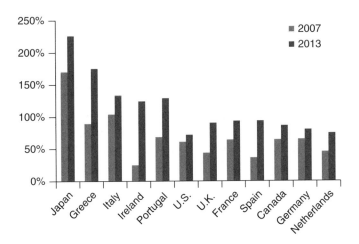

FIGURE 5.1　Growth in government debt since the global financial crisis (debt as a percentage of GDP)
Adapted from: Bloomberg

looking like the country might need a third bailout.[13] To top it off, the country's debt-to-GDP ratio went from about 110 percent in 2007 to nearly 170 percent, so what was the purpose of the first two bailouts? With the country entering its sixth year of recession and having record high unemployment combined with a rising poverty rate, it's impossible to see a way out for Greece other than defaulting.

Spain is in no better shape than Greece, yet, as of June 2014, 10-year Spanish bonds had a lower yield than 10-year U.S. Treasuries.[14] Spain, too, suffers from a record and unsustainable debt-to-GDP ratio, high unemployment, increasing poverty, and a stalled economy, yet bond investors feel that it is less risky than the United States.

COMPLEX DERIVATIVES THAT GREW OUT OF HAND

According to the Bank for International Settlements (BIS), the total size of the derivatives market has increased by $26 trillion since 2008, reaching $710 trillion at the end of 2013, or more than 10 times the world's GDP. Big banks, as you can imagine, have been disproportionately involved here as well. Just five banks are exposed to more than 40 percent of the total global derivatives market: Deutsche Bank, $72.8 trillion; JPMorgan Chase,

$70.1 trillion; Citigroup, $62.2 trillion; Goldman Sachs, $48.6 trillion; and Bank of America, $38.9 trillion.

Regulators seem to have turned a blind eye to this market, letting it grow beyond their capabilities of being able to regulate it. Much of the derivatives market is interest rate based, and the CDSs that brought us down in 2008 are as popular as ever.

Today, along with the popularity of CDSs, there has also been a return of some highly risky deals, which are downright junk and are currently being sold to investors. One of these is a deal by Blackstone Group, the world's largest private equity firm, and Deutsche Bank. Since mortgage-backed securities (MBSs) are the instruments of the past, they have come up with a new security called a *rent-backed security*. Since the financial crisis, Blackstone has been a big buyer of distressed homes across the United States. Over the past couple of years it has bought more than 41,000 homes for the purpose of converting them into rental units. In some cases, the renter would be the previous home owner, who defaulted on the property and lost it to foreclosure.

Blackstone, together with Deutsche Bank, has pooled the rental revenue from 3,207 of these homes and put it into a security to sell to investors. The total size of this security is $479.1 million.[15] Investors can choose how much risk they are willing to take by investing in different classes of certificates, which pay out different interest rates according to class and rating, as shown in Table 5.1.

What is surprising about these securities is that investors are not investing in the properties, nor will they be entitled to sell them if and when this scheme falls apart. Instead, investors are only entitled to the rental revenue stream and have no ownership in the homes. On top of this, the credit ratings on these securities and the interest rates being offered should be raising red

TABLE 5.1 Rating, Size, and Interest Rate on Blackstone's Rent-Backed Security

Class (Rating)	Initial Certificate Balance	Coupon Interest Rate
A (Aaa)	$278.7 million	1.31%
B (Aa2)	$34.3 million	1.51%
C (A2)	$47.1 million	2.01%
D (Baa2)	$31.5 million	2.31%
E (not rated)	$46.0 million	2.81%
F (not rated)	$41.5 million	3.81%

Sources: Moody's Investor Services, Deutsche-Bank Securities, and Bloomberg (http://www .bloomberg.com/infographics/2013-12-20/blackstones-big-bet-on-rental-homes.html)

flags. The highest class is rated triple-A and pays out a measly 1.31 percent interest rate, while the lowest two classes are not even rated yet pay out 2.81 and 3.81 percent, respectively. There are a lot of assumptions built up around these securities and how they were priced, one of which is the vacancy and default rates, which Blackstone assumes will be no more than 10 percent. Keep in mind that these homes are in states that have had the largest foreclosure rates in the country, including Arizona, California, and Florida. These states also continue to have weak economies and above-average unemployment rates. Any outcome outside of the assumptions will cause investors to lose money, beginning with the bottom classes and moving up to the top classes. Expect the outcome here to be no different than it was with the collapse of the subprime MBS market.

THE TRIGGER FOR A NEW FINANCIAL SYSTEM

Looking at the most recent financial crisis, the reasons why it happened, and the solutions that were applied, I can see that another financial crisis is just around the corner. The next crisis, however, will be on a much larger scale, primarily because this time the banks are bigger and have become more reckless, the debt in the system is larger, and the derivatives market is out of control.

Governments and central banks at this time are too afraid of the rising social unrest to be able to make a significant change to the financial system. Back in 1971, when President Nixon took the United States off the quasi–gold standard, canceling the Bretton Woods Agreement, the world did not face the challenges we face today. Although the United States was in the middle of the Vietnam War, its economy was on a stronger footing and debts were more manageable. The financialization of the global economy did not occur until after we entered into the current financial system by removing discipline from governments and central banks. This enabled them to go on a massive debt and financial engineering binge that has lasted 43 years.

Nevertheless, much like previous financial systems, this one will come to an end as well. Unfortunately, a change to the system will not come without a crisis to force it. This is why the next crisis will be the opportune time to evaluate the problems with the current system and come up with realistic solutions to develop a better and more just system.

Coming up in Part II of this book, I will discuss Islamic finance and why I believe it offers some real-world solutions that can help shape a better financial system.

SUMMARY

- The current bubbles formed in our financial system are being ignored primarily because the vast majority believe that government and central banks understand what is happening and will be able to fix whatever comes their way, or they feel that the 2008 financial crisis was too recent for another one to happen so soon.
- Overconfidence has bred complacency. We can see this by looking at the causes of the previous financial crisis and comparing it to where we are today.
- Easy-credit and subprime borrowers in the previous crisis were individual home buyers. Today the easy credit is with subprime governments, which have gone on a borrowing binge due to record low interest rates, and investors chasing the highest-yielding debt regardless of its risk.
- Too-big-to-fail banks are even bigger today and are taking on even more risk.
- Governments have led big banks to believe that they are too important to the financial system and will be bailed out any time a crisis arises.
- Big banks have taken their unethical and unlawful activities to a new level as governments fail to prosecute them for fear it will cause systemic risk in the financial system.
- Debt continues to rise even as consumers reduce their debt burden. Governments are convinced that debt needs to keep rising in order to get economies growing again.
- The derivatives market has grown out of control and is now bigger than it was before the last financial crisis.
- Our current financial system, which was born after the cancellation of the Bretton Woods Agreement by President Nixon in 1971, is coming to an end.
- Fearing rising social tensions and unrest, governments will not make meaningful changes to the financial system unless they are forced to by another severe financial crisis, which I believe is right around the corner.
- Discipline needs to return to the financial system, prohibiting politicians and bankers from becoming addicted to debt and financial engineering.

The Islamic Financial System

CHAPTER **6**

Overview and History of Islamic Finance

Looking back at past financial crises, we can see how debt plays a significant role in building up to a crisis as well as the ensuing pain it causes once a crisis is sparked. A high level of debt, however, is not the cause of a crisis; it is merely a symptom of other problems in the financial system. Take, for example, the global financial crisis of 2008. The high level of debt consumers were taking on was not the problem; it was a symptom of the loose lending standards that had become prevalent in the United States and elsewhere. There were three other problems in the system that led to the unsustainable increase in the level of debt: low interest rates, which encouraged more borrowing; lax regulation and oversight, which led banks to take on more risk and engage in fraud; and financialization of the economy, leading to engineering of new and complex financial products, such as credit default swaps (CDSs). This financial engineering not only gave the industry, and the economy, a false sense of security, it also resulted in an overbloated financial industry that continued to play a bigger role in the economy while productive industries, such as manufacturing, play a lesser role.

So if rapidly rising debt is a symptom of the problem, what can be said today, six years after the worst financial crisis the world has seen since the Great Depression? According to the Bank for International Settlements (BIS), the amount of debt globally has risen to more than $100 trillion in 2013, up from $70 trillion in 2007.[1] In other words, to save the global economy from the financial crisis, governments and central banks threw even more debt at the problem. Though this may seem to have calmed markets, it has only made the system more unstable and ensures that the next crisis will be even worse than the previous one. One of the clearest indications that this debt-for-growth path is not working is the fact that the additional $30 trillion in debt in the system since 2008 has done little to bring the world economy back to a normal growth level. The law of diminishing returns has caught up to this debt model.

What then are some solutions to this dilemma? I will discuss some of the solutions being proposed by economists and financiers in Chapter 11, but for now I would like to look at a financial system that is not being discussed: the Islamic financial system.

ISLAMIC FINANCE DEFINED

Islamic finance is a financial system that operates according to Islamic law. Islamic law, called *Shariah,* is derived from the Quran, the Hadith, and the Sunnah. The Quran, Islam's holy book, which Muslims believe to be the unalterable word of God, is said to have been revealed to the Prophet Muhammad (PBUH)* between 610 CE until his death in 632 CE. The Hadith is the narrative relating the actions and sayings of Muhammad. The Sunnah is the life and example of Muhammad. In addition to these three sources, Shariah also relies on *ijma, qiyas,* and *ijtihad. Ijma* is the consensus among religious scholars on issues not explicitly mentioned in either the Quran or the Sunnah. *Qiyas* is the use of deduction by analogy to provide an opinion on a case not referred to in the Quran or the Sunnah. *Ijtihad* represents a religious scholar's or jurist's independent reasoning relating to the applicability of certain Shariah rules on cases not mentioned in the Quran or the Sunnah.[2] When the basis of Shariah (Quran, Sunnah, and Hadith) is combined with *ijma, qiyas,* and *ijtihad,* it forms what is called *fiqh,* otherwise known as Islamic jurisprudence. *Fiqh* has played a leading role in the recent development of Islamic finance and Islamic banking around the world.

Although Islam has been around for more than a millennium, Islamic finance as an industry and a financial system is still very young, having been around for less than 40 years. Islamic theories of economics and commerce have been around as long as Islam itself. As Islam spread across the Middle East, Asia, North Africa, and later southern Europe, it brought with it a renewed interest in science and the acquisition of knowledge. This period, from the birth of Islam in the sixth century up to the twelfth century, is known as the Golden Age of Islam. During this age, the major Islamic capital cities of Baghdad, Cairo, and Cordoba became the main intellectual and learning centers for science, philosophy, and medicine. Muslim scholars advanced the knowledge gained from the ancient Greek, Roman, Persian, Chinese, Indian, and Egyptian civilizations and went on to make new discoveries in these fields. These advancements would later spark the European Renaissance.

Muslim scholars also worked on theories of economics and developed trading tools and contracts such as *sukuk* (promissory notes), mentioned

---

*Peace Be Upon Him.

in Chapter 1. By the mid-twelfth century, many scholars had presented key concepts of Islamic economics that are still relevant today.

The core concepts of the Islamic financial system are aimed at promoting trading and commerce, while at the same time promoting fairness and social justice. One of these key elements is the prohibition of interest (usury), known in Arabic as *riba*. Although Muslims are not allowed to pay or receive interest, business activities are encouraged, as is making a profit. Through Shariah and *fiqh*, economic activity is not restricted, but instead is directed toward responsible activities that benefit society as a whole. In other words, Islam allows for a free-market economy where supply and demand are decided by market forces, not dictated by a government. At the same time, it directs the function of the market mechanism by imposing specific laws and ethics to help the system run smoothly for the benefit of everyone.

A key purpose for imposing these laws and ethics is to promote social justice. As such, Islam tries to achieve social justice in the economy by prohibiting interest, defining the state's role in the economy, encouraging shared risk, and requiring *zakat*. *Zakat*, or almsgiving, is the practice of charitable giving by Muslims based on accumulated wealth and is obligatory for all who meet a minimum wealth requirement. It is considered to be a personal responsibility for Muslims to ease economic hardship for other Muslims and eliminate inequality for followers of Islam. The amount of *zakat* one has to pay is around 2.5 percent of total assets annually and is collected by specialized *zakat* foundations. These foundations can be found all over the world, including in non-Muslim countries, such as the United States and the United Kingdom. Those qualified to receive *zakat* funds include the poor, orphans, and those who have incurred overwhelming debts and are unable to satisfy their basic needs. This *zakat*, or wealth tax, as it is commonly referred to in the West, is the only tax Muslims are required to pay. However, Islam encourages charitable giving and helping the poor and needy outside of what is required by *zakat*.

As a result of Islam's laws on social justice, there is a misconception that Islam, or Shariah, places a limit on how much profit one can make. In reality, there is no limit on how much one can profit provided this profit is made within the guidelines stipulated by Shariah. Another misconception about Islamic finance is that it is only for Muslims and those not following Islam cannot benefit or participate in it. On the contrary, Islamic finance is open to all, as we shall see when we look at the spread of Islamic finance around the world.

A CLOSER LOOK AT *RIBA*

Islamic finance is a new and evolving industry. Islam, too, is open to evolution, particularly on matters related to trade and commerce.

Islamic jurisprudence, or *fiqh*, is divided into two parts: *fiqh al-ibadah*, which relates to matters of worship and prayer, and *fiqh al-mu'amalat*, which relates to trade and commerce. On matters of worship, Islamic jurisprudence is very straightforward. On such matters, the Quran, Hadith, and Sunnah are clear about what is permitted and what is prohibited. There is some room for interpretation, and this is where consensus, deduction, and reasoning (*ijma, qiyas,* and *ijtihad*) come into play. However, when it comes to *fiqh al-mu'amalat,* consensus, deduction, and reasoning play a much larger role. The reason for this is that the Quran only mentions what is prohibited in commerce and trade, such as the prohibition of *riba.* Hence, everything else is permitted, which leaves the door wide open for finance, trade, and business to evolve and develop.

In the Western world, finance is well-established and definitions are set in place. For example, *interest* is simply defined as a charge for borrowed money.[3] In Islamic finance, interest is considered a form of *riba.* There is, however, another term in the Western world that goes beyond this simple definition, and that is *usury,* which is defined as the practice of making unethical or immoral monetary loans intended to unfairly enrich the lender.[4] World religions throughout history, including Buddhism, Christianity, and Judaism, have outlawed usury and the charging of interest. It was not until recent history that the definition of *usury* became more flexible, coming to mean an exorbitant amount of interest. Under Islam, however, interest and usury have always been prohibited, and *riba* has an even broader meaning than interest and usury. *Riba* includes any increase given on an amount of money borrowed or any gift given in exchange. Under Shariah, there is only one form of lending that is permitted and that is an interest-free loan, also known as a benevolent loan, which tends to be given as a form of charity because the lender cannot ask for anything in return—only the return of the principal. For example, if a person were to take an interest-free loan and in return offered the lender a gift, such as a ride home or lunch, this would be considered *riba* and, therefore, unlawful. Such a broad definition of *riba* is mainly for the benefit of the poor and the less fortunate, as the aim of this prohibition is to stop people from becoming *debt slaves,* a term that has been making a comeback in recent years.

The literal definition of *riba* in Arabic is "effortless gain" or "the profit which is received without giving anything in exchange." *Riba* is prohibited because it is exploitive and produces a profit at someone else's expense. In a loan transaction, for example, the lender and the borrower are on unequal terms; the lender is guaranteed a profit while the borrower gains or loses money depending on the outcome of the transaction. Rather than being on equal terms whereby both parties share the risk, this lending creates injustice, which is what Shariah strives to avoid.

Islamic scholars are unanimous in stating the prohibition of *riba* since it is clearly mentioned in the Quran and Sunnah. However, with such a broad definition, the full meaning of *riba* is not set in stone, and some aspects of it have been open to debate. What might be defined as *riba* to one group of Islamic scholars may be deemed lawful by another group of scholars. Western lawyers tend to have a hard time understanding why Shariah varies from one part of the world to the next, or from one group of scholars to the next. Islamic scholars, on the other hand, would argue that this is one of the reasons Islamic finance is flexible and open to change in a world of fast-moving global finance. They also argue that setting in stone definitions and rules would only handicap the industry, which is still going through an evolutionary process. It is important, however, to note that, as one prominent Shariah scholar once told me, the vast majority of Shariah scholars agree on 90 percent of Islamic financial matters. What is open to debate is no more than 10 percent of what constitutes Islamic financial transactions, definitions, and contracts. Therefore, the view that Islamic finance lacks clear definitions and consensus among scholars is exaggerated.[5]

MODERN HISTORY OF ISLAMIC BANKING AND FINANCE

The decline of the Islamic empire and the rise of European powers from the thirteenth century on put the brakes on further development of Islamic finance for a very long time. It wasn't until the postcolonial era in the twentieth century that Muslim scholars and academics seriously began to revisit these topics. This set the stage for the modern Islamic finance industry to emerge in the 1970s.

Even before that, there were some attempts at launching interest-free banks. There was one in Malaysia in the mid-1940s and another in Pakistan in the late 1950s. Neither survived. In 1963, the Malaysian government set up the Pilgrim's Management Fund (also known as Tabung Haji) to help prospective pilgrims save for their once-in-a-lifetime pilgrimage to Makkah, a duty of every Muslim and one of the five pillars of Islam. Tabung Haji is still in existence today and has helped thousands save and even make a profit while saving for pilgrimage. In 1963, a savings bank, Mit-Ghamr, was established in Egypt. It was very popular and prospered initially, then closed down for various reasons, including mismanagement. However, this experiment led to the creation of the Nasser Social Bank in 1972.[6] Though the bank is still active today, its goals are more social than commercial and it does not adhere to Islamic finance principles.

The situation began to change in the 1970s, thanks in part to the Arab oil embargo, which led to the first oil crisis in 1973. The dramatic rise in the price of oil gave way to a massive transfer of wealth from developed countries to OPEC countries. Persian Gulf oil producers Iraq, Iran, Kuwait, Qatar, Saudi Arabia, and the United Arab Emirates were among the main beneficiaries of this massive wealth transfer.

As the economies of these countries became richer, along with the migration of educated Muslims to Western countries, Muslims' interest in their faith grew. With this came a new interest in finance and how it relates to their faith. In the early 1970s, Islamic intergovernmental organizations became more involved in discussing and researching the topic of Islamic economics and finance. The Conference of Finance Ministers of Islamic Countries held in Karachi in 1970, the First International Conference on Islamic Economics in Makkah in 1976, and the International Economic Conference in London in 1977 were the result of such involvement. The involvement of institutions and governments led to the application of theory to practice and resulted in the establishment of the first interest-free banks. The Islamic Development Bank (IDB), an intergovernmental bank established in 1975, was born of this process. The goal of the IDB is to foster economic and social development among member countries in accordance with Shariah principles. The bank operates similarly to how the World Bank operates. It grants interest-free loans, equity capital, and other forms of financing for productive projects in member countries as well as providing financial assistance for economic and social development.

The launch of the IDB officially set the stage for the launch of the world's first private Islamic bank. The Dubai Islamic Bank was set up in 1975 by a group of prominent businessmen from several countries in the region. Two years later, three other Islamic banks were launched: Faisal Islamic Bank in Egypt, Faisal Islamic Bank of Sudan, and Kuwait Finance House (KFH) in Kuwait.

Nearly 40 years after the establishment of the first Islamic bank, more than 700 Islamic financial institutions have come into being (Figure 6.1). In the mid-1990s, the global Islamic finance industry was modest and contained mainly in the Middle East and Malaysia. At that time there were approximately 144 institutions, with total assets approaching $150 billion. Today, assets of these 700 institutions have swelled to almost $2 trillion. Though many are in Muslim countries, there is a growing number of Islamic financial institutions in Western Europe as well as Asia and North America.

ISLAMIC BANKING AND FINANCE AROUND THE WORLD

Islamic banks have come a long way in a relatively short time and have captured a significant market share from their conventional rivals. Market share in some Muslim countries now approaches 50 percent and is growing at a faster rate than for their conventional counterparts, especially since the

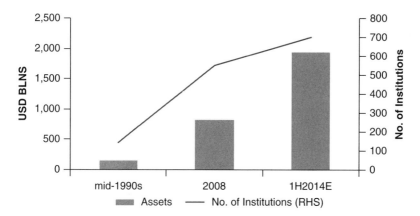

FIGURE 6.1 Growth in the number and assets of Islamic financial institutions around the world
Source: KFH Research

global financial crisis in 2008. The success and acceptance of Islamic banks has led to their spread in other countries beyond the Middle East, including non-Muslim countries (Figure 6.2).

Middle East

The Middle East has been a hotbed for the growth and development of the Islamic finance industry primarily as a result of the oil wealth of the

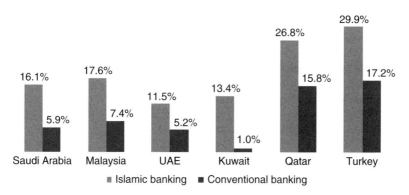

FIGURE 6.2 Growth of Islamic bank assets in select countries from 2008 to 2013 vs. their conventional rivals
Source: KFH Research

Gulf Cooperation Council (GCC)[†] countries. The Islamic Development Bank, which effectively launched the modern Islamic finance industry in 1975, has been successful on many fronts. Since its inception, it has funded and helped build countless infrastructure projects, worth billions of dollars, in member countries. The IDB also offers scholarship programs to help underprivileged students go on to colleges and universities around the world.

More recently, the IDB has stepped up its investment efforts in the wake of the financial crisis and has been focusing on infrastructure projects. The IDB is one of the few transnational organizations to be given a AAA rating by the leading rating agencies. In June 2014, the IDB announced two major initiatives. In the first initiative, the IDB has teamed up with the governments of Bahrain, Brunei, and Saudi Arabia to raise $2 billion for a new infrastructure fund for developing countries.[7] The second initiative has brought together the IDB and the Bill & Melinda Gates Foundation to set up a $2.5 billion fund to help the poor and fight disease in developing countries.[8]

The IDB is not the only success story in the Middle East. Since 1975, Islamic banks have popped up across the region, mainly in GCC countries, and they have captured a lot of market share from conventional banks. Figure 6.3 shows that Islamic banks in Saudi Arabia hold more than 51 percent of all banking assets in the country. In Kuwait, the figure is more than 45 percent, which is up from almost 32 percent in 2008. By the end of this decade I expect Islamic banks to be the leading financial institutions in their respective countries and to hold a majority of banking assets across the region. This is already happening in Kuwait and Saudi Arabia.

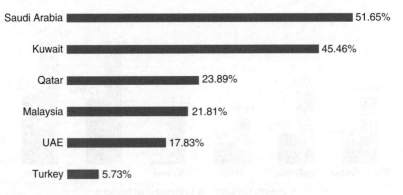

FIGURE 6.3 Market share of Islamic banks in select countries as of 2013
Source: KFH Research

[†]Gulf Cooperation Country (GCC) members include Bahrain, Kuwait, Qatar, Oman, Saudi Arabia, and the United Arab Emirates.

Kuwait Finance House, founded in 1977, was launched with support from the government. At first, few took the bank seriously. Many in the industry at the time referred to Islamic banking as an "experiment" that would fail. After all, few understood what Islamic banking would do differently than conventional banks. Many thought that it was simply religious marketing. KFH, as well as other upstart Islamic banks, lacked the skills and expertise to be able to compete with the well-established conventional banks. Ten years later, people stopped referring to it as an experiment and started to look at it as a viable niche industry, but never thought it would become much of a threat in the long run. By the end of the 1990s, conventional bankers were scrambling to figure out how Islamic banks were able to capture market share away from them. Today, these same conventional banks have either launched their own Islamic banking departments and subsidiaries or converted to full-fledged Islamic banks.

The National Bank of Kuwait (NBK) has maintained its position as the largest bank in Kuwait for decades. Its competitors in Kuwait were not even close to catching up with it in terms of size. Today, KFH has a larger asset base and would have easily overtaken NBK by other measures had it not been for the fact that NBK now owns a majority stake in Boubyan Bank, a competing Islamic bank. In 2007, Kuwait Real Estate Bank gave up on competing with its conventional rivals and became an Islamic bank, now called Kuwait International Bank. The Commercial Bank of Kuwait, another bank that has struggled to compete and has suffered since the financial crisis, is now considering becoming an Islamic bank, too. If it does convert, it will bring the total number of Islamic banks in Kuwait to six.

In Saudi Arabia, Al Rajhi Bank is one of the oldest and largest financial institutions in the country, having started out in 1957 as a money-changing operation capitalizing on the millions of pilgrims visiting Makkah every year and needing money-changing services. The company went on to become one the largest banks in Saudi Arabia and one of the largest in the region. The Al Rajhi family today is one of the wealthiest families in the Middle East.

The success of Al Rajhi bank drove other banks to compete with it on the Islamic finance front. Some, such as HSBC Saudi Arabia, also known as Saudi British Bank (SABB), launched dedicated Islamic banking branches, while others are in the process to become full-fledged Islamic banks, such as National Commercial Bank (NCB). Over the last decade, two more Islamic banks were launched in Saudi Arabia: Bank Albilad and Alinma Bank, bringing the total number of Islamic banks in the country to four. This is in addition to a wide range of Islamic financial service companies that exist.

Bahrain embraced Islamic finance early on, as it developed as a regional banking center in the late 1970s and was successful at attracting regional and global financial institutions to set up operations there. Regulators spotted the potential of Islamic banking early and realized that they needed to find a niche in order to better compete in the global marketplace. Needless to say, Islamic banking, insurance, and other related financial services took off in the 1980s as Islamic finance experienced its first boom.

Global financial institutions at the time chose Bahrain as the place to test-launch their Islamic financial services. In 1996, for example, Citibank launched a dedicated Islamic bank called Citi Islamic Investment Bank. It was the first Western financial institution to launch a dedicated Islamic subsidiary, giving recognition and credibility to the industry. In 2002, UBS followed suit and launched Noriba Bank, a wholly owned Islamic investment bank under a separate brand. However, with limited success over the years, UBS decided to finally fold its activities into the UBS group, effectively closing down Noriba. Other banks and financial services firms, such as asset managers and insurance companies, also used Bahrain as a launching pad for their entry into Islamic finance.

Bahrain became the de facto Islamic financial center for many years, until Dubai launched a rival offshore financial center—the Dubai International Financial Centre (DIFC)—in 2004. In true Dubai fashion, it spent a lot of money on marketing and image building. The DIFC became wildly successful. Today, Dubai is the de facto financial center not only for the Middle East but also for South and Central Asia as well as East Africa. It has stolen the title of regional Islamic financial center away from Bahrain and has its sights today on becoming the global Islamic financial center.

Having launched the first Islamic retail bank in the world gave Dubai an edge when it came to targeting Islamic financial services. Where Bahrain targeted global financial institutions to offer offshore financial services, Dubai targeted these institutions to offer onshore financial services. With it came their other business, too, sucking it away from Bahrain. The political turmoil in Bahrain since 2011 helped accelerate its decline as a financial center.

HSBC, for example, was one of the early players in Islamic finance, along with Citibank, but HSBC chose to launch global Islamic banking services, including retail banking. Dubai became the bank's global center for Islamic banking and currently offers the most comprehensive range of Islamic financial products and services of any global financial institutions. Its closest rival would probably be Standard Chartered Bank. The bank's philosophy is similar to that of HSBC in catering to the needs of the markets where it has a presence.

With 21 of the 25 largest financial institutions in the world having a presence in the DIFC,[9] it's no surprise to see that a majority of them are active in Islamic finance in some form, including BNP Paribas, Credit Suisse, Deutsche Bank, Goldman Sachs, and JPMorgan Chase, even though they do not offer these services in their home markets.

In the domestic market, Dubai and its six other sister emirates that make up the United Arab Emirates (UAE) have seen tremendous growth in Islamic financial services. Ironically, after the launch of Dubai Islamic Bank in 1975, the country did not see another Islamic bank launch for another 22 years. Once Abu Dhabi Islamic Bank (ADIB) was set up in 1997, it sparked a near renaissance of Islamic banking activity in the country. Not only did banking regulators allow new Islamic banks to be set up, they also allowed conventional banks to offer Islamic banking services alongside their conventional banking offerings. Again, there is a debate in this matter, which is: Can an interest-based financial institution truly offer segregated financial services that have not mixed with or touched *riba*? The debate is ongoing, but countries such as Kuwait and Qatar strictly do not allow banks to commingle their funds; they are either conventional institutions or Islamic institutions—they can't be both. The UAE and Malaysia, on the other hand, see no issue in the matter, leading many banks to offer Islamic services as a way to stop Islamic banks from taking their market share.

There are currently seven Islamic banks operating in the UAE, including Sharjah Islamic Bank (SIB), which was the first conventional bank to convert to an Islamic bank back in 2002. Its former name was National Bank of Sharjah. In addition to these seven banks, a host of other local and international banks compete for local and international Islamic financial business, making the UAE banking market extremely competitive.

Across the Middle East, Islamic banking has taken hold and is growing. One would expect Islamic banks to have a presence in all Muslim countries, but this is not the case. Due to political and social turmoil in these markets, Islamic banking has always been looked upon with caution, if not outright hatred. In Iran, Iraq, Jordan, Qatar, Sudan, and Yemen, Islamic banking is well established. However, in Algeria, Libya, Morocco, and Syria, there have been attempts at launching Islamic banks, but regulators in those markets have still not authorized them. Libya and Morocco are said to be authorizing them soon, while Syria was expected to open its first Islamic bank just as its civil war began in 2011.

Egypt, Oman, and Turkey have had a love–hate relationship with Islamic finance from the beginning. One would expect Egypt, in particular, to have a thriving Islamic finance industry, being one of the largest Muslim countries, but ongoing political and social issues in the country have kept Islamic banking's growth limited. Abu Dhabi Islamic Bank, however, has recently established a presence in Egypt, as well as Iraq, in an attempt to go after untapped markets for Islamic finance.

In Oman, the government had always been against Islamic banking and refused to allow it until the Arab Spring uprising in 2011. One of the key grievances protesters had was their wish for Islamic banking in their country.

So the government conceded, and today Islamic banking is up and running in Oman.

Turkey, on the other hand, has allowed Islamic banking activities in the country since 1985, but did not allow them to be called Islamic. Instead, the government preferred the term *participation banks*. Demand for Islamic banking services in Turkey came from the domestic population, but it wasn't until investors from the GCC started setting up "special finance houses" in the country that the industry took off. In 1985, Bahrain-based Al Baraka Banking Group set up Al Baraka Turk, the first participation bank in the country. It was followed by the launch of Faisal Finans Kurumu by Saudi-based Faisal Finance in that same year. In 1989, Kuwait Finance House opened the doors of Kuveyt Turk Participation Bank. Local players soon followed: Anadolu Finans (1991), Ihlas Finans (1995), and Asya Finans (1996).[10] Although participation banks currently hold less than 6 percent of the total banking assets in Turkey, as shown in Figure 6.2, the sector has been growing at a rate of almost 30 percent over the past five years, well ahead of the conventional sector.

Asia

In Asia, the Islamic finance industry has been concentrated in Malaysia. Though Islamic finance has spread to other countries in the region, such as Brunei, Indonesia, Singapore, and Thailand, Malaysia remains the driving force in Asia for Islamic banking and has become one of the most developed and competitive Islamic financial markets.

The first Islamic financial institution in Asia was Tabung Haji, established in Malaysia in 1963. In what was at the time a low-income country, it would take the average income earner 10 to 15 years to be able to save enough for the pilgrimage. Tabung Haji's aim was to reduce this time as well as help more Malaysians save for and afford the trip. Today, the firm manages more than $13 billion in assets from over 8 million depositors.[11]

The first Islamic bank in Asia was Bank Islam Malaysia Berhad (BIMB), launched in 1983 after the Malaysian government signed into law the Islamic Banking Act in that same year.[12] The act gave Bank Negara, the country's central bank, the authority to supervise and regulate Islamic banks as it does with the country's conventional banks. The success of Tabung Haji and the awareness it built up over the years prior to the launch of Bank Islam helped it get off to a good start.

It was not until 10 years later that the Islamic financial services industry in Malaysia took off. In 1993, following the success of Bank Islam, the Malaysian government decided to open up the industry to spur further development and competition. Unlike governments and regulators in the

Middle East, the Malaysians actively and aggressively promoted the development of the industry, both on the national level and on the international level. The introduction of the Islamic Banking Scheme in 1993 by Bank Negara allowed, for the first time, existing conventional banks to offer Islamic banking services using the infrastructure and branches they already had in place.[13] The government and Bank Negara saw this option as being the most effective and efficient way of increasing the number of institutions offering Islamic banking services. These institutions, however, were required to separate the funds and activities of Islamic banking from those of the conventional banking business to ensure that there would not be any commingling of funds.

Following these developments, it's no surprise that Malaysia quickly developed and became the Islamic financial center in Asia and one of the leading Islamic financial centers in the world. Today, there are more than 21 Islamic banks operating in the country, many of which are subsidiaries of conventional banks. There are also international banks offering Islamic banking services (HSBC and Standard Chartered) and foreign Islamic banks (KFH and Al Rajhi) that have entered the Malaysian market in the past eight years.

With strong support from the government, Bank Negara, along with other financial market regulators, have developed the most advanced Islamic financial services industry in the world. In addition to the high number of Islamic banks in the country, there are also more than 16 Islamic insurance companies (known as Takaful) and reinsurance companies (re-Takaful) operating in the market. Its financial markets have also developed well ahead of markets in the Middle East. Malaysia boasts the largest number of Islamic mutual funds of any other country, currently standing at over 250, and the largest and most active secondary market for the trading of Islamic financial instruments, such as *sukuk*.

Other financial centers in Asia—namely, Singapore and Hong Kong—have looked at Malaysia's success with envy. Though both these financial centers dwarf the size of Malaysia's market, the success and rapid growth of Islamic finance around the world have attracted their attention. To date, Singapore has been ahead of Hong Kong in tapping into this market. In 2007, the Islamic Bank of Asia was launched, the country's first Islamic bank, albeit an investment bank and not a retail bank. Singapore's status as the leading private banking center in the world has helped it attract Islamic high-net-worth assets to the private banks operating there. Local banks such as DBS and OCBC offer Islamic private banking services, and international fund managers such as Franklin Templeton, Noruma, and Amundi offer a wide range of Islamic funds for investors across Asia.

In September 2014, the Hong Kong government jumped into the Islamic finance market by issuing a landmark $1 billion in *sukuk*

(Islamic asset-backed securities). Demand from investors was high and has since sparked interest from other non-Muslim countries in the *sukuk* market.[14] Brunei and Indonesia, with majority Muslim populations, and the Philippines and Thailand, with significant Muslim populations, have established Islamic banks. In the case of Brunei and Indonesia, there is renewed interest from government and regulators to get the industry moving after seeing Malaysia's success. Indonesia in particular has a lot of untapped potential, which is now attracting interest from Malaysia and the Middle East. The Philippines, a majority Catholic country, set up Amanah Islamic Bank in 1990. Thailand, a majority Buddhist country, set up the Islamic Bank of Thailand in 2002. Both banks are aimed at catering to the Muslim minority populations in their respective countries.

The development of Islamic finance in Asia does not stop there. Islamic finance is well established in Bangladesh, Pakistan, and Sri Lanka. Non-Muslim countries in Asia have also been looking for ways to tap into this market. Japan and South Korea, countries with negligible Muslim populations, have indicated their interest in accessing the Islamic capital markets for *sukuk* and other financial instruments. To them, the Muslim investor is viewed as an alternative source of capital and a way to diversify their investor base.

Europe

Islamic finance made its way to Europe earlier than most would have expected. The first Islamic financial institutions in Europe were in Switzerland and Luxembourg, not because of demand for Islamic banking in these countries, but rather as a result of Islamic financial institutions in the GCC looking for reputable offshore jurisdictions in which to base some of their operations. Dar al-Mal al-Islami (DMI), one of the earliest Islamic financial groups, set up Takaful SA in Luxembourg in the 1980s, along with a private bank in Geneva, Switzerland, which today is called Faisal Private Bank.

With the rapidly rising wealth of GCC countries in the 1980s and 1990s, Swiss private banks developed a lucrative business in managing money for the new high-net-worth clients from these countries. The growth of Islamic banking during this time caught their attention, and they began experimenting with offering these clients some Islamic banking services, such as asset management, investment funds, cash management, and trust services, all in compliance with Shariah. All the major Swiss banks at one time or another were offering some level of Islamic banking services, including Credit Suisse, Pictet & Cie, and UBS. Over time, some of these banks dropped their Islamic banking offerings while others launched new ones. Overall, Swiss banks have had mixed success in Islamic finance. Their mediocre success in this field was primarily the result of their lack of commitment and enthusiasm. It was never their intention to develop products and services to compete with their bread-and-butter private banking business but, rather, a way to entice clients to stay with them by offering them a few Shariah-compliant services.

Swiss banks today are still following this business model with the same level of success. They will probably never jump into Islamic finance with both feet, especially now that they have bigger issues to deal with, such as claims they help clients evade taxes in their home countries. Their business model today is under threat, and the country is losing its stature as a private banking center and tax haven. Countries such as Singapore have taken advantage of the cracks in the Swiss banking model, which can only be beneficial to Islamic finance in the long run.

The first true Islamic bank in Europe was launched in 2004 after the United Kingdom passed laws allowing for the regulation and licensing of Islamic banks and financial institutions. The Financial Services Authority (FSA) was put in charge of licensing and regulating Islamic financial institutions in the country. Shortly after the law was passed, the Islamic Bank of Britain (IBB) was born as the first Islamic retail bank in the Western world. Since then, five other Islamic banks have been licensed in the United Kingdom: Bank of London and the Middle East (2007), European Islamic Investment Bank (2006), QIB UK (2008), Gatehouse Bank (2008), and Abu Dhabi Islamic Bank UK (2012). The Islamic Bank of Britain is the only retail Islamic bank. The other five banks are licensed as investment banks.

IBB, however, was not the first bank to offer Islamic financial services in the United Kingdom, nor is it alone in serving the retail market today. In 2002, the United Bank of Kuwait (UBK) was the first and only bank in the United Kingdom offering an Islamic mortgage solution.[15] The bank was not an Islamic bank but, rather, a conventional bank owned by investors from Kuwait, among others. Seeing pent-up demand for an Islamic mortgage product in the West, the bank's management decided to offer a first-of-its-kind Shariah-compliant mortgage product through its branch network in the United Kingdom as well as in the United States. This was a pioneering move at the time. Following the bank's merger with Al-Ahli Commercial Bank of Bahrain, the group rebranded as Ahli United Bank.[16] The bank maintains a presence in the United Kingdom to this day and still offers its Islamic mortgage product. After the merger, however, the bank decided to close down its U.S. operation.

Competition today in the U.K. Islamic mortgage market is strong. IBB may be the only full-service Islamic retail bank in the market, but it faces tough competition from no less than 20 other financial services companies.[17] In addition to Ahli United Bank, other banks offering Shariah-compliant mortgage solutions include HSBC, Royal Bank of Scotland, and Lloyds TSB.

The U.K. government has also been making a bold push into Islamic finance. In June 2014, it issued its first *sukuk* (asset-backed) security on the market. The issuance was relatively small at £200 million, but it attracted orders of over £2 billion.[18] Although this move caught a lot of attention in the media, it was not the first *sukuk* issued by a European government. In 2004, the German state of Saxony-Anhalt issued a €100 million *sukuk* and was listed for trading in Luxembourg.[19]

In other parts of Europe, Islamic finance has yet to establish itself. Luxembourg already lists many of the U.S. dollar–denominated *sukuk* and mutual funds, but it would now like to attract new business. Laws in Luxembourg have since been modified to attract more Islamic investors to the country. In 2013, investors from the GCC announced plans for launching an Islamic bank, to be called Eurisbank, capitalized at €60 million.[20] Another notable development in continental Europe is the expansion of Kuveyt Turk Participation Bank into Germany. The bank is currently upgrading its representative office in Mannheim, Germany, to a full-fledged bank in order to target the large Turkish population living there. France, on the other hand, has been quiet on Islamic finance. Even though all its international banks are active in Islamic finance overseas, it is not something French regulators (or the bankers themselves) would like to see marketed in France.

The United Kingdom is clearly ahead of other European countries in Islamic finance, and it has been able to maintain its role as one of the leading Islamic financial centers even with all the competition from Dubai and Malaysia. The United Kingdom has traditionally been the preferred banking center for the Middle East, and the country's embrace of Islamic finance will push it further ahead of any potential European rivals.

North America

The seeds of Islamic finance were planted early in North America. Though there are no Islamic banks in the United States and Canada, community-based Islamic investment and finance companies have been around since the 1980s. In Canada, for example, the small but growing Muslim population in Toronto set up the Islamic Housing Co-Operative 1980, which is still active today and is called Ansar Co-operative Housing Corporation. The cooperative's goal is to serve Muslims living in Canada, by pooling their funds to enable them to offer home financing solutions. Banks at the time were not interested in serving this market. Other Shariah-compliant mortgage providers popped up over the years, including a company called UM Financial, which went bankrupt in 2011 under a cloud of shady activities.[21] This damaged the reputation of all other Islamic financial services companies operating in Canada and has been a major setback to the industry. Prior to this, community leaders and investors were in discussion with regulators to allow for an Islamic bank to be licensed along the same path as in the United Kingdom. However, the headlines the UM Financial fiasco attracted put the brakes on this for the foreseeable future.

Islamic finance has been more successful in the United States. The industry there also got its start through community-based groups that went on to form financial services companies. One of the first such groups was the North American Islamic Trust (NAIT), founded in 1973 as a not-for-profit endowment fund to help build, finance, and manage the growing demand for mosques in the country. In 1986, NAIT was responsible for helping to start the first Islamic mutual funds in the United States, which are managed by Saturna Capital, based in Washington state. The firm currently manages close to $3.5 billion in three Islamic mutual funds,[22] with a vast majority of investors being non-Muslim.

Another early pioneer in the United States is Lariba American Finance House, founded in 1987 in Pasadena, California.[23] The group's aim was to help Muslims buy a home or invest in a business in accordance with Shariah principles. The company is still active today and has gone on to purchase Bank of Whittier, a local bank in California. The bank is not an Islamic bank, since regulators in the United States do not issue Islamic banking licenses; it currently operates as a conventional bank that also offers Shariah-compliant services, such as home financing.

The 1980s and 1990s saw a wide range of companies and community-based initiatives looking to offer Islamic financial services. In 1996, the Ameen Housing Co-operative was launched in Palo Alto, California, and was modeled after the housing cooperative in Toronto. In 2001, I joined HSBC to manage the launch of its Islamic banking initiative in the United States, beginning in New York state. We successfully launched in March 2002 and attracted a lot of headlines for the move, especially in light of the tragic events on September 11, 2001. While I was there, we launched other banking services to meet the needs of the Muslim market and went on to develop investment solutions as well. Less than a year after I left the bank in 2004, however, HSBC decided to close down the Islamic banking department. I attributed this to the new management that arrived with the bank's acquisition of Household International. Suffice it to say that the Household team did not have the same commitment to Islamic finance. In Chapter 3, we saw what a disaster the Household acquisition was for HSBC.

With HSBC out of the market, there were still plenty of players vying for the Muslim market in the United States. Even though United Bank of

Kuwait was the first bank to offer a Shariah-compliant mortgage solution in the United States, it was not until HSBC entered the market that the industry began to professionalize and move beyond community-based initiatives to nationwide initiatives. At the same time HSBC entered the market, three other firms entered to compete with HSBC on the East Coast and Lariba on the West Coast: Devon Bank in Chicago, University Bank in Michigan, and Guidance Residential in Reston, Virginia. Based on my information from these companies, it is estimated that the size of the U.S. Shariah-compliant mortgage market is well over $5 billion today.

While these firms operate on Main Street, on Wall Street there is even more Islamic financial activity. From Goldman Sachs and JPMorgan Chase to the leading law firms in Midtown Manhattan, bankers and lawyers are hard at work structuring billions of dollars' worth of Islamic financing deals. Many of these deals are not in the United States, but there is still plenty of Islamic financing done in the country for international investors. In 2004, Liberty Aerospace, a small Florida-based aircraft manufacturer, was acquired by Kuwait Finance House in an Islamic private equity deal valued at $60 million.[24] KFH has been investing in the United States for decades, primarily in real estate such as multifamily housing and warehousing facilities. It also owns part of the Ritz-Carlton Residences in Chicago.[25] Other, more common, names that have at one point been owned by Islamic investors include Caribou Coffee Company, Church's Chicken, Yakima Products, and Southland Log Homes.[26]

The fast pace at which Islamic finance developed around the world has been impressive. Although there have been some setbacks and not everyone has been so accepting of it, the rapid growth of this industry deserves a closer look. An industry that went from zero to $2 trillion in a 40-year span merits a detailed review and analysis to see what it has to offer.

SUMMARY

- Islamic finance is a financial system that operates according to Islamic law, called Shariah.
- Shariah is derived from Islam's holy book, the Quran, along with the sayings of the Prophet Muhammad (Hadith) and his actions (Sunnah).
- Islamic jurisprudence, or *fiqh,* is based on Shariah as well as deductive reasoning and analogy to form a consensus of opinion on matters not covered in Shariah.
- The main purpose for imposing these laws on commerce and trade is to remove injustice and inequality in financial dealings.
- One of the most prominent laws in Islamic finance is the prohibition against charging interest, also known as *riba.*

- *Riba*, however, has a much broader meaning than "interest" alone. It also includes usury or any benefit or advantage one person may have over another in a financial transaction.
- The only form of lending allowed in Islam is an interest-free loan, or benevolent loan, whereby the lender is only entitled to the return of the principal.
- The lender and the borrower are on unequal terms because the lender is guaranteed a profit while the borrower gains or loses.
- One of the aims of this prohibition is to stop people from becoming debt slaves.
- Modern Islamic finance was officially born in 1975 with the launch of the Islamic Development Bank, followed by Dubai Islamic Bank.
- Today, the industry has grown to include more than 700 institutions worldwide, controlling nearly $2 trillion in assets. It has been capturing market share from conventional banks.
- It is expected that Islamic banks will overtake their conventional counterparts in many markets where they are active, as this is already happening in Saudi Arabia and Kuwait.
- The Middle East has been a hotbed for the development of Islamic finance. As such, Islamic banks have come to dominate some of these markets. To compete, conventional banks have been forced to convert or launch their own Islamic banking operations.
- In Asia, Malaysia is the center for Islamic finance and is well ahead of other financial centers in terms of product offerings and depth. However, Malaysia in not alone in having Islamic financial services. The Islamic banking and finance industry is very active in Southeast Asia.
- In Europe, the United Kingdom is the leader in Islamic banking. Not only has it authorized Islamic banks to operate there, but it has also gone on to issue Islamic asset-backed securities, called *sukuk*.
- Much of the Islamic financial activity in North America was community based in the 1980s and 1990s until HSBC launched its Islamic banking operation in 2002. Since then, the industry has developed rapidly, but banking regulators have yet to authorize the licensing of Islamic banks.

CHAPTER 7

The Key Principles of Islamic Finance

The prohibition against *riba* is a fundamental aspect of Islamic finance, and this alone sets it apart from conventional finance. However, it's not enough to say that Islamic finance is interest-free finance. There is more to it than that. The reason behind the prohibition against interest, and *riba* as it is broadly defined, is to remove injustice and inequality from financial matters. To do so, Shariah has stipulated some ethical guidelines to follow.

As mentioned in Chapter 6, when it comes to trade and finance, everything is permissible unless it is explicitly prohibited by Shariah, leaving the door wide open for financial creativity and for free markets to operate. Some of the other prohibitions include industries that Muslims must avoid because they conflict with the tenets of Islam and Shariah. These industries include the following:

- *Gambling*: This includes all forms such as games of chance, lotteries, and, in modern times, speculation. The premise for this prohibition is based on chance: A person would pay an amount of money for a chance to win a larger amount of money if the outcome is in his/her favor. If not, the money paid is lost and no value was created in the process. In contrast to investing in, say, a start-up company, the risk of large profits or losses is there, but the investment is used for a productive purpose. If the venture works out, the return is high, and if the venture fails, the investment is lost. The risk/reward trade-off is at the center of Islamic finance, as we shall see later.
- *Pornography*: In modern times Shariah scholars have also included sectors in media, advertising, and fashion industries as part of this prohibition due to their promotion of sex, promiscuity, and nudity as part of their business model.
- *Alcohol*: The production of, trade of, investment in, and consumption of alcohol products is forbidden. The Quran clearly states that all

"intoxicants" are forbidden, so this goes beyond alcohol and includes intoxicating drugs as well. There is some debate, however, on certain forms of medical drugs such as strong painkillers that have intoxicating effects. Some scholars view medicinal drugs as acceptable. I'm not sure, however, on their view of medical marijuana, which has been a recent topic of debate in the United States.

- *Pork*: The production, trade, investment, and consumption of pork and pork-related products such as lard and gelatin are forbidden. Many non-Muslims are aware of Islam's prohibition against pork, similar to the Jewish prohibition. As with Jewish traditions, Muslims must also slaughter their animals using certain methods to deem them acceptable, or *halal,* as it is known. *Kosher* and *halal* are similar terms, and this is why in the United States, for example, you will see that Jewish slaughterhouses will certify halal meats as well. What is not widely known, however, is that Muslims are also forbidden to eat any carnivorous animals such as dogs, cats, eagles, lions, tigers, and so on.

- *Conventional finance and insurance*: The obvious reason for this restriction, of course, is that their business model is based on paying and receiving interest. This includes all conventional banks regardless of whether they have an Islamic banking department, finance companies, and mortgage companies, as well as companies that derive a significant portion of their revenue from interest or that pay a significant portion of their expenses in interest.

- *Weapons and defense*: Though not strictly forbidden, this is a gray area, since using weapons for defensive purposes is permitted—though weapon and defense companies don't discriminate among their buyers as to who is buying for defensives purposes and who is not. As such, a majority of scholars prefer to avoid investing in or participating in such activities.

- *Tobacco*: This is also a gray area, since tobacco is not explicitly forbidden in Shariah. However, there is consensus among scholars that anything harmful, even though it has not been explicitly mentioned in Shariah, should be avoided.

- *Environmental concerns*: The same consensus applies here. If something is harmful to the environment, it should be avoided.

- *Hospitality and entertainment*: Investing in or participating in these industries is not prohibited unless the industries are engaged in one or more of the other activities listed here—alcohol, pornography, gambling, or pork. As you can see, a vast majority of Western hospitality and entertainment companies are out of bounds for Muslims to invest in or participate in.

This list might seem too long or too strict, but on the flipside, look at all the industries that are wide open for Muslims to invest in: software, technology, telecommunications, health care, food production, farming, automotive, energy, aerospace, building and construction, real estate, transportation, education, utilities—not forgetting Islamic banks, finance companies, and insurance companies. So, then, according to Islamic finance, what are some of the ethical rules one must follow to avoid injustice and inequality in a trade or financial transaction? Islamic finance is not one-sided; it does not only look out for the interest of the buyer over the seller, or the receiver of capital over the provider of capital, or even the depositor over the bank. It aims to be fair to all parties involved in a transaction. Here are some of the key ethical rules that must be followed:

1. *You cannot earn a return or profit unless you're willing to take some risk.* There is no riskless return. Anyone willing to invest their money must be willing to accept a loss if it doesn't work out. As with capitalistic principles, the higher the risk one is willing to take, the higher the return they can potentially earn. In business school we are taught that government bonds are risk-free. Under Shariah, this would not be acceptable. Lending is another financial instrument that is not designed to take a loss. There is only one form of lending in Islamic finance, and it is, as mentioned earlier, interest-free and must be paid back. These interest-free loans, however, are not designed for business transactions; they function more as charity. I can't imagine a bank having a successful business model based on giving out interest-free loans.

2. *There is no guaranteed return.* Under Shariah, returns cannot be guaranteed, since a business or venture can fail. If the business fails, then there is no return to investors. Establishing a fixed rate of return is acceptable, such as rental or lease payments that are fixed each month, but to guarantee them means that if your renters default, you are still on the hook to make the payments to your lender or investor. Investors must realize the potential risks of an investment and weigh it against their return or appetite for return, and then make a decision based on this. In conventional finance, if you borrow money, you are expected to pay it back with interest regardless of how your business or venture works out.

3. *You cannot lose more than you invest.* How can you lose more than your investment in conventional finance? In most cases you can't. If you invest in the stock market, the maximum you can lose is the amount of your investment. Investments in corporations or limited liability companies (LLCs) are designed to shield investors from losing more than their investment. However, when leverage is added to the mix, investors can

lose a lot more. Buying stocks on margin or borrowing money to buy an investment property can easily lead to losing more than your investment. During the most recent financial crisis, the financial term *underwater mortgage* became a household name. As the property market took a nose-dive, millions of home owners ended up owing more on their house than they had put in, meaning that if they sold their house at the current market value, not only would they lose all their equity but they would also owe the bank an additional amount of money, since banks, being lenders, do not take losses on loans. In Islamic finance, you cannot lose more than what you put in. So in the case of a dramatic drop in your home value, you can lose your entire investment, but not more than that. The bank or finance company would also take a loss.

4. *All investors are treated equally.* One investor is never favored over another. In conventional finance, preferred shares are commonly used to give these investors a priority claim on a company's profits over investors in common stock. In Islamic finance, this is not allowed. All investors in shares are treated equally as other shareholders.

5. *You cannot sell what you do not own.* In conventional finance this is allowed. Imagine that you borrow your neighbor's car, then turn around and sell it, and then you give him/her the amount you sold it for minus a commission for yourself. This is not a situation that would occur normally, but in financial markets it happens every day, and is called *short-selling.* You bet that a stock price will fall, so you borrow shares from another investor and sell them without ever owning them. If the price drops, you buy the shares at a lower price and give the investor his/her shares back, keeping the profit from the price drop to yourself. If it goes the other way and the share price rises, the investor can force you to give back the shares so they can sell them and make a profit, leaving you with the loss since you will have to buy shares at a higher price in order to give them back. Short-selling is another example of being able to lose more than you invest.

6. *In order for your money to earn a profit, it must be invested in something productive.* Hoarding money or having wealth sit idle is discouraged. Money cannot earn a return sitting idle. Actually, money cannot earn a return unless it is invested. This also goes back to points 1 and 2, meaning that you must be willing to take on some risk in order to get a return, which cannot be guaranteed.

7. *There must be transparency* in any financial dealing, such that ambiguity and uncertainty are removed or minimized. If you are buying a car or a house, all defects and issues must be disclosed, allowing a potential buyer to make a decision based on all the information available. The same goes for investors looking to acquire or invest in a company. A simpler way

of saying this is that you cannot pay for something without knowing the price. This happens frequently in high-end restaurants, where the prices are not disclosed up front. Under Shariah, price is one of the key elements that must be disclosed before a transaction can take place. There are cases where uncertainty cannot be removed from a transaction, such as natural disasters or during the recent financial crises when credit markets froze. Events like these are hard to foresee, and Shariah does not expect them to be eliminated, as they are risks that one must take into consideration before investing.

8. *All forms of gambling must be removed from a transaction.* Casino-style gambling and lotteries are obvious, but there are other forms of gambling. Going back to the scenario with your neighbor: Instead of borrowing his car, you make him an offer to buy his car tomorrow, but only if your favorite football team wins the game this evening. This is not a valid offer under Shariah, since the sale will take place only if a chance event occurs. In recent times there was a company that gained notoriety and a lot of business for allowing people to bet on chance events and the stock market. Intrade, set up in 1999, kick-started what was to be called the prediction market. Much like sports betting, Intrade allowed "traders" to bet on chance events, such as presidential elections, hurricanes, or stock index closing prices. These were all-or-nothing bets, meaning that you either won or lost. All forms of chance betting are prohibited in Islamic finance. Intrade was shut down in 2013 following investigations into its trading activities.[1]

9. *Money is not a commodity.* It cannot be discounted or sold in advance or at a markup. It cannot earn a return on its own by being lent out.

This list is not exhaustive, but you can see how Shariah guidelines are aimed at leveling the playing field for parties involved in trading or a financial transaction. You can probably think of more scenarios in modern-day finance where the application of these rules would make sense. Accepting risk when investing under these terms might seem as though it would make the financial system riskier, but, on the contrary, by having investors and lenders reevaluate their investment decisions based on taking on more risk, they will become more prudent in their investment decisions and less willing to lend to riskier ventures. Following these rules would also remove some of the reckless behavior in the market by eliminating gambling and other forms of betting. Allowing gambling in financial markets makes the system riskier. We saw this during the last financial crisis, when banks were (and still are) taking on big bets in derivatives only to see them fall flat on their faces, leading to the biggest financial bailout in history.

What needs more attention, however, is Shariah's definition of money. Money plays a huge role in our financial system, and a lot of emphasis is placed on the time value of money. Understanding how Shariah views money and its time value is paramount to understanding Islamic finance.

DEFINITION OF MONEY ACCORDING TO SHARIAH

If money is not a commodity, then what is it? To understand what Shariah defines as money, let's first consider the definition of a commodity. A commodity is a good whose price is determined by the market's supply/demand dynamics for it. Commodities are often substances that come out of the ground and that maintain roughly a universal price. A commodity is fungible, meaning that there is no differentiation between a commodity produced in one country and the same commodity produced in another country. An ounce of gold produced in South Africa is identical to an ounce of gold produced in Russia. The price of gold is universal and fluctuates daily based on global supply and demand.

Commodities in general can be split into two categories: hard commodities and soft commodities. Hard commodities are aluminum, copper, crude oil, gold, iron ore, palladium, platinum, and silver. These commodities are mined and typically do not go bad or expire. Soft commodities, on the other hand, do expire and include agricultural products such as coffee, corn, rice, salt, soybeans, sugar, and wheat. Hard and soft commodities share a characteristic in that they can be stored and transported. There is another class of commodities—energy commodities—which includes electricity, gas, coal, and oil. Electricity is the odd one of the bunch in that it is either impossible or uneconomical to store and, therefore, must be consumed as soon as it is produced. In modern finance, currencies are also considered commodities and are traded as such. They fit the criteria in being fungible, but they are not considered a good. Nevertheless, they are treated as commodities and traded globally on exchanges in the same way hard and soft commodities are traded. Shariah, on the other hand, doesn't see it this way and considers money to be money and not a commodity.

What, then, is Shariah's definition of money? *Money* is defined as something generally accepted as a medium of exchange or a means of payment. It is also a unit of account, meaning that when you are considering buying a new car, it is much easier to pay in dollars than in pounds of wheat or barrels of oil. Money is a unit of account because it is accepted universally in an economy as a means of payment and a measure of value. Money plays an excellent function as a unit of account because it is divisible (dollars and cents), easily stored, and easily transported. Another important characteristic of money in our society is that it is a store of value[2]—and this is where Shariah differs on the definition.

According to Shariah, money is a medium of exchange and a unit of account, but it is not a commodity, since it cannot be used or consumed directly without exchanging it for something else. It is also not a store of value, since it has no intrinsic value in itself. It cannot be utilized in direct fulfillment of human needs. You can't eat money, build with money, or use money to power your car.

In the early Islamic period, gold and silver were used as money. This is not to say that paper money has no place in Islamic finance; on the contrary, Shariah doesn't place a limit on what money can be, since it is merely a reference point, a tool used to transact in commerce and a way to settle payments. Thus, paper money, and digital money today, are acceptable forms of money under Shariah.

A feature of money in Islamic finance, unlike in conventional finance, is that it cannot be bought and sold at a premium or discount, since it has no intrinsic value. Doing so would be considered *riba*—incurring a gain or loss on something that has no value in itself. As such, currency trading is allowed but only if it is on the spot market, which means that the trades must be immediate, without any time delay or premium/discount. Gold and silver are also considered to be money under Shariah and are treated the same as currencies. They likewise can be traded only on the spot market. This renders the trading of currencies, along with gold and silver, using futures, forwards, and options out of bounds for Islamic investors.

DOES TIME VALUE OF MONEY EXIST IN ISLAMIC FINANCE?

A dollar today is preferable to a dollar sometime in the future. This concept is easy enough for most people to grasp without the use of models and mathematics. The definition of *time value* of money is simply this: Money's value changes with time. Getting paid today is worth more to you than getting paid at a date in the future because there is inflation in the financial system, which eats away at your money's value over time. The longer you wait to get paid, the less it's worth, as inflation takes part of it away from you. There is also increased risk that you will not get paid if the person or company owing you the money defaults, runs off, or goes bankrupt. Therefore, most people would rather enjoy their money today rather than waiting to enjoy it sometime in the distant future.

The next logical question is whether Shariah and Islamic finance recognize the time value of money. If money has no intrinsic value, it can't earn a return. This means that money can't "make" more money. It also means that the concept of compounded interest does not exist in Islamic finance.

If there is no time value of money in Islamic finance, how does it place value on a person's wealth over time, since *time value* of money is a fundamental financial theory and a basic element in our current monetary system? The time value of money does exist in Islamic finance, but it is totally different from the theory we were taught in college. The main reason for this is that Islam's definition of money differs from that in the conventional system. From the Shariah perspective, money can earn a return only if it is converted into a productive activity. By this I mean that when money is invested in an asset, venture, company, or other productive activity, then it can earn a return because now it is being used to produce value and is subject to risk (i.e., profit and loss). If you have money sitting idle at the bank and want to earn a return on it, you can, for example, invest it in a rental property to earn a return. Money sitting idle does not entitle it to earn a return.

Islam recognizes time value, but not on money sitting idle. The concept of paying now or paying later at a higher price is well established in Islamic finance. Many of its financial instruments are based on this. Islamic finance differentiates between paying now and paying at a date in the future. If you were to buy something today and pay later, it would cost more than paying on the spot—there is no debate on this point between conventional finance and Islamic finance. The time value Islam places, however, is not on the money; it's on the good or asset the money was converted to. If I sell you my car today, I will ask you to pay $10,000. However, if you can't pay me $10,000 today, you can pay me $500 per month for 24 months. This adds up to $12,000 over the two-year period, and this is perfectly acceptable because the purpose of the transaction was to sell the car and not to lend money.

We will get into more detail on this when we go through the main financial instruments used in Islamic finance. The main point I want to make here is that there is time value in Islamic finance.

ISLAMIC FINANCIAL INSTRUMENTS

In conventional finance, there are auto loans, home mortgages, corporate lending, bonds, private equity, and venture capital, among a host of other financial tools and instruments. These instruments also exist in Islamic finance, albeit in different forms. In some cases the concept is similar but with a slight variation. This slight variation is what differentiates Islamic finance from conventional finance. It is also this slight differentiation that changes the transaction from being *riba*-based to *riba*-free. Some may think that these slight changes in the structure of a transaction are trivial, but in Islamic finance they are very relevant. I will try to explain them as we walk through the instruments. One thing to point out, however, is that Islamic finance tends to "Arabize" the definitions, which, in my opinion, makes no difference to the structure or meaning. So instead of using Arabic terms for these instruments, I will refer to them for the most part in English so as to try to avoid any confusion. One term, however, that is difficult to translate is *riba,* but I think the broad definition given earlier helps clarify its full meaning.

It's also important to mention that for any Islamic financial instrument to be used and gain acceptance in the market, it must be reviewed and approved by an independent panel of Shariah scholars. These scholars ensure that the structures and instruments are in line with Shariah rules and guidelines. Once approved, they issue a ruling (also known as a *fatwa*) stating their approval. Think of this as you would an accounting and auditing firm. Every year they review a company's financial reports and issue a statement on whether the company's financials are correct and in compliance with the accounting rules. The Shariah approval process is similar. Every bank and financial institution, regardless of whether it is an Islamic financial institution or a conventional institution, must have its Islamic financial products, structures, and instruments reviewed and approved by an independent Shariah panel.

That being said, the following six instruments have been universally accepted by Shariah scholars and are at the core of Islamic finance today. Understanding how they work will help you better understand Islamic finance and how it tries to implement its ethical and social justice rules.

Trust Financing (*Mudaraba*)

One of the simplest financing structures in Islamic finance is trust financing, known as *mudaraba* in Arabic. Trust financing is simply as it says: One party entrusts its money or investment to another party, whose role it is to use the money to invest in a Shariah-compliant project or activity. The returns, if any, are split between the parties. This is illustrated in Figure 7.1.

The investor or provider of capital in this case would provide all the money or capital to the venture, while the investment manager (or entrepreneur) would provide their skills and experience to make the venture successful and earn a return. If the venture is profitable, both parties share in the profits, which must be agreed to in advance, before the start of the venture. For example, 80 percent of the profits go to the investor since they are the sole provider of the capital, and the remaining 20 percent go to the manager or entrepreneur since they are providing their time

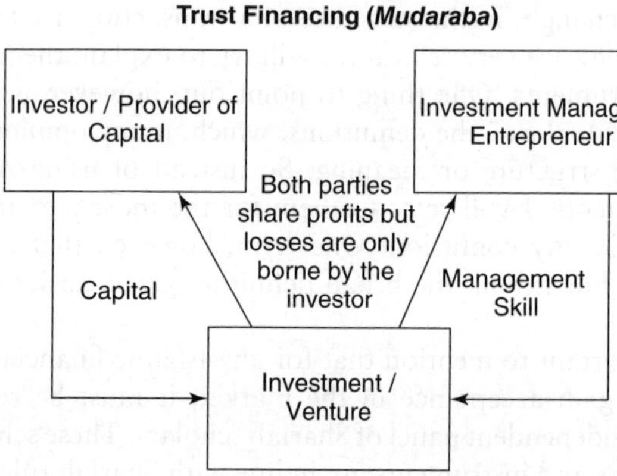

Trust Financing (*Mudaraba*)

FIGURE 7.1   Illustration of trust financing

and skills (also known as sweat equity). However, in the case of a loss, the sole provider of capital is also the sole loser of capital. Since the manager/entrepreneur did not put up any capital, they cannot lose any capital. This goes back to ethical rule number 3, mentioned previously. The manager/entrepreneur in this case can lose only the time and effort they spent working on the venture.

Some might think this is crazy, since what investor in their right mind would agree to it? Well, this type of structure exists today in our financial system, and it is very popular. Think of the relationship you have with your mutual fund or 401(k) plan. You provide all the money to invest, and the fund manager invests it on your behalf (because you have entrusted the manager with it). The fund manager uses their skills and experience to earn you a return. If the outcome is successful, you earn a return and the manager keeps their job. Hopefully, the manager gets more of your money to invest, since they collect a fee based on a percentage of money invested. If the outcome of the investments is a loss, all of it is borne by you and the other investors in the fund, not the fund manager. They might lose you and others as clients. If they continue to lose clients on a regular basis, that is the risk they take.

Hedge funds, on the other hand, take trust financing to a higher level, which is also in line with Islamic finance. Hedge funds not only invest your money and earn a fee based on a percentage of money entrusted to them, but also take a percentage of the profits, if any, which goes back to the 80/20 example just explained. You get 80 percent of the profits, and the hedge fund manager gets 20 percent, plus their management fee, giving them a huge incentive to earn a return for you. This setup is perfectly Shariah compliant, provided that the investments are done in a Shariah-compliant manner, which they, unfortunately, usually are not. Hedge funds tend to invest in interest-based instruments, derivatives, and short-selling, among other non-Shariah-compliant instruments. This structure, however, is compliant and is used more broadly in Islamic finance than in conventional finance.

Beyond fund management, trust financing is used in Islamic finance to fund angel investments and manage real estate investments, endowments, and other types of investment portfolios.

Cost-Plus Financing (*Murabaha*)

Being one of the Islamic financial instruments that is friendliest to conventional financial institutions and one of the most loved by lawyers for its simplicity, cost-plus financing, known as *murabaha,* is probably the most widely used Islamic financial instrument today. This has been the case since modern Islamic finance took off in the 1970s, the reason being that it is easy to understand and easy for non-Islamic financial institutions to use, because, once executed, it becomes an IOU, which financial institutions love putting on their books. This is illustrated in Figure 7.2.

Cost-plus financing is also referred to as *deferred-payment financing,* which goes back to the concept of the time value of money. Using the car purchase example again: A person (the buyer) would like to buy a car but doesn't have enough money to buy it today. The car costs $10,000. The car dealer or seller is not in the financing or lending business, so they want

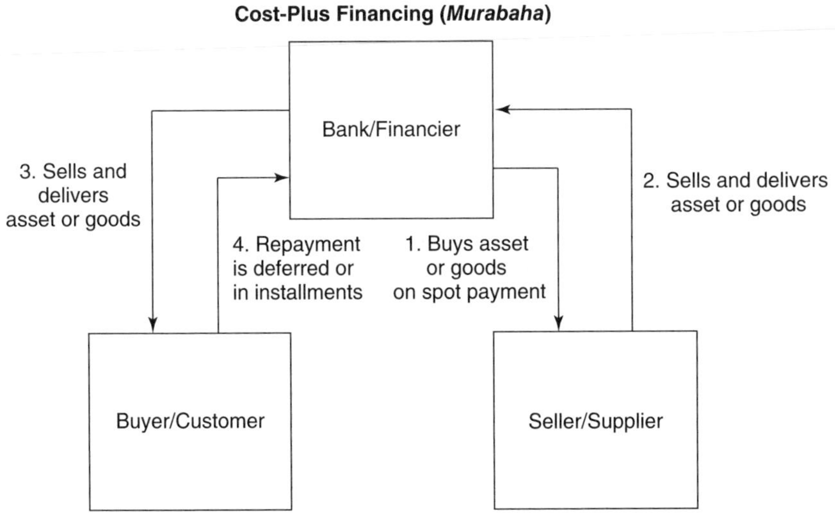

FIGURE 7.2 Illustration of cost-plus financing

$10,000 for the car up front. The buyer then needs to find a way to buy the car but pay for it at a later date or in installments. The buyer finds an Islamic financial institution that is willing to buy the car from the seller and resell it to the person in installments. The institution offers to buy the car for $10,000 and immediately resell it to the buyer for $12,000. It agrees to receive $500 per month for the next 24 months instead of the lump sum. So, for agreeing to pay over time, the person/buyer must pay more. There is a price for paying over time, and this is perfectly acceptable under Shariah rules.

The reason it is acceptable is because the financial institution did not loan the person money and ask for a return of the money over time plus a profit (interest) on top of it. Instead, the institution acted more like a wholesaler than a banker. It bought the car first and then resold it at a higher price. This is the definition of wholesaler. In doing so, the institution also took more risk acting as a car buyer and seller than simply selling/lending money. This physical activity is what differentiates this transaction from a lending transaction. The return the institution is asking for is based on the sale of an asset, for which it seeks a return.

Cost-plus financing is widely used because the structure is simple. More important to conventional institutions engaged in this type of financing is that, once the asset is bought and sold, what's left is an IOU, which the institution places on its books as money owed. However, Shariah places some rules on money owed, the main rule being that money owed (i.e., a debt) cannot be sold to someone else or traded at a premium or discount. If you borrow $1,000 from your father, he cannot go and sell it to your uncle for $950. Now you owe money to someone else, to whom you never intended to owe money in the first place. On top of this, your father sold it at a discount so that your uncle will be making $50 in the deal.

Even with the interest-free lending that is allowed in Islamic finance, which is more of a form of charity, the loan cannot be sold to another party. Money owed can only be repaid to the person (or legal heir, in case of death) or entity giving the loan. For a conventional financing perspective, this makes it impossible to create asset-backed securities off cost-plus financing receivables, which has put a monkeywrench in seeing them morph into other financial tools, as other instruments have recently. However, some more liberal-thinking Shariah scholars have allowed the sale of these receivables based on the fact that the initial purchase and sale transactions were compliant and used for a productive activity; therefore, the sale of the receivables is acceptable. This is not the mainstream view and has been applied primarily in Malaysia, which is seen as the more liberal center for Islamic finance.

Partnership Financing (*Musharaka*)

Partnership financing is as simple as it sounds. In modern finance, we refer to this as private equity and venture capital. This type of partnership or equity financing is at the heart of the Islamic principle of risk sharing. This is illustrated in Figure 7.3.

In partnership financing, there must be at least two partners; otherwise, it defeats the purpose of being called a partnership. There is no maximum number of partners allowed in this structure. Each partner contributes capital to the venture. Profits and losses in the venture are shared according to each partner's capital contribution. If a partner invests in 10 percent of the capital, they are entitled to receive 10 percent of the profits. The maximum loss they can take will equal the total amount they contributed and nothing more.

It is important to note that there are cases where one partner can receive a higher percentage of profits from another partner contributing the same amount of capital. In this case, one partner will be contributing their time/labor and experience, similar to trust financing. This doesn't automatically apply, however, and must be agreed to in advance. As with all Islamic financial activities, everything must be agreed to in advance. There is no limit to the amount of profit one can make and no strict rules on how much each partner can contribute or share in profits. As long as it is agreed to in advance, there are numerous ways to structure a transaction or, in this case, a partnership.

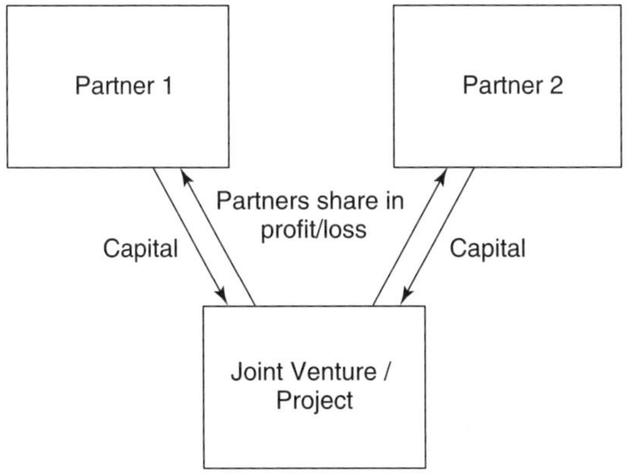

Partnership Financing (*Musharaka*)

FIGURE 7.3   Illustration of partnership financing

Partnership financing might seem like the obvious choice for the most widely used Islamic financial instrument; on the contrary, it has only become more popular in recent times. Islamic finance in its early years was very sensitive to taking on a high amount of risk. This is why cost-plus financing took off first. Venture capital and private equity–type activities were slow to take off because of this risk aversion. Another factor that plays a significant role in the slow start is that the industry lacked qualified people who could manage this type of financing. Only recently has it taken off and is now seeing a lot of growth, especially on the securitization front. Islamic finance loves securitization, since it's an asset-based industry. Once assets are in place, it's easy to package them together and sell shares in them to other investors. Making derivatives off of them, such as CDSs, is, of course, not permissible.

Leasing (*Ijara*)

After cost-plus financing, leasing is the most frequently used financial instrument in Islamic finance. Most people are familiar with leasing—one party rents or pays for the right to use another party's asset or property. Figure 7.4 illustrates how it works in Islamic finance.

There are basically two types of leasing: leasing with the intent to own at the end of the period and leasing with the intent of returning to the owner at the end of the period. The former is called a *financing lease*, and the latter an *operating lease*. These two exist in conventional finance, but Islamic finance uses them to finance a broader range of assets whereas conventional finance

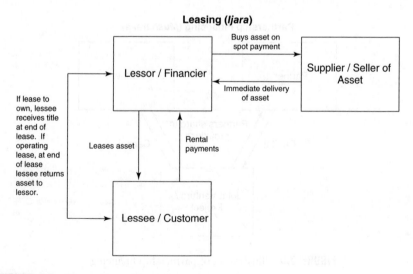

FIGURE 7.4   Illustration of leasing

tends to prefer lending. Lending is preferred in conventional finance because financial institutions do not like being in the business of owning assets, not to mention regulatory and tax factors that also provide a disincentive for them to get into the leasing business.

For Islamic finance, however, leasing is a key business. You might think of leasing as the relationship between a landlord and tenant, or in terms of a car-leasing transaction. Islamic finance goes beyond these to offer leasing on a wide range of assets from land and toll roads on the institutional side to computers and home financing on the retail side. Using leasing to finance the purchase of a home is actually quite common. Since lending money to buy a home is not allowed, having the financial institution buy the home and lease it to you is one of the common solutions. Similar to a mortgage, after paying for the house for a preagreed number of years, it becomes yours without any further liens or claims by the financing company. In similar fashion to home mortgages, home leasing assets can be securitized into pools of leased assets, which can then be sold to investors seeking income-generating investments.

What makes securitizing and selling off leased assets acceptable and selling mortgages not acceptable is the fact that leasing is not a lending transaction. The lessor (financial institution) owns the asset and the lessee (renter) pays the lessor for the right to use the asset. The lessor has full title to the asset and the lessee has the right to use, which does not prohibit the owner from selling the asset to another party if they wish. A mortgage, on the other hand, is a moneylending transaction whereby the financer holds a lien against the property until the debt is fully repaid. In Islamic finance, the owner of an asset has the flexibility to buy, sell, or trade the asset. Selling or trading an asset at a premium or discount is also permitted. This is why leasing has taken off to become one of the leading asset classes in the industry.

Forward Sale (*Bay Al-Salam*)

Forward sales, much like the other instruments described in this chapter, date back to the early Islamic period, when farmers were in need of financing to grow and harvest their crops. Figure 7.5 illustrates the straightforward nature of this transaction.

In a forward sale, a farmer, for example, would seek financing to grow and harvest crops for the season. The financial institution would agree to buy the crops in advance, giving the farmer the money now to start working. The financial institution would have locked in the price of the crops, most likely below the current market price, giving them a profit once they receive the harvest. The risk, of course, is that the farmer will have an issue with delivering the crops for various reasons such as disease or drought, as well as the risk of the price of the crop dropping below what was paid.

FIGURE 7.5 Illustration of forward sale

This type of instrument is used today not only in the farming industry but also in manufacturing, where the manufacturer would need financing to produce products and/or to buy raw materials. The financial institution would buy the end product before it's produced at a lower price than the manufacturer currently sells on the market. In many cases, the manufacturer would also put the financial institution in touch with their clients to secure advance sales of the product, thus reducing the risk to the financial institution and increasing the chances of the manufacturer getting the financing they need.

Construction Financing (*Istisna*)

Another familiar term is *construction financing*. Real estate developers cannot live without it. Islamic finance, too, uses this in a similar fashion, as illustrated in Figure 7.6.

An example of construction financing is one party with land (customer) wanting to construct a building on it. The customer finds a developer (manufacturer) willing to build it, but the customer doesn't have the money to pay the developer in advance. The customer finds a financial institution willing to offer financing and promises to buy the building from the institution once construction is complete. Once agreed, the financial institution pays the developer in stages as the building is constructed. Upon completion of the construction, the developer is fully paid and the financial institution owns the building. It then sells the building to the customer, who then pays back the institution. The payments are typically in installments and are agreed to in advance in terms of the amount and duration. The financial institution, of course, will have sold the constructed building to the customer at a higher cost than it paid to the developer.

In this case, the financial institution would have two reasons to justify earning a profit. First, it paid for the construction of the building, which it

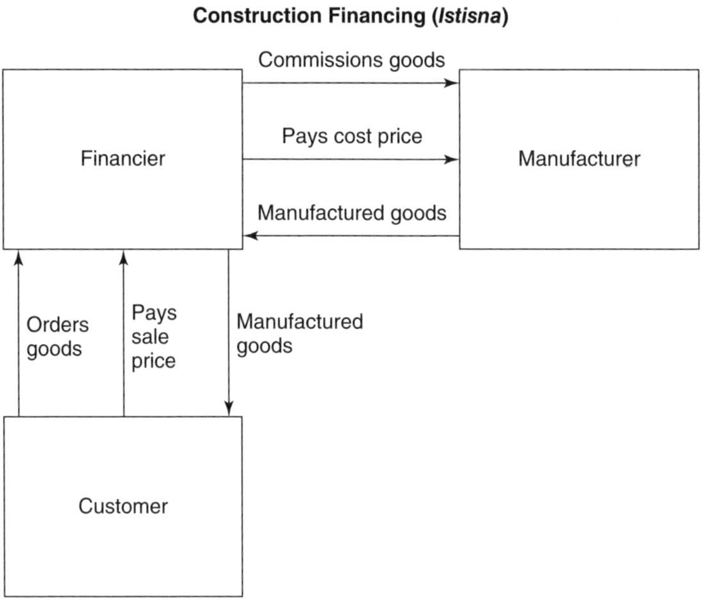

Construction Financing (*Istisna*)

FIGURE 7.6   Illustration of construction financing

now owns and, second, it agreed to repayment in installments instead of a lump sum.

This type of financing is not only used in construction of buildings but is more commonly being used in infrastructure development projects such as the building of roads, hydroelectric power plants, and other large, capital-intensive projects. In such cases, more than one financial institution would be in involved in partnering on the project.

Sukuk and Other Financial Instruments

In addition to the six instruments just described, there are others that are used in modern Islamic finance. Of these instruments, the most commonly used are *sukuk*, as they are known in its plural form. (In singular form, it is simply *sukk*.) *Sukuk* were briefly described in Chapter 1 as an early form of paper money used during the Golden Age of Islam, which basically constitute promissory notes. They were later adopted in Europe, where they were referred to as *cheques*.

In modern Islamic finance, *sukuk* regained popularity in the late 1990s in Malaysia, eventually making their way to the Middle East and other parts of the world roughly around the year 2000. They initially took off in Malaysia for two reasons. First, Malaysia was a rapidly growing country with the need for a deep capital market and access to capital. Second, Malaysia is seen not only as liberal when it comes to Islamic finance but as an innovator in developing and accepting new forms of financing. It also helped that the government was the most supportive in the Islamic world for the development of Islamic finance and had long established rules and regulations for Islamic banking and capital markets.

Sukuk did not take off in the Middle East until they had proven themselves in Malaysia. Islamic banks witnessed their success firsthand through the projects being financed by *sukuk,* including the new toll roads, metro systems, and the acceptance of *sukuk* as an alternative to issuing government and corporate debt.

So what are *sukuk* today and how are they used? *Sukuk* still can be considered a form of a promissory note, but they more closely resemble a security interest in an asset. The best way to describe *sukuk* as they are used today is to say they are asset-backed securities. Even though they are referred to as Islamic bonds, because they tend to behave like bonds in some respects, they are not bonds. Bonds are debt securities, and *sukuk* are not a debt; they are ownership interest. *Sukuk* must be tied to an asset. Investors who buy *sukuk* are buying a share of the assets in the *sukuk* pool. The pool can consist of one asset, such as an airplane, or multiple assets, such as a pool of homes, making them equivalent to mortgage-backed securities. Owners of *sukuk* have rights to the underlying asset and actually have ownership in them, unlike bonds, where investors have claims to interest payments and the principal and hold collateral as security against these payments.

There are various ways to structure *sukuk* using one of the six instruments previously described. *Sukuk* are just a way to pool assets and sell stakes in them to multiple investors; they are not a financial instrument. The underlying instrument could be any one of the six instruments mentioned earlier, and this is why *sukuk* were not included among the structures. Chapter 8 offers some examples of how *sukuk* are being used not only in Islamic countries but also in Western countries.

With the rapid development of Islamic finance over the past few decades, new financial instruments are constantly being developed. Some new instruments have been designed to mimic conventional financial instruments such as money market funds, call options, and financing based on few, if any, assets. I won't get into much detail about them, since they are not widely used and there is still some controversy over their structure. Shariah scholars tend to view instruments that were designed to mimic conventional ones with skepticism.

Two such instruments are the *arboun,* which literally means "retainer" or "deposit," and *tawarruk,* which means "monetization." An *arboun* is a tool aimed to mimic the effects of a call option. In the conventional form, buying a call option gives the buyer the right, not the obligation, to buy the asset or stock in the future at a stated price with a stated term (one month to more than one year, in some cases). What the buyer is paying for is a *premium*, or price for the option. If the asset or stock goes the buyer's way during the term of the option (i.e., before it expires), then the buyer executes the option, buying it at the option price and selling it at the lower price and making a profit. If the asset or stock falls in price, then the buyer lets the option expire, losing the premium the buyer paid.

Let's put this in an example to see how it works. The example is for the purchase of shares in a publicly listed company. Options for shares are sold in lots of 100 shares, so 1 option is 100 shares and 10 options are 1,000 shares. An investor thinks that shares of XYZ company are going to rise within three months. Shares of the company are currently trading at $10 per share. The investor buys one call option (100 shares) to buy XYZ company at $11 per share over the next three months. The cost of this option is $1 per share, also known as the *option premium*. So the investor pays $100. If, within the next three months, the shares rise to $15 per share, the investor executes the option, meaning the investor buys the shares at $11 and sells them at the market price, which is now $15. The difference of $4 gives the investor $4 × 100 shares = $400, which leaves the investor with a total profit of $300 after deducting the cost of the option. If the stock price stays at $10 or drops, the investor simply lets the option expire and loses the $100.

The reverse of this is a put option, whereby the buyer purchases the right to sell an asset or stock at a set price within the option term. It's like short-selling, but cheaper for investors since they are only on the hook for the premium (the cost of the option).

In Islamic finance, options do not exist in this form because paying a premium for a right is not Shariah compliant. A right, promise, or any other intangible agreement cannot be paid for. Rights, promises, and agreements are free; you can only pay for goods or assets. Thus, a dilemma is created for Islamic investors looking to mimic the effects of options. The solution is to use an *arboun*, an old Islamic instrument that was brought back to life. An *arboun* mimics the effects of a call option by giving the buyer the right to buy an asset or stock at a stated price on a set date. The difference here is that the buyer does not pay a premium to buy the asset or stock; the investor makes a down payment while promising to pay the rest at a fixed date in the future. The investor cannot execute the option at any time, only at the expiration date of the *arboun*. So if it's a stock and it has risen in price, the investor pays the remaining amount to take possession of the stock and then immediately sells it at the market price, earning a profit. If the shares fall in price, the investor forfeits the promise to purchase the stock, losing the deposit.

Tawarruk is a way for a person or entity to borrow money without having an asset or property in mind. Since Islamic finance is asset based, any financing must be tied to an asset, such as buying a house or investing in a business. If the person or entity is looking for cash and not to buy or invest in an asset at the time, some financial institutions offer *tawarruk*. With *tawarruk*, the financial institution would advance the client cash by selling commodities on the client's behalf, giving the client the proceeds of the sale. The client would have promised to purchase the said commodities over time, since the client did not have the money at the time. Thus, the client pays back the financial institution in installments for the cash advance received from the sale.

Shariah scholars are not unanimous in their acceptance of the *arboun* and *tawarruk* because they don't see the real economic benefit. In the case of the *arboun*, they agree on the concept of making a down payment to purchase an asset, but they do not like the fact that it is designed to enable investors to speculate on stocks and to walk away from a promise if the stock doesn't go their way. For *tawarruk*, scholars view the cash advance from the commodity as a backdoor to *riba*, since the investor had no intention to engaging in commodity trading other than to receive money up front with a plan to repay it in the future.

There are several other cases of new financial instruments being developed, but acceptance of them is not universal among Shariah scholars. A lot of the recent innovation has been looked on by Shariah scholars with skepticism. They are open to developing new tools and investment solutions but not at the expense of introducing *riba* into the transaction or giving up on some of the ethical principles. Not every conventional financial instrument has an Islamic finance equivalent simply because they tend to include one or more of the prohibited elements mentioned earlier. In many cases, a conventional equivalent is not needed, since Islamic finance already has the right instruments and tools to serve the market. It is also important to note that many conventional instruments are designed around debt, speculation, and gambling. All the new financial instruments being designed on Wall Street are destabilizing to financial markets and increase the risk in the system. Derivatives are the clearest example.

SUMMARY

- There is more to Islamic finance than the prohibition of interest and *riba*.
- Islamic finance has established rules based on Shariah, which prohibit engaging in or participating in certain industries such as gambling,

alcohol, pork, conventional finance, and insurance. Other industries that are not prohibited but are discouraged include weapons and defense, tobacco, and entertainment.

- There are ethical rules that must be followed to ensure there is no *riba*, injustice, or inequality in financial matters. These include:
  - Earning a profit or return must be based on accepting some risk.
  - Profits and returns cannot be guaranteed.
  - You cannot lose more than you invest.
  - All investors are treated equally.
  - To sell it, you must own it first.
  - To earn a return, money must be invested in something productive.
  - There must be transparency.
  - All forms of gambling must be removed from a transaction.
  - Money is not a commodity.
- Islam does not view money as a commodity, since it defines money as a means of exchange and a unit of account but not a store of value. Money has no intrinsic value.
- Therefore, the time value of money does not exist in Islamic finance, but the concept of time value does.
- There are six main financial instruments that are used in Islamic finance today:
  1. Trust financing, which is similar to the relationship between a fund investor and a fund manager.
  2. Cost-plus financing, whereby the financial intermediary acts like a wholesaler.
  3. Partnership financing, which is along the lines of equity investing, such as private equity and venture capital.
  4. Leasing, which includes both operating leasing and financial leasing.
  5. Forward sale, which started out as a way to help farmers finance their crops, but has wider uses today, such as in the manufacturing industry.
  6. Construction financing, which is used in infrastructure finance in addition to construction.
- There are other tools and instruments used in Islamic finance, the most popular of which are *sukuk*, which are Islamic forms of asset-backed securities. They have become a driving force behind the growth of Islamic finance in recent years.
- Other financial tools have been developed in recent years but are not widely used or accepted, as there is still some controversy regarding their acceptance under Shariah.
- Shariah scholars are open to developing new tools and instruments but not at the expense of sacrificing key Shariah principles.

CHAPTER 8

Islamic Financial Instruments as Alternatives

Over the past 40 years, Islamic banks and financial institutions have been racing to develop a full range of financial products and services to match the offerings of conventional banks. In some cases, Islamic banks have been able to beat conventional banks at their own game by launching more competitive products. The proof of this is in the degree to which Islamic banks have taken away market share and continue to take away market share from their conventional counterparts. If Islamic banks had been underperforming and offering subpar products, then their conventional competitors would not have needed to resort to launching competing Islamic financial products to stop the erosion of their market share. In some cases, conventional banks have thrown in the towel and either converted to Islamic banks or set up dedicated branches and subsidiaries in order to offer Islamic products and services.

In Malaysia, the most advanced Islamic financial market, nearly every bank, insurance company, mutual fund company, and financial institution offers a range of Islamic products and services. Though there are only a few pure Islamic banks in the country, every bank either has a dedicated subsidiary, which offers Islamic banking services, or offers both conventional and Islamic services in its branches. CIMB Bank is the largest bank in the country, having a dedicated Islamic banking subsidiary, CIMB Islamic. Maybank the largest bank overall, offers a full range of Islamic products and services across its branch network. Even firms whose traditional clients have not been Muslims are getting involved in this market. The most notable are Hong Leong Bank, a Malaysian-Chinese owned bank catering to Malaysia's large ethnic Chinese community, which launched Hong Leong Islamic Bank in order to grab a slice of the growing Islamic banking business, and Public Mutual, one of the largest mutual fund companies catering to the Malaysian-Chinese community. Public Mutual has become one of the largest Islamic fund managers over the past decade.

In the Middle East the trend has been similar. Even though banking regulators there have taken a different approach to Islamic banking, the industry has nevertheless become a major force in the markets where Islamic banking is active. In Saudi Arabia, for example, Islamic banking currently makes up more than 50 percent of the country's banking system, as mentioned in Chapter 6. In Kuwait, this figure is quickly approaching the 50 percent mark. Regulators in these countries chose not to allow conventional banks to offer Islamic banking services, preferring instead to keep Islamic and conventional banks separate. One argument supporting this decision comes from the fact that Islamic banks by their nature would not be able to offer conventional financial services. Therefore, this would put them at a great disadvantage if conventional banks were allowed to compete on their turf when they would be barred by Shariah restrictions from competing on the conventional turf.

An example of the differing outcomes of Islamic banking regulation in Malaysia versus Saudi Arabia and Kuwait can be seen by the number of Islamic banks operating in each country. In Malaysia, there are only two pure Malaysian Islamic banks, whereas in Saudi Arabia there are four and in Kuwait there are five. A question that often arises is, which regulatory environment offers a better financial system in the long run? This question has been discussed and debated in the Islamic finance industry for many years, but for the purpose of our topic, we will not get into it here.

The question we need to ask is how Islamic banks, given all of their prohibitions and religious guidelines, offer competing financial products to conventional banks. In this chapter, we take a look at the three areas where Islamic finance is most active to see how the guidelines stipulated by Shariah, along with the key Islamic financing structures, are incorporated to develop banking and financial products. These three areas are consumer banking, corporate finance, and government finance.

CONSUMER BANKING

The consumer or retail banking side has been the most active in the development of the Islamic finance industry. This goes back to the roots of modern Islamic finance, beginning with the launch of Dubai Islamic Bank in 1975, the first true Islamic bank. The foundation of this bank, as well as the other early entrants into Islamic banking, was to serve the retail market by offering basic savings and financing alternatives. In doing so, these banks established the foundation of a new financial system, creating an alternative to the established one.

The basis of this system was built upon risk sharing and a profit/loss relationship between the bank and its customers. The key products offered by Islamic banks include deposit, savings, and investment accounts on the deposit side, and consumer, auto, and home finance on the financing side, known as the lending side in conventional banking.

Deposits, Savings, and Investments

Since there is no return or profit without the potential for taking a loss, how do depositors in a bank feel secure and know that their money is safe? To understand how Islamic banks treat deposits, you must first understand how conventional banks treat deposits. When you deposit your money into a checking or savings account, you are effectively giving your money to the bank in the form of a loan. This is why bank deposits show up on the liabilities side of a bank's balance sheet. Once your money is deposited, it becomes the bank's money, and the bank can use it as it pleases, within the guidelines and rules prescribed by banking regulators. Since the money is now the bank's money, the bank can impose restrictions on how you use it. In January 2014, for example, HSBC Bank in the United Kingdom began imposing restrictions on customer cash withdrawals over £5,000. The bank stated that it needed to know how the money was going to be used before authorizing the withdrawal.[1]

With Islamic banks there are three main forms of deposits. The first, and most basic, is a current account or checking account. Similar to an account at a conventional bank, this account does not earn any return; it is simply an account used for routine transactions and cash needs. From a Shariah perspective, a deposit account cannot be used in the bank's investment activities and is treated as money entrusted to the bank for safekeeping. Therefore, money held in current accounts is not subject to the profit/loss arrangement. Depositors in these accounts can rest assured that their money will not be used by the bank.

However, when it comes to the other two main types of accounts, savings and investment, the profit/loss arrangement comes into play. Savings accounts in Islamic banks, which include time deposits (aka certificates of deposit), are used to fund their trading and investment activities and are subject to profit and loss. Investment accounts tend to be focused on a specific investment area, such as real estate projects, and are subject to higher risk. They are also subject to higher potential returns as a result.

The way savings account holders receive their profits on their accounts is based on the overall profitability of the bank. Every Islamic bank sets its own guidelines for the amount of total profits paid out to account holders. After the end of the year, once the annual financials are finalized, account holders receive their profits based on the bank's total profits and each account holder's average annual balance. Another way to look at this is to view savings account holders as stakeholders in the bank's activities and ultimate profitability. In return for having a stake in the bank, account holders receive a dividend based on the bank's year-end profit.

Conventional banking analysts have a problem with this, since they cannot accurately calculate Islamic banks' cost of funds. In conventional banking, a bank's cost of funds is simply the interest cost it pays to its depositors and account holders. This enables them to calculate the bank's profitability based on a spread between the interest rate the bank charges on its loans and the rate it pays account holders. For Islamic banks, the cost of funds, to analysts' frustration, cannot be determined up front since the final cost will not be known until after year-end, when the financial results are calculated. The cost of funds, however, can be calculated by the spread between what the bank charges for its financing activities and what it paid out to its account holders at the end of the year.

Islamic banks typically have more savings accounts than any other account because over the years savings accounts have been proven to be a low-risk way to earn a return. There are two main reasons for this. First, while theoretically a savings account holder can lose money if the bank loses money, in practice this has not been the case. For the most part, Islamic banks have been able to maintain a steady growth in profitability over the years, and in years in which they have had trouble they have been fortunate enough to have the local government support them—and bail them out, in some cases—so that account holders would not take losses on their accounts. While this cannot go on indefinitely, for the time being there is a common belief that any type of deposit or savings account will be protected from loss. As with all other financial and economic beliefs, this works for now until one day when it doesn't.

The second reason Islamic banks have attracted a lot of savings account holders is that they have historically paid out higher returns compared with conventional bank returns. In Kuwait, for example, Kuwait Finance House has consistently paid out higher returns on savings accounts than its conventional competitors. In 2013, National Bank of Kuwait, the country's largest financial institution and KFH's main competitor, paid out 0.625 percent on savings accounts.[2] KFH paid out more than double this rate, at 1.31 percent.[3] The difference here is that account holders at NBK knew up front what return they would earn, while account holders at KFH did not know until after year-end. This consistent payout of higher returns, coupled with the government's support for the country's banking sector overall, has enabled Islamic banks, such as KFH, to grow their account base at a faster rate than their conventional counterparts. In KFH's case, deposits grew by more than 569 percent from 2001 to 2013, increasing from KD 1.775 billion ($6.2 billion) to KD 10.104 billion ($35.3 billion), respectively.[4] The year 2014 might be the year KFH holds more customer deposits than NBK, which, as of 2013, stood at KD 10.719 billion ($37.5 billion).[5]

This scenario is being played out not only in Kuwait but across the board where Islamic banks operate. Though growth in savings accounts has been impressive, Islamic banks would prefer having fixed-term deposits to better manage their investment activities. This is why they aggressively offer time deposits ranging from one year to five years. These term deposits, similar to conventional banks' certificates of deposit, offer higher rates of return as a result of locking in their deposits for longer periods. The same condition, however, applies here: Term depositors will not know for sure what their returns will be until after the period is over; all they know is that whatever profits are paid out will be higher than those to savings account holders, as the time value is in their favor here.

Similarly, investment account holders stand to earn even higher returns over the period of their investment, but they will also be subject to loss if the underlying investment or project loses money. As a result of the higher risk associated with these accounts, they tend to be the smallest portion of an Islamic bank's overall customer accounts.

Consumer, Auto, and Home Finance

Consumer finance plays another major role in Islamic banks' profitability. In conventional lending, banks primarily offer their customers secured and unsecured credit. Secured credit is credit or a loan tied to the asset it was used to purchase, such as a car or a house. Unsecured credit is not tied to an asset but, rather, to an individual or company's credit standing. Islamic banks have a problem with this form of financing, since they cannot lend out money. There must be an underlying asset or product that needs to be purchased by the bank and resold or leased to the customer. How, then, do Islamic banks offer consumer credit such as credit cards?

Islamic banks do offer credit cards, but they are the smallest part of their overall financial portfolio. The credit cards work on a deferred payment basis using primarily a cost-plus financing structure. Credit cards are not very attractive to Islamic bank consumers for two main reasons. First, Islamic banks do not give out high credit limits and tend to base the limit on the customer's monthly salary—usually equal to one month's salary or a little more, but not much more. This tends to discourage consumers from using them, since the amount they can purchase with them would be limited. Second, the structure itself is not very attractive. In order for the bank to offer credit using cost-plus financing, the bank must be the entity selling the consumer the goods. Thus, the credit card is structured to act as the bank's agent in purchasing the goods and reselling them instantly to the consumer at a higher price. So the repayment is always in installments and there is always a markup, whereas with a traditional credit card, purchases can be paid off right away to avoid interest charges or the customer can choose installments with interest. With the Islamic credit card, the markup and installments are built in and the consumer must follow the repayment plan.

In addition to these two issues, Islamic banks cannot package credit card receivables and sell them off in the market as asset-backed securities, since selling of receivables is a form of debt, which cannot be resold. Therefore, banks tend to keep credit card portfolios small relative to their overall financing book. Credit cards are used more as a way to offer a service to customers rather than using them to earn high profits. What is more common at Islamic banks are prepaid cards: The customer fills up a card with whatever amount they intend on using, say while traveling, and then uses up that amount over time. These cards are interest-free and banks earn a small fee for issuing the cards and/or a small annual fee. Again, these are not moneymaking products but a way to serve the needs of their customers.

What is more lucrative for the banks is consumer, auto, and home financing. Consumer finance products are fairly diverse in what they can be used for—from the purchase of a computer to buying furniture. The customer applies for the financing at the bank, and the structure is typically cost-plus financing or lease to own. Auto financing is probably the highest-volume business for Islamic banks. There are four ways banks get involved in auto financing. Since Islamic banks must own the vehicle before they can resell it or lease it to the customer, over the years Islamic banks have ventured into having huge auto showrooms and their own inventories of vehicles. Thus, the bank can sell a vehicle to a customer who pays cash and still make a profit on the cash sale since the bank would have purchased the vehicles in bulk at a wholesale price. The banks are also able to compete on price with the auto dealerships, since, in some cases, they would have received similar pricing from the manufacturers. For a conventional bank to get involved in the buying and selling of vehicles would be out of the question, but for Islamic banks, it is part of their business model.

The other three ways Islamic banks offer auto financing are by offering cost-plus financing, lease-to-own agreements, and operating leases. The terms of the financing and installments are comparable to what conventional financing would end up being, and, in some cases, Islamic financing can be cheaper. In other cases, conventional banks would not be able to compete with Islamic banks. This is mainly on the operating lease structure, since conventional banks are not in a position to own a fleet of vehicles once the operating lease ends. For Islamic banks, this is an additional moneymaker, since they have the ability to sell the used vehicles through their showrooms and have favorable sales terms with auto wholesalers to get rid of the used-car inventory. As a result of these financing options, Islamic banks have been able to become a major force in the auto finance industry in the markets where they are active.

Home finance or real estate finance is another area where Islamic banks are very active, since real estate is an ideal asset for Islamic financing structures. It also allows for easy securitization. The construction financing structure is obviously used here, but the most common form of home financing is lease to own, not only in the Middle East but also in Asia, Europe, and the United States. This is where the bank buys the property and leases it to the customer over a period of time. At the end of the term, the title is transferred to the customer. During the lease period, the bank (or the investors, if the property was part of a securitization) is the owner of the property and the payments made to the bank represent rent plus an amount to buy out the bank over time. During the term of the lease, the bank is the sole owner of the property and the customer is a renter but also has rights to the property and a stake in it should he or she decide to terminate the lease early. Any increase or decrease in the property's value is passed on to the customer, similar to conventional home financing. All the details of the lease are disclosed up front so that the customer has a clear understanding of the structure along with the terms of how their equity stake in the property is built up over time. Nearly every bank offering an Islamic home financing solution offers leasing for its simplicity and clear ownership and legal structure.

Another structure that has been gaining popularity is the partnership financing structure. This structure is probably the most attractive to home buyers. Under partnership financing, the bank and the home buyer are partners in the property purchase. This is an all-equity transaction, and no debt is used. The home buyer's down payment is their equity stake in the venture, and the bank's financing is its equity stake. So, for example, if the property costs $200,000, the home buyer puts down 10 percent, or $20,000; the bank would "invest" $180,000 and own 90 percent of the property. The home buyer using the property would pay the bank rent plus an amount to buy out the bank's equity stake over time. So, over the course of 30 years, the bank's stake would slowly be reduced from 90 percent to zero, at which point the home buyer would be the sole owner of the property. This is also known as a *diminishing* partnership structure, since one partner's share diminishes over time.

The beauty of this structure is that any increase or decrease in the property's value is shared by the partners according to each one's percentage of ownership. If the property declines in value, then both parties take a loss according to their ownership stake. In this case, the parties cannot lose more than they invested in the property, so an underwater mortgage scenario would not be possible. If the home owner buys out the bank over the term of the agreement until the bank's ownership is zero, then, of course, the bank will not have any stake in the property's increase or decrease in value.

There are ways to structure this to limit the loss to one party should the other decide to sell early at a loss. There could also be a minimum period established before the property could be sold, such as three, five, or seven years, as well as a mutual agreement on how and when it can be sold. Since the structure is a partnership, the home owner could also find a buyer for his or her stake so that the bank would not have to realize a loss if that were the case. The reverse is also true: The bank could decide to sell its stake and get out of the agreement. The most likely scenario here would be if the bank created asset-backed securities from multiple home investments and sold them to investors. The flexibility of this structure makes it an attractive solution to both home buyers and banks. It is also attractive for investors seeking to invest in a diverse pool of residential real estate in the form of a real estate investment trust (REIT) or asset-backed securities. I think that this debt-free form of home financing will become more popular after the next financial crisis hits borrowers and lenders.

Partnership financing is still relatively new, and few institutions offer it. One institution that does is Guidance Residential in the United States, which has been using this structure for more than 10 years. There are other structures that can be used for home financing, such as cost-plus financing, but they have become controversial and unpopular. HSBC Bank in the United States used the cost-plus financing structure to offer Islamic home financing from 2001 to 2005 because, being a large conventional bank, it had legal issues with the leasing structure. The main issue was that, by offering home leasing, the bank would become a landlord and responsible for numerous properties. The potential liability and legal issues with leasing made it an unattractive solution to offer. It was also easier for the bank to record a debt on its books from the cost-plus financing rather than recording a lease. The cost-plus structure was the closest structure to a conventional loan; thus, it was a better fit for the bank at that time.

From a Shariah perspective, cost-plus financing is really intended for short-term financing and not as a long-term financing solution, since the charge for the cost-plus (i.e., the markup) in the transaction is built into the repayment. Any early repayment would mean that part of the markup would have to be rebated to the customer. Think of this as paying off your credit card early. When you do so, you are no longer liable for any interest charges, since the balance has been paid off. However, under cost-plus, if you pay off early, you are still liable for the remaining balance. In essence, the bank in a cost-plus structure acts as a wholesaler. So, in the case of home finance, they would have bought the house for you at, for example, $200,000 and sold it to you for $300,000 over the agreed repayment term. If you decided to pay off early, you could do so, but the full amount would still be due, since the bank's sale price was $300,000. Asking for a discount for paying early would raise questions about *riba* from a Shariah perspective because the price would have already been agreed to at the onset of the agreement. Receiving a discount for paying early before the end of the term would mean that there was a time value of money in the transaction, which constitutes *riba*. Also, once the cost-plus transaction is executed, meaning that the sale and purchase have already taken place, what is left is an IOU from you to the bank, which is a debt (you owe the bank money for selling you the house, which already took place; there is no asset left). A debt, under Shariah, cannot be resold or discounted, as this would mean there was *riba* in the transaction.

In HSBC's case, the bank offered a rebate for early repayment so that it would act more like a conventional mortgage and satisfy U.S. banking regulators, but this only highlighted the Shariah permissibility of a cost-plus structure for home financing. Cost-plus financing is best suited for short-term financing needs where early payment stands little chance of becoming an issue. This is why leasing and the partnership structure are better suited for these types of transactions: An asset is always involved from start to finish and not a debt, which can then be bought, sold, and even discounted.

There are other financial products that have been launched and developed over the years, including education finance and medical finance solutions. In addition, a full range of investment and retirement funds are available to Islamic investors not only in the Middle East but also in Asia, the United States, and parts of Europe.

CORPORATE FINANCE

Companies seek out banking relationships every day to help finance their business and operations. Much of what is done on the corporate finance side is lending based, such as the issuance of loans and bonds. However, there are alternatives to lending being offered by Islamic banks, which, in the end, offer companies similar benefits. Companies tend to look for ways to finance the purchase of assets and materials as well as to fund their underlying business operations. With the exception of offering unsecured credit, Islamic banks can offer companies financing facilities to match those of conventional lending.

Alternatives to Lending

As long as a company has assets, an Islamic financing solution can be structured. A lot of the corporate lending is used by companies for expansion, to build new facilities, purchase new equipment, or acquire another company. In all these cases, an Islamic alternative exists to alleviate the company from choosing the debt route. In many of these cases, Islamic banks would use leasing to structure the transaction for the company. If the company was looking to build a new facility or purchase new equipment, a leasing arrangement could be used by the bank to build the facility or purchase the equipment and then lease it back to the company. If the company needed working capital to support its ongoing operations, leasing could also be used. In this case, some of the company's assets would be sold to the bank. The bank would pay for the assets, giving the company access to the capital it needed. The bank would in turn lease the assets back to the company, which would pay the bank in monthly installments.

As you can see, there are similarities in outcomes between this type of financing and a conventional loan. In both cases, the company received the capital it needed and would probably be making similar payments. However, what differs here are the flow of the transaction and the role of the banks. In the case of the conventional bank, it offered the company a loan (i.e., it gave the company money) and asked for it to be repaid with interest. In doing so, the bank put a lien on some of the company's assets until the terms of the loan were fully satisfied. In the case of the Islamic bank, it bought assets from the company, giving it money for the purchase. It then leased the same assets back to the company for an agreed repayment and term. The conventional bank merely acted as a lender while the Islamic bank acted as a buyer of assets and a lessor. This physical possession of assets and lease-back are what differentiated the Islamic bank from the conventional bank, which in no instance got involved in ownership of assets.

Aside from providing an alternative to lending, Islamic banks tend to be heavily involved in real estate–based financing as well as the issuance of *sukuk*. Venture capital and private equity also play key roles in Islamic finance, but much like conventional finance, venture capital and private equity tend to be too risky for banks and are better served by specialized companies and investment vehicles.

One of the main criticisms of Islamic banks by banking analysts and ratings agency analysts has been their heavy exposure to real estate. This is true—ownership and investment in real estate are major parts of Islamic banking activity, as physical ownership of assets (and real estate) needs to take place in order for the transaction to meet Shariah requirements. What Islamic banks are not given credit for is the fact that their ownership and investment in real estate take place in lieu of them taking liens on assets in exchange for loans.

A common form of corporate lending that is out of bounds for Islamic banks is receivable financing, also known as *factoring*, whereby a company sells its outstanding receivables (i.e., moneys owned to the company by its customers) to a bank or factoring company in return for getting repaid faster.

On the corporate side, when a company sells its products to other companies, which are its clients, it is common for the company to offer payment for the products sold over a period of 60 to 90 days, or more in some cases. If companies do not offer these terms, they fear that their customers will go to their competitors. It is also a sign of financial weakness if a company cannot offer its customers simple short-term repayment terms. Companies, however, may be short on cash and need repayment over a shorter period. Therefore, they sell their receivables at a discount to a bank or factoring company. The bank relies on the credit quality of the customers to determine the likelihood of their repaying on time or repaying at all. Based on this, they offer to buy the receivables at a discount to the actual amount owed by the customers. There is usually an implied interest rate in the sale of receivables so that both sides can determine the cost or expected return from the transaction.

Factoring has become a major source of financing globally and has weathered the financial crisis virtually unscathed, growing at double-digit rates since 2008. Today, the total size of the factoring market globally is estimated to be over $3 trillion.[6] Fortunately or unfortunately, there is no Islamic financing alternative to factoring since a receivable is an IOU, which cannot be sold or discounted.

Another important fact to note is that Islamic banks do not have derivatives exposure, which most conventional banks have, especially to hedge against interest rates. Analysts' failure to account for and understand the underlying risks of derivatives will play out in the years to come, which should add additional support to the Islamic banking model in the future.

Sukuk

Sukuk, as described in Chapter 7, has evolved into Islamic finance's version of asset-backed securitization. As financial engineering took off in the 1990s, Islamic finance looked for ways it could also innovate and develop new financing instruments to compete in the global market. The solution was asset securitizations that led to a multi-billion-dollar finance sector. This sector has been growing at a double-digit pace since the *sukuk* craze took off around the year 2000.

As shown in Figure 8.1, *sukuk* were virtually nonexistent prior to 2000. They initially took off on the corporate banking side as a way for companies to issue alternatives to bonds. This is why *sukuk* are referred to as "Islamic bonds" today, even though they are not, by their definition, bonds.

There are a few reasons why *sukuk* took off and a few reasons why *sukuk* have a long way to go to reach their full potential. *Sukuk* can be very diverse and flexible in their use, which makes them appealing for a wide range of industries, especially those that are asset intensive. They have

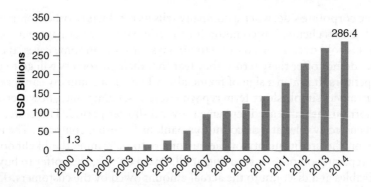

FIGURE 8.1 Growth of the global *sukuk* market from 2000 to June 30, 2014
Source: KFH Research

been used to help finance hospitals, oil and gas companies, manufacturing companies, public utilities, and real estate, to name a few.

Sukuk, for the most part, are structured according to one of the six financing structures described in Chapter 7, though a majority of *sukuk* issued to date have been in the form of cost-plus financing or leasing. Unlike corporate bonds, which have terms ranging up to 30 years, *sukuk* were initially used in short-term and more lately in medium-term financing ranging from one year to seven years. This, however, has started to change, as demand for *sukuk* has risen dramatically over the years, especially since the global financial crisis in 2008. Today, there are a growing number of long-term *sukuk* issued by companies as well as perpetual *sukuk,* which have a specified term that keeps renewing after the initial term ends. This also means that the principal is not repaid unless there is a callable feature on the issue, which allows this instrument to behave more like equity capital that pays a dividend. This has been attractive to Islamic banks, such as Dubai Islamic Bank and Abu Dhabi Islamic Bank, the first such issuers, who saw it as a Shariah-compliant solution to boost their capital base. Other companies are starting to issue perpetual *sukuk,* such as Malaysian Airlines, which issued a RM 2.5 billion perpetual *sukuk* in 2012.[7]

The airline industry was one of the early industries to adopt *sukuk* financing. Emirates airline has been one of the leading players in this field. In 2005, Emirates issued a $550 million seven-year *sukuk* to finance the construction of its corporate headquarters and has been using *sukuk* ever since to finance its purchase of new planes. In 2014 it announced plans to issue $4.5 billion in *sukuk* for such purposes.[8] *Sukuk* issuance has not been limited to companies in the Middle East and Malaysia; Western countries have also shown interest in issuing *sukuk.* One of the most notable is GE Capital, which issued $500 million in *sukuk* at the height of the financial crisis in 2009 to support its aircraft leasing business. The five-year issue has been traded on NASDAQ-Dubai, one of the main exchanges for the trading of *sukuk*.[9] The growing popularity of *sukuk* can be seen by the diversity of its applications. Another example is the $1 billion five-year *sukuk* issued by Abu Dhabi's Tourism Development and Investment Company to build museums in the Emirate.[10]

With such broad and appealing uses for *sukuk*, one has to wonder why the market hasn't grown faster than it has. According to Bloomberg, the global debt market has reached $100 trillion,[11] yet the *sukuk* market has yet to reach 1 percent of this size. There are a lot of research and published reports on *sukuk* and the reasons they haven't taken a big enough slice out of the global debt market to date. Suffice it to say that it is a combination of legal and regulatory hurdles that need to be overcome in order for *sukuk* to be attractive in many developed markets. One of these issues is the fact that there can be more than one purchase and sale transaction within the *sukuk* structure, triggering double taxation in some cases. These are also reasons why potential issuers in developed markets are pushing to get their regulators on board with *sukuk*. Their primary reason is to tap into a new source of funding that *sukuk* can unlock for them, as they see a saturated market on the corporate bond side. Some see a limit to how much larger the global bond market can grow.

Sukuk, on the other hand, can't seem to satisfy the demand from all the potential buyers. There has been extremely high demand to buy the *sukuk* issued so far. The fast-paced growth of Islamic finance has led to a shortage of fixed-income instruments for banks and other investors. The downside to this is that the high demand for *sukuk* has created extremely low trading volume in them, because investors snap them up and hold them to maturity. This is unlike the situation with corporate bonds, which are actively traded. One of the main features of *sukuk* is their tradability. The shortage of them has, on one side, strangled the trading activity in them and, on the other side, led companies and governments in developed markets (the same markets that are currently drowning in debt) to look at *sukuk* with great interest. Conventional banks and multinational corporations are already issuing *sukuk*. Some of the notable names other than GE Capital include British supermarket chain Tesco, Goldman Sachs, Nomura Holdings, Toyota, and, more recently, Bank of Tokyo-Mitsubishi UFJ, which in June 2014 announced plans to issue a $500 million multicurrency *sukuk*.[12]

Venture Capital and Private Equity

Though venture capital and private equity have been around quite possibly as long as business activity has been around, it was not until after

World War II that they were organized as niche industries within the finance sector. Prior to this, venture capital and private equity were reserved mainly for wealthy families. Investors such as Laurance S. Rockefeller, J. Pierpont Morgan, J.H. Whitney, and Eric M. Warburg were some of the early pioneers who helped create the industry we have today.[13] Thanks to the Glass–Steagall Act, which separated commercial banking activities from investment banking activities, venture capital and private equity funding after World War II came from specialized investment firms set up specifically for finding and managing early-stage investments, corporate buyouts, and other forms of private equity. In the early 1960s these specialized firms began setting up private equity funds, and in the early 1970s venture capital firms began popping up in Silicon Valley to capitalize on the new investment opportunities in the technology space. Firms such as Kleiner Perkins Caufield & Byers (KPCB) and Sequoia Capital, founded in 1972, are among the largest and most well-known venture capital firms today.

In Islamic finance, venture capital and private equity started out in similar fashion. Though equity investing and risk taking are, by definition, the ideal investment vehicles for Islamic investors, the sector has been slow to take off. Much like the case with conventional finance, early investors into private equity and early-stage companies were wealthy families. As Islamic finance began to gain acceptance in the market, Islamic forms of private equity began to appear on the institutional side. It took two decades for private equity to emerge as an industry on both the conventional side and the Islamic side. The first Islamic private equity firms began appearing in the mid-to-late 1990s. The first such firm was Bahrain-based First Islamic Investment Bank, which later became Arcapita, followed by Gulf Finance House, also based in Bahrain. A host of other firms soon followed, emerging not only in the Middle East but also in Malaysia. Since the investment opportunities in the Middle East were few and far between, these investment firms looked to developed markets, primarily in Europe and the United States, to deploy their investment capital. Over the next two decades they would invest billions of dollars in acquiring companies and other assets in these markets.

From 2004 to 2009, I worked for one of these new Islamic private equity firms. I was tasked with setting up an office in Chicago and hiring an investment team to begin scouting for and investing in U.S.-based companies. The reason for this was twofold. First, Islamic finance at the time lacked the necessary talent to be able to manage such investments. Second, deal flow in the Middle East was still low and there weren't a sizable number of companies in which to invest. The most developed private equity market in the world was the United States. The firm saw its entry there as a way to build up its expertise in the field while at the same time being able to show its investors that it had access to U.S. private equity investments, all of which were structured in accordance with Islamic finance principles.

We were not the first Islamic firm to jump into the United States. Kuwait Finance House had been investing in U.S. real estate and private equity since the mid-1980s, and Arcapita entered the United States in 1997. What differentiated us from the other Islamic firms operating there is the fact that we tried to source as much capital from the United States as possible. The sizes of our investments were relatively small, ranging from $5 to $20 million, but went up as high as $100 million in a couple of cases. The issue for us was the size of our parent company in Bahrain, which was small, as it was also a newly established bank. In order to make private equity work for us, we had to find partners in the United States willing to invest with us or offer us financing that met Shariah guidelines. This was no easy task. There are literally hundreds of specialized finance companies and funds in the United States that serve the private equity industry and whose purpose is to offer leverage (in other words, debt) for private equity acquisitions.

Private equity today can be a bit misleading, since most of the financing is done using debt. Leveraged buyouts (LBOs) became popular in the 1980s during the height of the junk bond craze. The firms KKR became a household name after its acquisition of RJR Nabisco in 1989. The $25 billion deal was 1 part equity and 23 parts debt.[14] This megadeal set the tone for the rest of the industry. I would say that today nearly all private equity deals involve some debt, with a vast majority of the debt being multiple times more than the equity. So to call it private equity is misleading. It should be renamed "private debt."

Thus, the challenges we faced were enormous; we were operating in a multi-billion-dollar industry with a few million dollars in hand and going around asking conventional lenders to give us Shariah-compliant financing for our deals. We weren't very successful initially, and the team really had to think long and hard about the career choice they'd made. After being declined many times by potential lenders and seeing the puzzled looks on their faces, we finally got a break from one of the local private equity lenders in Chicago. Like us, they were a small firm and saw this as a way to build a niche for themselves. They also saw this as an opportunity to attract more Islamic investment companies from the Middle East.

The financing terms and structures we used were based on cost-plus and leasing using the target company's assets as the basis for the financing. It worked well. The limit we had was based on the company's assets, which would theoretically limit our financing to 100 percent of the assets. In reality, however, our typical transaction was 50 percent equity and 50 percent Shariah-compliant financing from our conventional lending partner. The conventional lender often reminded us that by limiting the amount of leverage we were willing to take we were also limiting our potential return. Most firms use as much debt as possible in order to generate higher equity returns once the acquired company grows its revenues and profits. If the company doesn't perform as planned, however, investors in the company could end up losing more than they invested. Think of this as your mortgage being underwater. The lender liked our conservative approach, and we ended up attracting more lenders willing to meet our terms as a result of our investment philosophy.

The bigger payoff that I saw was when meeting with potential target companies. Private equity is an extremely competitive business in the United States. It is common for companies to go through a bidding process, with the highest bidder winning the company. In other cases, companies were being sold by the owners and founders of the business. It was in their best interest to see their company grow and prosper in the future. In every case where we had a chance to meet the business owners and explain our investment philosophy, the owners overwhelmingly preferred our model over the conventional model. We were never able to compete in the bidding process, but we found our niche in targeting business owners who saw us as business partners and not buyers.

On the venture capital side, Islamic finance has yet to make significant inroads. There are some efforts at promoting venture capital in the Middle East, but they are not specifically targeting Islamic finance. In Europe and the United States, Islamic investors have invested in early-stage venture companies. As with conventional venture capital, it will take more time for a proper industry to form on the Islamic side.

GOVERNMENT FINANCE

Up until recently, governments looking to finance their domestic projects and budgets had no choice but to seek out conventional finance through the issuance of bonds and other forms of debt. After the establishment of the Islamic Development Bank (IDB) in 1975, governments in member countries, many of which are among the poorest countries in the world, gained access to funding for necessary infrastructure projects. These projects would have been out of reach for them without the IDB's help, or they would have had to pay a high price to get them funded conventionally through the other intergovernmental agencies, such as the World Bank. Since its founding, the IDB has approved funding and assistance to more than 7,909 projects worth over $97.8 billion, $10.4 billion of which has been approved in the past two years alone.[15] The IDB uses several Islamic financial instruments to fund its projects, including construction finance, leasing, and partnership finance. The bank has launched specialized funds, such as the $2.5 billion fund in partnership with the Bill & Melinda Gates Foundation mentioned in Chapter 6, as well as billions of dollars in *sukuk* sold to investors worldwide.

Since the development of *sukuk* in the late 1990s and their mass acceptance as a viable Shariah-compliant funding alternative to conventional bonds, governments have played a major role in the growth of the *sukuk* market. Of the $286 billion in *sukuk* in the market, over half has been issued by governments. In the first half of 2014 alone, governments issued more than $38 billion in *sukuk*.[16] The largest government issuer of *sukuk* is the Malaysian government, but there is an increasing number of government *sukuk* being issued by Bahrain, Saudi Arabia, and the United Arab Emirates. The wealthy governments in the Middle East have not had much need to tap into debt or *sukuk* markets, as they are flush with revenues from their oil exports.

The most interesting development on the government finance front is the entry of non-Islamic countries into the market. The German state of Saxony-Anhalt was the first Western government to issue *sukuk* back in 2004. It issued €100 million backed by the buildings of the Ministry of Finance. The U.K. government, after years of discussion and debate, finally issued its first *sukuk* in June 2014. These landmark *sukuk* were relatively small in size, only £200 million, but this was seen as a first step toward issuing a lot more in the future. The five-year term will pay investors a yield of 2.036 percent, in line with what comparable U.K. government bonds pay. However, investors in these *sukuk* will receive rental payments based on the lease of three central-government properties. In this structure, ownership of physical assets (the buildings) was transferred to a special entity specifically set up to own the assets. Certificates in this entity were then sold to investors, who have beneficial ownership in the building and will receive rental payments (income) from the U.K. government. This is a classical *sukuk* leasing structure, which was put together by HSBC Bank. Certificates in this entity (the *sukuk*) can then be traded on an exchange and sold to other investors, much as other tradable securities are. Demand for this issue was extremely high; investors placed orders worth £2.3 billion for this £200 million issue.[17]

The U.K. government had two main reasons for getting involved in the *sukuk* market. First, it wants to maintain its leadership position as the world's Islamic financial center. The U.K. government just signaled to the market that it is committed to doing so. Second, Western governments saddled with increasingly high debt loads are in great need of finding new funding solutions and a new investor base. The U.K. government just tapped into a new source of funding. *Sukuk* investors are not only in Islamic countries, they are spread all over the world. Western pension funds and insurance companies are active investors in *sukuk*. They like their asset-backed nature and view these instruments as a way to diversify their portfolios away from bonds and into other income-generating investments. Nearly 39 percent of investors in the U.K. *sukuk* came from the United Kingdom, and 24 percent from Asia. The remaining 37 percent of investors came from the Middle East.[18]

With the success of the U.K. *sukuk* followed by the successful issuance by the governments of Luxembourg and Hong Kong, we can expect to see a rush of *sukuk* issuance by non-Islamic governments in the coming years. This trend will only accelerate as more of these governments look to Islamic finance as a way to expand and diversify their funding base.

SUMMARY

- In the span of 40 years, Islamic banks and financial institutions have raced to develop a full range of products and services to be able to compete with conventional institutions.
- The proof of Islamic banks' success at offering real financial alternatives is the fact that Islamic banks are continuing to eat away at conventional banks' markets share in nearly every market where they operate. In some cases, such as in Saudi Arabia and Kuwait, Islamic banking has taken over 50 percent of the market or close to it.
- The three most active areas of Islamic finance are consumer banking, corporate finance, and government finance.
- Deposits and savings differ greatly in how they are treated by Islamic banks compared with conventional banks. Unlike conventional banks, where deposits are treated as loans from customers, Islamic banks treat deposits as money entrusted to them; therefore, deposits cannot be used to make money.
- Savings and other investment accounts in Islamic banks must be subject to profit and loss if they are to pay a return, which is another difference between Islamic banks and conventional banks.
- Islamic banking offers alternatives to consumer finance such as auto loans and home mortgages, but is not able to offer unsecured credit, which is popular around the world today. Instead, Islamic banks prefer tying financing to the purchase of specific goods or assets, such as the financing of computers and furniture.
- As a result of Islamic banking's nature, banks have gotten more involved in finance, especially in auto finance, where they are active in the purchase and sale of vehicles directly to their customers. In some cases, Islamic banks maintain their own inventories of vehicles and have their own showrooms.

- In corporate finance, Islamic banks offer alternatives to lending, namely, lease finance and short-term cost-plus financing. Islamic finance, however, is not able to offer receivable financing, known as *factoring*, due to its non-Shariah-compliant nature.
- *Sukuk* have been a driving force on the corporate side. The industry was virtually nonexistent until 2000. Since then, the *sukuk* market has grown to more than $286 billion in issuance from major corporations around the world, including Western and Asian corporations.
- Venture capital and private equity are at the core of Islamic finance, and there is a growing niche market here for such investments. Much like the conventional side of the industry, Islamic venture capital and private equity have taken similar paths to development over the past two decades.
- Due to the lack of investment opportunities in the Middle East, Islamic private equity firms have looked toward the United States and Europe to deploy their private equity capital.
- The Islamic Development Bank (IDB), launched in 1975, was the first intergovernmental agency set up to help member countries finance their government projects, all on a Shariah compliant basis.
- The IDB has financed and supported projects worth more than $97.8 billion since its inception.
- The bigger picture, however, is in the government *sukuk* market. More than half the existing *sukuk* market consists of government-issued *sukuk*. In the first half of 2014 alone, more than $38 billion worth of government *sukuk* were issued.
- Government-issued *sukuk* are expected to play a major role in the coming years as non-Islamic governments tap into this market as a way to seek out a new investor base.
- To date, five non-Islamic countries have issued *sukuk*: Germany, Hong Kong, Luxembourg, South Africa, and the United Kingdom.
- Not all investors in *sukuk* are Islamic investors; many Western pension funds and insurance companies like the asset-backed nature of *sukuk* and seek them out as a way to diversify away from bonds.

CHAPTER 9

Criticisms, Shortcomings, and Misconceptions of Islamic Finance

Islamic finance is not free of criticism, nor should it be. Any financial instrument, tool, or system should be open to critique and criticism in order to have an open debate on its merits and interworking. This allows for growth and improvement versus a closed system. Islamic finance also has its own limitations and shortcomings, which have so far restricted Islamic finance mainly to Muslim countries. Even though Islamic finance is active all over the world, including Europe and the United States, its presence outside of the Islamic world remains small and fragmented.

Some questions that come up frequently when discussing Islamic finance in the West include: If Islamic finance is such a great system, why hasn't it been able to effect any changes in the current financial system? Why are all the countries around the world, including Muslim countries, still on the conventional financial system? Answers to these questions are at the heart of the Islamic finance debate. However, there are also some misconceptions around the world about what Islamic finance is and what values it strives to achieve. I think it's important to address these in addition to some of the criticisms and shortcomings.

Throughout the course of my career, I have come across five main criticisms, shortcomings, and misconceptions on Islamic finance, as follows:

1. Islamic finance supports and is linked to terrorism.
2. Islamic finance is for the benefit of Muslims and is part of Shariah's agenda for world domination.
3. Islamic banks are not safe.
4. Islamic finance is a marketing gimmick.
5. Islamic finance cannot be a stand-alone financial system since it is too dependent on the conventional one.

In this chapter, I would like to go over each one of these misconceptions in some detail, beginning with the one I hear most often: Islamic finance supports terrorism. For those people who are not involved in Islamic finance or have never heard of it—which is a vast majority of the world's population—having someone tell them that Islamic finance is the way terrorists get their funding wouldn't cause them to think twice or challenge this view. Unfortunately, the words *Islam, Islamic,* and *Muslim* have developed negative connotations in the media and are often associated with terrorism and violence. You rarely read any headlines that cast these words in a positive light. This is why I think it's important to address this issue first and clarify the misconception surrounding Islamic finance.

MISCONCEPTION #1: ISLAMIC FINANCE IS LINKED TO AND SUPPORTS TERRORISM

I grew up in the 1980s between the United States and Kuwait. It was a good time back then because you could easily differentiate between the good guys and the bad guys. The bad guys were the communists, namely, the U.S.S.R., Eastern Europe, Cuba, China, and North Korea. This was the Cold War. If you were a communist country or a country associated with communism, you were the enemy. Iran should be included, since it had close ties to the U.S.S.R., and there was that U.S. Embassy incident during the country's revolution in 1979. Libya, the Irish Republican Army (IRA), and the Palestine Liberation Organization (PLO) should be added to the list as well, since they were the terrorists at the time.

Flash forward to 2014, and the bad guys have changed, except for Cuba, Iran, and North Korea, which have stayed the same pretty much since the 1980s. Today, the Muslims are the enemies, China is the world's main trading partner and the manufacturer for the world, Eastern Europe is a great summer vacation destination, and the U.S.S.R. has been broken up into more than a dozen countries. These new countries are all considered friendly, except for Russia, which, as of 2014, seems to be headed toward the "enemy" category again for its annexation of Crimea and its opposing views on the West's meddling in the political situation in Ukraine.

What happened over the past 30 years to change all of this? When did Islam and Muslims become the enemies? U.S. President Ronald Reagan in a March 8, 1983, speech delivered to the National Association of Evangelicals in Orlando, Florida, said:

> They [the U.S.S.R.] preach the supremacy of the state, declare its omnipotence over individual man and predict its eventual domination of all peoples on the Earth. They are the focus of *evil* in the modern world . . .

Two years later, in his February 1985 State of the Union Address, President Reagan said:

> We must not break faith with those who are risking their lives . . . on every continent, from Afghanistan to Nicaragua . . . to defy Soviet aggression and secure rights which have been ours from birth. Support for freedom fighters is self-defense.

The unquestionable enemy at the time was the U.S.S.R., and anyone who stood up against them was on the side of good. The freedom fighters Reagan was referring to were the Afghan mujahideen. Not only did he call them freedom fighters, he also supported them with weapons and military training to help fight the Soviets. On November 9, 1989, the Berlin Wall came down and, with it, communism, the Soviet Union, and the end of the Cold War. It was a new world, which was to bring about peace and prosperity everywhere.

Up until that point I had never heard of Islamic terrorism. In 1989, when you heard the word _terrorist_, you would think of Libya, the IRA, or the PLO, not "Muslim extremist group" or "Islamic terrorists." With the fall of communism, the world had no major enemy. It wasn't until August 2, 1990, that the world would unite behind a common enemy again. It was the day Saddam Hussein rolled his army into Kuwait, taking over the country and its oil wells. I remember this time well, as I was involved in Operation Desert Storm to remove Saddam from Kuwait. Iraq was sold via the media as having one of the strongest armies in the world at the time—1 million strong or so. It took roughly 100 hours for the United States and its coalition forces to defeat Saddam's army. The swift war was a great testing ground for military hardware, but Saddam's quick defeat left the world again with no major enemy. It didn't take long, however, to find a new one. On February 26, 1993, terrorists detonated a truck bomb in the parking garage of the World Trade Center in New York City. Muslim extremists were behind this attack. It was the first time I had heard of Muslim terrorists. In the 1970s and 1980s the news was filled with terrorist attacks headed by the PLO, which was primarily fighting against Israel for Palestinian territory. Though many Palestinians are Muslim, the PLO was not an Islamic organization. There was also the occasional story of an IRA attack in Northern Ireland or England. So to hear of Islamic terrorism was a wake-up call.

It turns out that the fall of the U.S.S.R. also led to the ending of its occupation of Afghanistan, which it had invaded in 1979. Afghanistan struggled to form a functional government with lasting peace after the Soviets left, but civil war broke out. The mujahideen, Reagan's freedom fighters, split into militias fighting each other. The thousands of Arab fighters who volunteered to fight the Soviets went back home to find nothing else for them to do that fit their skill set. This caused problems for governments across the Middle East, as returning fighters, having little opportunity, started to rebel against their governments. Saudi Arabia was particularly vulnerable, as hundreds, if not thousands, of Saudis had fought in Afghanistan. Not only did these returning fighters cause problems in their home countries, they also became mercenaries who went on to fight holy wars in other countries around the world, including in Bosnia, Chechnya, and Algeria.

The 1990s is when the radicalization of Islam began and Islamic terror-ism appeared. To get a good understanding of how Islamic extremism flour-ished in Muslim countries, one has to look no further than the demographics. Muslim countries, which I consider to be any of the 57 countries belonging to the Organization of Islamic Cooperation (OIC), are faced with an enormous demographic problem. They have above-average population growth with a huge young population that has fewer and fewer economic opportunities. Islamic extremist groups capitalized on the growing youth frustration with their governments. This allowed them to convince an increasing number to join their cause.

Out of the chaos in Afghanistan and the rise of Islamic extremism, groups such as Al-Qaeda found a comfortable home in Afghanistan to base their activities. The country was increasingly being run by a new group of thugs known as the Taliban, or "the students" in English. The Taliban were formed and funded largely by Pakistan as a way to buffer the ongoing violence in Afghanistan and keep it from spreading into Pakistan and as a way to exert its influence over the country. Nobody disputed how bad the Taliban were. Women's rights, human rights, and pretty much all other rights were thrown out the door when the Taliban came to power. The one positive thing the Taliban managed to do while in power was to drastically reduce the trade in the country's main cash crop. The Taliban banned the trade in poppies, the main ingredient in heroin, which was wildly successful, especially as Afghanistan was the largest poppy producer in the world.[1]

With all their strict laws and their disregard for human and religious rights, the Taliban were still not considered to be the enemy by the United States or other Western powers. In 1997, the Taliban were considered to be friendly. They were even invited to Houston, Texas, to meet with oil executives to discuss the terms of an oil pipeline, which was to run through the country.[2] It wasn't until September 11, 2001, after the terrorist attacks in the United States, that the Taliban were labeled an enemy and Islamic terrorism took over the spotlight. The Taliban became the enemy after refusing to hand over Osama bin Laden, the head of the Al-Qaeda terrorist group comprising former Mujahideen fighters, said to be responsible for the attacks. Overnight, Islam and Muslims were equated with terrorism and terrorists.

In his January 29, 2002, State of the Union Address, President George W. Bush said:

States like these (Iran, Iraq, North Korea), and their terrorist allies, constitute an axis of *evil*, arming to threaten the peace of the world.

The terrorist allies he was referring to were the Taliban. This was the beginning of the buildup that would eventually lead to the invasion of both Iraq and Afghanistan. In the span of just over a decade, the word *evil* went from being associated with communism to being associated with Islam.

What does this have to do with Islamic finance? For starters, it was widely believed that the terrorists responsible for the September 11 attacks used Islamic banks to move their money around. It was also believed that terrorist groups used Islamic banks to raise funds to support their causes. In a report titled "National Commission on Terrorist Attacks," published in August 2002 by the National Commission on Terrorist Attacks Upon the United States (also known as the 9-11 Commission), no Islamic financial institution was found to be involved in funding or supporting the attacks. The commission found that the attackers used Dresdner Bank, Citibank, Standard Chartered Bank, and the Saudi British Bank (HSBC's affiliate in Saudi Arabia) to wire money to their U.S. bank accounts. For the most part, however, the attackers did not use bank accounts at all to funnel their money. Instead, they opted to use traveler's checks and money-transfer shops such as Western Union to finance their activities in the United States.

While Islamic financial institutions were not involved in funding the attacks, the same cannot be said about some of the Islamic charities. When looking into the source of funding for these terrorist organizations, the commission found that most of these terrorist groups, such as Al-Qaeda, got their funding from Islamic charities across the Middle East. The lax oversight of these charities, coupled with the fact that most of them had no idea their funds were being siphoned off to terrorist groups, was the main reason these groups were getting funded, according to the commission. Weaknesses in banks' know-your-customer (KYC) policies were also cited as reasons the terrorists were able to move money into the United States without detection.

Since then, governments in the Middle East have reined in their charities and begun keeping a closer watch over their activities. They also have imposed stricter KYC policies on banks, which was in line with the moves made by banking regulators in Europe and the United States. In 2013, for example, Kuwait enacted a law criminalizing terrorist financing, which calls for the immediate freezing of terrorist assets, and the creation of a Financial Intelligence Unit to monitor financial activities.[3] The commission's report, however, did little to change the misconception of Islamic finance in the Western world.

Islamic finance continued to be looked upon with skepticism and suspicion even as non-Muslim countries began allowing Islamic finance to open up in their countries. The United Kingdom has been the most aggressive in terms of opening up to Islamic finance, but other countries such as Luxembourg, Singapore, Hong Kong, and even Russia have been allowing and even encouraging Islamic finance to establish itself in their respective countries.

Skeptics cite the Bank of Credit and Commerce International (BCCI) and Arab Bank as two high-profile examples of Islamic banks involved in terrorist funding and money laundering. At the height of its operation in the 1980s, BCCI operated more than 400 branches in 78 countries. It was owned by Pakistani and Middle Eastern investors who used the bank for all sorts of activities from personal loans to money laundering. It was purposely set up in multiple jurisdictions to be able to move money around for its clients and away from banking regulators. One of the bank's high-profile clients was the Central Intelligence Agency (CIA). The CIA used multiple accounts at BCCI to fund the Afghan mujahideen. Oliver North was said to hold several accounts at the bank, which were used to finance weapons transfers leading up to the Iran-Contra scandal.[4] The bank was closed by regulators in 1991 and made headlines around the world not only for its size, which was estimated to include more than $20 billion in assets, but also due to the level of criminal activities.[5] The bank's main investors may have been from Pakistan and the Middle East, but the bank in no way was an Islamic bank, nor did it ever refer to itself as one.

Arab Bank is one of the oldest and largest financial institutions in the Middle East, headquartered in Amman, Jordan. The bank operates more than 600 branches in 30 countries. The bank was sued in the United States in 2004; the suit alleged that the bank helped route funds from Hamas in Palestine, which in turn went to fund the group's terrorist activities in Israel. In September 2014, the bank was found to be liable for knowingly supporting terrorism.[6] Arab Bank, however, is not an Islamic bank; it is a conventional bank and always has been. The bank does own an Islamic bank called the Islamic International Arab Bank, which was set up in 1998.[7] In my research, I could not find any news linking this bank to the current case against Arab Bank.

If it were 1980 and a bank called Communist Bank of Europe were to be set up, headquartered in Warsaw, I'm sure it would get the same reaction by the media as some Islamic banks get today. The fact is, Islamic banks face the same challenges when it comes to monitoring their clients' activities, and a few bad apples always seem to fall through the cracks. When it comes to money laundering and terrorist financing, the big global banks seem to be bank of choice for these groups, not Islamic banks. There has been no evidence to support the claim that Islamic banks support terrorism or help finance their activities. The misconception lies in the recent history of how Islam and Muslims replaced communism to become the new enemy of the West.

Islamic banks and financial institutions face the same challenges in dealing with money laundering and terrorism financing as any other financial institutions. In most cases, regulators in jurisdictions where Islamic banks are active follow the same guidelines in handling these challenges as regulators in Europe and the United States.

MISCONCEPTION #2: ISLAMIC FINANCE IS FOR THE BENEFIT OF MUSLIMS AND IS PART OF SHARIAH'S AGENDA FOR WORLD DOMINATION

Islamic finance naturally established itself initially in predominantly Muslim countries. In the 1970s Islamic finance existed exclusively in the Middle East and Malaysia, but in the 1980s it began to follow its investors to other parts of the world, including Switzerland and the United Kingdom. At the time, the push toward Europe was at the request of investors seeking to deploy some of their capital there for safekeeping. Their goal was the protection of their wealth outside of their homelands, which always seem to have some ongoing political turmoil. The early Islamic financial institutions set up in Europe were not designed to attract European investors.

Early in the 1970s and 1980s, many believed Islamic finance to be an experiment that would not last. Those involved in Islamic finance at the time did not have the confidence to aggressively market themselves or their institutions. Once these institutions had a stronger footing and a track record of offering investors good returns, they went on to expand their client base. As mentioned in earlier chapters, Islamic finance quickly began to grab market share from conventional financial institutions, leading the conventional banks to either become Islamic banks themselves or start offering Islamic financial services. This would not have been possible if only Muslims were allowed to participate.

Islamic finance is based on a set of values, rules, and guidelines open to all. To hear someone say that Islamic finance is only for Muslims is as absurd as hearing someone say that sushi is only for Japanese. Those who are skeptical of this should ask a more logical question: Why would a non-Muslim be interested in Islamic finance?

The true test of whether Islamic finance is a viable alternative to conventional finance is when non-Muslims see the value in it or benefits from it. The reasons typically cited by non-Muslims for choosing Islamic finance are because they view it as being more ethical and fair, they like the risk-sharing nature, or they have had bad experiences in conventional finance and wanted to find an alternative. Islamic banks and financial institutions around the world, regardless of whether they are in a predominantly Muslim country, have growing numbers of non-Muslim customers.

In Malaysia, for example, Hong Leong Islamic Bank, a Malaysian-Chinese owned bank, estimates that 50 percent of its customer base is non-Muslim.[8] Across the Middle East, where Islamic finance is most active, Muslim and non-Muslim customers have a choice about the financial institution they choose. Both types of customers are increasingly choosing Islamic finance, not only because of the range of services but also because Islamic finance in some cases is cheaper than conventional finance. An example is Kuwait Finance House in Kuwait, which is the largest car leasing company in the country. As a result of the volume of leasing it does, it is able to offer better financing terms than its conventional counterparts.

The Islamic Bank of Britain, the only Islamic retail bank in the country, has a growing number of non-Muslim customers. The bank actually benefited during the financial crisis, as non-Muslims opened accounts there as a way to protect themselves from the fallout resulting from bank closures and government takeovers.[9] They viewed the Islamic bank as a safe haven due to its lack of exposure to toxic assets and counterparty risk.

Along similar lines, Saturna Capital, manager of the Amana mutual fund family in the United States, witnessed an increase in the number of investors as a result of the financial crisis. Launched in 1986, the Amana funds are a family of three mutual funds run in a Shariah-compliant manner, meaning they do not invest in sin industries, banks, finance companies, insurance companies, and highly leveraged companies, among others. As investors pulled out of these companies, looking for safe havens, assets under management in the Amana funds swelled. From 2008 to 2014, assets in these funds more than doubled, reaching $3.6 billion.[10] Though it is difficult to get an accurate assessment of the percentage of non-Muslims in these funds, Saturna estimates that about two-thirds of the assets are owned by non-Muslim investors and cites their investment philosophy and good track record as the reason investors chose them.

I have read articles and seen interviews with Islamophobes who believe that Islamic finance is a back door to allow Shariah to take over Western countries. They see the opening of Islamic financial institutions in their country as the first of many calculated steps by Muslims to begin imposing Shariah law. I find this hard to believe, as Islamic finance currently makes up less than 1 percent of the global finance industry. This is minuscule by any standard, yet we are to believe that Islamic finance is coming to take over? I haven't seen or heard their explanation of how they see this playing out.

In addition, if you look at the statistics on the members of the 56-member Organisation of Islamic Cooperation (OIC), you will see that they are all developing countries, and some are among the poorest in the world. Their total GDP makes up around 5 percent of the world's total. Most of these governments are also not interested in seeing Islamic finance dominate their own economies, much less plan for a takeover of global finance. In talking to Shariah scholars, there is a consensus that "world domination" is not a concept Islam or Shariah adheres to. Any person or group talking about world domination does not speak for Muslims in general and is not in line with the overall Shariah consensus on the matter.

People involved in Islamic finance would tell you that they see it as an alternative system based on a set of rules and guidelines designed to be fair and equitable to all. It's about being inclusive and not exclusive, regardless of one's beliefs.

MISCONCEPTION #3: ISLAMIC BANKS ARE NOT SAFE

Being just shy of 40 years old as I write this, I have seen the Islamic banking industry experience its fair share of ups and downs. Islamic banks are seen as inherently riskier than conventional banks because of their business model. They share risk with their clients; they work on a profit-and-loss basis, not a guaranteed-return model (i.e., interest); they buy and sell assets and get involved in the ownership of assets instead of money lending. These activities are out of the question for conventional banks because they are too risky!

There have been some well-publicized cases of Islamic financial institutions running into trouble. In 2010, for example, the Islamic Bank of Britain needed to be recapitalized during the financial crisis due to mounting losses from its business activities. The bank was bailed out with a £20 million capital injection from Qatar International Investment Bank. The fresh capital brought the Qatari bank's stake to 88 percent and, with it, a new strategy and expansion plan.[11]

In the Middle East, dozens of Islamic finance companies fell into trouble as a result of the financial crisis, which caused real estate values to drop. Two prominent companies in the region defaulted on payments and were near bankruptcy. The Investment Dar in Kuwait, which made headlines in 2007 for its acquisition of luxury automaker Aston Martin, defaulted on a $100 million *sukuk* payment. This pushed the company to the brink of bankruptcy and forced it to scramble to raise money and restructure $3.7 billion in other *sukuk* and financing.[12] The other well-publicized company was Gulf Finance House, which was one of the largest Islamic investment banks based in Bahrain. The bank was overextended in real estate investments and private equity deals. When the financial crisis hit, the value of its investments plummeted and the bank began hemorrhaging cash. In 2010, shareholders approved a plan to raise $500 million in new capital to rescue it from bankruptcy.[13] Many Islamic retail banks were overly exposed to these finance companies either by owning shares in them or by providing them financing, but no Islamic retail bank was closed or went under during the financial crisis.

In some of these cases fraud was involved. In North America, there were two headline-grabbing fraud cases involving Islamic finance: one in Toronto, Canada, and one in Chicago, Illinois. UM Financial was a Toronto-based Islamic home finance company. It was not a bank and did not have its own capital to provide home financing; therefore, it relied on a Canadian bank to provide a funding line. UM collapsed during the financial crisis, and fraud was found within the company—specifically, misappropriation of C$4.3 million in home finance payments due to the funding bank. There was also the strange case of 32 kilos of missing gold and silver bars.[14] In Chicago, Sunrise Equities Inc., a Muslim-owned property developer, was indicted in 2010 along with its owners for allegedly running a $44 million Ponzi scheme. Muslim investors in the company's real estate projects, as well as several local Chicago banks, were defrauded in this case. Sunrise marketed itself as an Islamic finance company offering investors Shariah-compliant investment returns.[15]

In all cases where fraud was involved, Islamic finance was used as the marketing tool to lure unsuspecting investors. These investors eagerly sought suitable Islamic investment solutions whereby they could invest their hard-earned income. As a result of these incidents, Islamic finance has left a bad impression in some communities. This is unfortunate, since these fraudulent companies in no way adhere to Islamic principles.

The global media attention Islamic finance gets when there is a company in crisis or when fraud is involved hits this small industry hard. This leads some to view Islamic finance as a high-risk industry. Needless to say, the bailouts, fraud, and criminal activities of conventional finance pale in comparison. As of August 2014, the U.S. Justice Department is said to have recovered nearly $37 billion in settlements from the big banks for their role in selling questionable mortgages up to the financial crisis.[16] This does not include the billions of dollars paid in fines and for other fraudulent charges, including money laundering.

One way to see whether Islamic banks are safer or riskier than conventional banks is to look at their credit rating by one of the three leading credit-rating agencies. In Table 9.1 you will see the ratings assigned to some of the key Islamic banks in the Middle East along with the top global financial institutions. The Islamic banks are shaded in gray.

TABLE 9.1 Credit Ratings of Islamic Banks vs. Global Banks as of August 2014

Banks	Fitch		Moody's		S&P	
	Rating	Outlook	Rating	Outlook	Rating	Outlook
HSBC Plc	AA−	Stable	Aa3	Negative	A+	Negative
National Bank of Kuwait	AA−	Stable	Aa3	Stable	A+	Stable
Bank of NY Mellon Corp	AA−	Stable	A1	Stable	A+	Negative
Al Rajhi Bank	A+	Stable	A1	Stable	A+	Stable
Kuwait Finance House	A+	Stable	A1	Negative	A−	Stable
UBS AG	A	Stable	A2	Negative	A	Negative
Abu Dhabi Islamic Bank	A+	Stable	A2	Stable	NR	NR
Ahli United Bank of Kuwait	A+	Stable	A2	Stable	NR	NR
Deutsche Bank AG	NR	NR	A3	Negative	A	Negative
Barclays Plc	A	Stable	A3	Negative	A−	Negative
Qatar International Islamic Bank	A	Stable	A3	Positive	NR	NR
Goldman Sachs	A	Stable	Baa1	Stable	A−	Negative
Boubyan Bank	A+	Stable	Baa1	Stable	NR	NR
Gulf Bank	A+	Stable	Baa1	Positive	BBB+	Positive
Dubai Islamic Bank	A	Stable	Baa1	Stable	NR	NR
Bank of America Corp.	A	Negative	Baa2	Stable	A−	Negative
Citigroup Inc.	A	Stable	Baa2	Stable	A−	Negative
RBS Plc	A	Negative	Baa2	Negative	BBB+	Negative

Source: Bloomberg, KFH Research

As you can see, Islamic banks are rated fairly well. Al-Rajhi Bank, Kuwait Finance House, Abu Dhabi Islamic Bank, Ahli United Bank of Kuwait, and Qatar International Islamic Bank all have higher credit ratings than Goldman Sachs, according to Moody's. Bank of America, Citigroup, and Royal Bank of Scotland pose greater credit risks and have a higher chance of defaulting than the Islamic banks listed in Table 9.1.

Another way to look at this is to do some in-depth research on Islamic bank risk and look into past failures. Luckily, a recent research report was published on this exact topic. In June 2012, a research paper titled "Failure Risk in Islamic and Conventional Banks" was published by researchers at Lancaster University and Cass Business School in the United Kingdom. The researchers wanted to see if Islamic banks have a higher risk of failure compared with conventional banks in the same country. The researchers detailed their findings after studying 421 banks (both conventional and Islamic) in 20 countries in the Middle East and the Far East from 1995 to 2010.

The research concluded that Islamic banks were 55 percent less hazardous than conventional banks in the same country. What is interesting is that they found Islamic banks to have higher operational risk because of their business model of acquiring assets and risk sharing on the profit and loss side. However, a direct result of this business model is the removal of moral hazard, which is quite apparent in conventional finance. Let's not forget that up to the financial crisis Wall Street banks were selling subprime mortgages to their clients while at the same time betting that they would lose. This is still happening today.

The research also found that Islamic banks had lower leverage and a lower concentration of investments in the banking sector. Islamic banks by their nature avoid leverage, but some conventional banking analysts lump their financial activities into the leverage category in order to compare them with conventional banks. They also tend not to borrow and lend to each other, so this is why there would be a low concentration in the banking sector. While they are quite often criticized and chastised by rating agencies for their high concentration in the real estate sector, they are not commended for their low exposure to other banks. Counterparty risk is a big issue for banks. The contagion effect of banks falling like dominoes after the Lehman Brothers failure is what led regulators and rating agencies to pay close attention to counterparty risk. Conventional banks are overexposed to other banks more than they were before the financial crisis, while Islamic banks are underexposed. The exposure Islamic banks have to other banks is mainly through their treasury activities, whereby an Islamic bank would park some of its excess cash at one of the global banks such as Deutsche Bank. Deutsche Bank, in turn, would invest this cash on the Islamic bank's behalf in order to generate a Shariah-compliant return. This is usually done through commodity trading. Nevertheless, the Islamic bank becomes exposed to Deutsche Bank in the event of a Deutsche Bank failure.

At the end of the report, the researcher concluded that banking regulators and rating agencies are placing unwarranted regulation and requirements on Islamic banks, fearing that they are riskier. They suggest that Islamic banking is misunderstood by these regulators, which is evidenced by the way regulators have asked some Islamic banks to raise their capital as a consequence of placing higher risk on Islamic banks' financing activities. They have also required Islamic banks to hold larger cash reserves, even though their financial activities typically come with ownership of assets (i.e., collateral), which should reduce the requirement for high cash reserves.[17]

We might have to wait until the next financial crisis before regulators and rating agencies reexamine the risk assessment of Islamic banks. In the meantime, rating agencies will continue to underrate Islamic banks while looking the other way at conventional banks that are now exposed to over $710 trillion and counting in derivatives.[18] Islamic banks' exposure to derivatives is nearly zero. It's not quite zero because they are exposed to conventional banks by way of their commodity trading and investment activities. In a crisis scenario where the derivatives market blows up, conventional banks' capital will be wiped out many times over. No bailout would save them from the trillions of dollars in collapsing derivatives. Islamic banks would only be exposed to the portion of cash and capital they have parked at conventional banks, so they would be hurt but not wiped out. This is the banking model conventional banks want to avoid because they say it's too risky!

MISCONCEPTION #4: ISLAMIC FINANCE IS A MARKETING GIMMICK

I often hear people say that Islamic finance is nothing but a marketing gimmick used to attract Muslim customers and investors. Lawyers who have worked on structuring Islamic financial transactions, whether in New York, London, or Dubai, would say that Islamic finance's handicap is that it follows the letter of the law and not the spirit of the law. There have been cases where conventional lending documents have been used to write Islamic financing contracts, with the only change being replacing the word _interest_ with _profit_ and then sending them off to be signed. Though I'm sure this has happened more than a few times, it is not standard practice. Shariah scholars have been criticized for not being as hands-on as they should be, especially early in the industry's development. Thus, word-editing conventional lending documents and then rubber-stamping by Shariah boards is no longer the case.

I still must agree somewhat with lawyers' view that Shariah has been focused more on the letter of the law than on the spirit of the law. In focusing on the legal documents, too much time and effort has been spent making sure there are no holes from a Shariah perspective. This focus shifts attention away from the purpose and intent of the transaction itself. The bigger issues, however, are the deficiencies in Islamic financial practice versus theory. Islamic finance theory is based on the Shariah principles described in

Chapter 7. As it turns out, in practice Islamic finance is not applied according to all the stipulations and principles of Shariah, especially in non-Muslim countries. The main assumption in the theory is that all Islamic finance principles and Shariah requirements can be applied in the market. In practice this is very challenging even in Muslim countries. Many of the world's legal systems operate on the basis of either common law or civil law; few countries operate under Shariah law, and even then it can be challenging because, as stated, the practice differs from the theory. It's also important to note that regardless of whether a country applies Shariah law, the world is on a conventional financial system. As a result, Islamic finance has had to adjust to its legal surroundings.

An example of this is the way Shariah scholars have allowed investment in the stock market. In addition to weeding out the prohibited industries, such as casinos, pork producers, and banks, there is a stipulation that Muslims can only invest in stocks of companies with a little conventional debt, not zero conventional debt. The threshold that has been set is 30 percent, so companies having a debt-to-equity ratio or debt-to-asset ratio in some cases above 30 percent are prohibited from being included in the acceptable universe of stocks. Shariah clearly stipulates that paying or receiving any amount of interest is prohibited. If Shariah scholars had not applied their deductive reasoning and consensus as described in Chapter 6, then they would not have allowed any investment in the stock market. In today's global marketplace, it would be extremely difficult to find a publicly traded company that did not receive any interest on its bank account or cash holdings or pay any interest on loans and credit lines. In order to permit Muslims to benefit from investing in stocks, scholars bent the rules, allowing for exposure to companies with low debt levels. This ended up being a sound financial decision as well, since history has shown us that companies with low debt are better at surviving financial storms than companies with high debt.

The bending of the rules and adjusting to the surroundings have sometimes affected people's perception of Islamic finance. They see these adjustments and exceptions as watering down Shariah rules. Some have shied away from Islamic finance because they cannot see or feel a difference between Islamic and conventional finance. Therefore, they opt for the conventional route because they know it and understand it. The reasoning behind this decision is that if Islamic finance and conventional finance cost the same, then what is the difference? Wouldn't I be better off sticking with a big-name bank if the cost is equal? Why would I expose myself to the risk of doing business with a small Islamic financial institution?

This is best illustrated with an example. Let's go back to the cost-plus financing structure, known as *murabaha*, to see how it compares with a conventional loan in a car financing transaction (Figure 9.1).

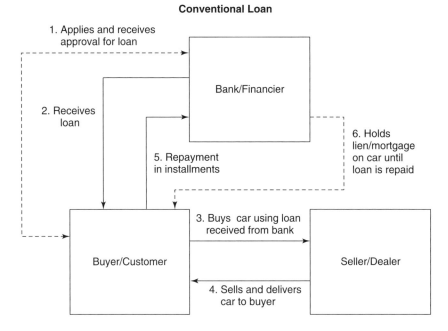

FIGURE 9.1 Conventional loan diagram

With a conventional auto loan, you find the car you like at the dealer or through a private seller, you negotiate the price and agree to buy it for $20,000, then you go to your bank and apply for a loan. The bank tells you the annual interest rate on the loan is 5 percent and asks you if you are making a down payment. In this case you don't put anything down. The bank then asks you how long you want the term of the loan to be. You say four years, meaning the car will be fully paid after 48 monthly installments. If your credit is good, the bank gives you the loan; it either gives you a check or deposits the money in your account. You then go back to the dealer/seller, pay for the car, and take possession. The car is now yours, but the bank usually holds a lien on the car until the loan is fully repaid. In some cases the bank doesn't hold anything other than your good credit. You then pay the bank a monthly installment of $460.60 for the next 48 months, which includes repayment of the principal plus interest. After 48 months, you would have paid a total of $22,108 in payments, so $2,108 was the total interest on the loan.

In a cost-plus financing transaction (Figure 9.2), you find the car you like at the dealer or through a private seller, you negotiate the price and agree to buy it for $20,000, then you go to your Islamic bank or finance company

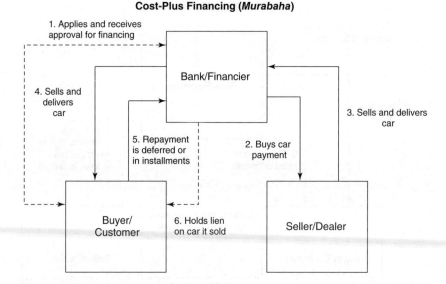

FIGURE 9.2 Cost-plus financing diagram

and apply for financing. You tell the bank that you will not be making a down payment and you want to pay off the financing in four years. After a review of your credit, the bank agrees to buy the car from the seller on your behalf and sell it to you for $22,108. The $2,108 is the bank's profit for buying the car from the seller and reselling it to you. The bank goes to the car seller or nominates you to act on its behalf to purchase the car. Once the car is sold to the bank, the bank sells it to you for the agreed terms. You take possession of the car and make a monthly payment of $460.60 for the next 48 months. The bank will hold a lien on the car it sold you until all the payments have been made.

You can see how the cost-plus financing method can be controversial. A lot of people can't see, and definitely can't feel, a difference when using this method versus a conventional loan. However, a closer look at both transaction diagrams shows that in a conventional loan the bank had no role in the car purchase and no relationship with the seller. It also did not sell an asset in order to make its profit. It gave the buyer money and asked for it to be repaid. This is interest. In the cost-plus transaction, the bank was directly involved in the transaction. You can see this by the two sales that took place. The first sale is from the original seller to the bank, and the second sale is from the bank to you. The bank in this case acted as a middleman or wholesaler that buys an asset at a lower price and sells it to you at a higher price. This is profit.

Skepticism and criticism of this transaction comes from two sides. First and foremost, both methods cost the same, so how can this be Shariah complaint? Second, did the bank really have to create more paperwork by buying the car first and selling it to me seconds later? Wouldn't it have been easier if the bank just gave me the money to buy the car? On the first side, Shariah does not stipulate what price to charge, nor does it say that it cannot cost the same as conventional financing. Just because two items cost the same doesn't mean that they are either acceptable or unacceptable. Case in point: A bottle of Evian water can cost $5 and a cheap bottle of wine can cost $5. Does this make both of them prohibited for Muslims to consume since both items cost $5? The reason for the equal cost is simply a competitive business decision and is not stipulated by Shariah.

The real difference is on the second side. Yes, in an Islamic financial transaction, the bank or finance company needs to own the asset before selling it to you. There is no way around this. This is at the core of Islamic finance. If this is a marketing gimmick, then ask a conventional bank to finance your next car using the cost-plus method. I will be surprised if they agree to it because, right away, the bank will notice that it must buy the car first and then sell it to you. The bank will most likely respond by telling you that they are not a car dealer, they are a bank. They have money to sell you and not cars. They will also see the inherent risk in getting involved in buying and selling assets instead of simply selling money. This direct involvement in the transaction, coupled with the fact that the Islamic bank takes on additional risk in doing the cost-plus financing, is the difference between one transaction being permitted and the other prohibited. It's the difference between *riba* and profit. The bank's customer may not see it or feel it, but the bank does.

I used the cost-plus example because it's probably one of the transactions most people point to when trying to show you that Islamic finance is more of a marketing gimmick than a real financing alternative. If I use the example of leasing or partnership finance, the difference between Islamic finance and conventional lending becomes more apparent.

MISCONCEPTION #5: ISLAMIC FINANCE CANNOT BE A STAND-ALONE FINANCIAL SYSTEM SINCE IT IS TOO DEPENDENT ON THE CONVENTIONAL ONE

The argument goes something like this: Islamic finance is not a stand-alone financial system because it needs conventional finance to operate. I just mentioned that one of the criticisms of Islamic finance is that it is operating in a conventional financial world. Therefore, far from being perfect, Islamic finance has to adjust to the realities around it and work within the box it was put in. So to say that Islamic finance is not a stand-alone financial system is true. But to say it can't be is another question.

To predict whether Islamic finance will one day be a complete financial system is beyond me. There are too many variables and "what-ifs" to conclude either way. If we look at the examples we have today to see how it's working out, I would say that Islamic finance as a model financial system looks dismal. Iran, Pakistan, and Sudan claim to operate a 100 percent Islamic financial system. What they claim and what reality is are two different things. Though not model economies by any stretch of the imagination, two of them are considered to be rogue nations—Iran and Sudan—and the third is nearing failed-state status. In order to make Islamic finance fit into their economic model they've had to make modifications that mainstream Islamic bankers would not consider to be Shariah compliant. Keep in mind that even though internally these economies might be trying to operate under an Islamic financial system, the reality is that they still must deal with the outside world, which doesn't fully subscribe to Islamic finance. Once you add in all the corruption and cronyism, I find it hard to see how Islamic these economies really are. I don't remember seeing corruption and cronyism on the list of Shariah principles.

Looking at countries where Islamic finance and conventional finance operate together, such as Malaysia, Bahrain, Saudi Arabia, and the UAE, you will see that Islamic finance is dependent on conventional finance. Islamic banks' parking some of their funds at global banks, as described in the earlier example, is not done by choice. They generate lots of cash and need to place it globally not for safety but to be able to generate returns on it. This is done mainly through commodity trading, which is a global business run out of the world's key financial centers. They also need to invest outside of their countries due to the limited opportunities available at home. Once this capital is in international markets, it's operating in the conventional space, even though specific instructions (Shariah guidelines) will be given on how it is to be used.

Therefore, as Islamic finance currently stands at less than 1 percent of the global financial industry, it needs conventional finance to operate. This is not to say that the rest of the world can't borrow some of Islamic finance's principles and apply them. After all, recent history has already shown Islamic finance to be more stable, ethical, and equitable than conventional finance. The current shortcomings of Islamic finance in no way diminish what it stands for or what it strives to achieve. As we head into the next financial crisis, maybe conventional finance can borrow some of the Islamic principles to build a better system. I hope it's not too late to start the discussion.

SUMMARY

- Islamic finance has its fair share of criticisms, shortcomings, and misconceptions.
- The top five are:
  - Islamic finance supports and is linked to terrorism.
  - Islamic finance is for the benefit of Muslims and is part of Shariah's agenda for world domination.
  - Islamic banks are not safe.
  - Islamic finance is a marketing gimmick.
  - Islamic finance cannot be a stand-alone financial system since it is too dependent on the conventional one.
- Looking back at the recent history of the fall of communism and the rise of radical Islam gives you a better understanding of how Islamic finance has been perceived to be linked to terrorism.
- Islam does not believe in the concept of world domination, and Islamic finance is open to all.
- Rating agencies dispel the myth that Islamic banks are not safe, while recent research concludes that Islamic banks are actually safer than conventional banks.
- It is understandable that some may not be able to see or feel the difference between an Islamic financial transaction and a conventional loan, but the differences are there. Conventional banks would not take on Islamic financing because they deem it to be too risky or outside of their business model of selling/lending money.
- Islamic finance makes up only a fraction of the global financial system and needs conventional finance in order to operate. However, this does not diminish the fact that conventional finance can apply Islamic financial principles to build a better system for the future.

The New Financial System

CHAPTER 10

Preventing Future Crises—Real-World Solutions from Islamic Finance

With a better understanding of Islamic finance and a look back at the history of money, financial systems, and financial crises, let's see if there are any lessons to be learned from Islamic finance. I'm not suggesting that Islamic finance take over the global financial system, but I would like to see its concepts and philosophy become accepted as offering ethical solutions to issues we face repeatedly in our financial system.

Before looking at possible solutions, we must first define the problems in our current system and understand why we keep going from crisis to crisis. We must also look at the reasons these crises are increasing in severity and why nothing has been done so far to fix the problems. The big question in the end is, what will it take for our financial system to change? Once these questions are addressed, we can see what solutions, if any, Islamic finance has to offer.

In Part I, I covered the history of money, past financial systems, financial crises, and the buildup to the next major crisis. The main cause of the boom-and-bust cycle of our financial system is the foundation upon which it is built. If the foundation is bad, the entire system is bad and can be fixed only if the foundation is replaced. The foundation of our financial system is money—fiat money—which is supported by the ever-growing mountains of debt. Our fiat money system is held together only by government promises. History has shown us that governments break these promises 100 percent of the time, yet we keep hoping that the next time will be different.

For our economies to grow, they must be pumped with an ever-increasing amount of debt. By now it should be obvious that much of it will never be repaid. If the overall level of debt in the system stays constant or, god forbid, drops, then the systems crashes, as you can see from Figure 10.1.

The current global financial system began in 1971, after the United States dropped out of the Bretton Woods Agreement, which removed any backing of the U.S. dollar other than the government's promise. The rest of the world followed, creating our fiat money system. The results of being on this system for the past 43 years can be seen by the divergence between GDP growth and debt growth shown in Figure 10.1. Overall debt in the United States, both government and private, has shot up at an increasing rate since 1971. The slight blip on the debt line in 2008 was the result of the global financial crisis. Thus, a decline in overall debt leads to a recession. It also leads to a decline in the money supply, since new money is issued only on the back of new debt, regardless of whether it is government debt, corporate debt, or consumer debt. Every new paper or digital dollar coming into the market is a result of another dollar in new debt being issued. Without bigger and bigger mountains of debt, the system collapses. This is why governments and central banks stepped in with such force during the most recent crisis; they took on the role of debt issuers, since corporations and consumers were overloaded with debt. This trend continues to this day, with governments taking on more debt than they can ever repay in the hope that all the new debt will kick-start economic growth. This should be the clearest sign of the fragility of our system and the brick wall it is headed toward.

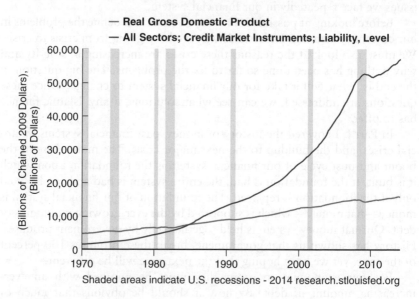

FIGURE 10.1   U.S. GDP growth vs. total debt growth from 1970 to 2014
Source: Federal Reserve Bank of St. Louis

We are most likely to hit the brick wall sooner than later. The pumping of fresh debt into the system is having less of an effect on the economy than it had in the past. One dollar of new debt in the system today does not yield the same economic growth as it did in the past. Thus, even more debt is needed to push the economy forward. The Federal Reserve has been frustrated at the lack of growth from all of its quantitative easing (QE) programs. Since 2008, the Fed has pumped nearly $4 trillion in new cash into the economy—about a fifth of annual U.S. gross domestic product—yet the effects have been lackluster at best.

One of the few positive effects of the Fed's QE has been the stock market, but as can be seen in Figure 10.2, the rapid rise in the stock market comes with strings attached. The stock market rise is directly correlated to the rise in margin debt—people and institutions borrowing money to buy stocks. The Fed's cheap money has gone into the stock market and other higher-risk assets seeking to earn higher returns. This is one of the reasons the stock market lately goes up when there is bad economic news and goes down when there is good economic news. Investors worry about the day when the Fed will pull the plug on the cheap money. Thus, market fundamentals have gone out the door and been replaced by untested Fed policies. Looking at

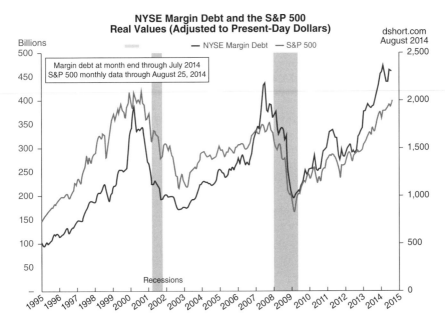

FIGURE 10.2   S&P 500 Index vs. NYSE margin debt from 1995 to August 2014
Source: Advisor Perspective (www.dshort.com)

Figure 10.2, which shows the two most recent bubbles, would you invest in the stock market at this time or pull your money out?

One of the unforeseen consequences of the Fed's policies is the crash in the velocity of money. Velocity of money measures the rate at which money changes hands and moves around in the economy. An increasing rate tends to indicate a healthy and growing economy. Too much of an increase, however, could indicate rising inflation or even hyperinflation. A drop in the velocity tends to happen in recessions. However, notice in Figure 10.3 that the velocity of money has collapsed. The reason for this collapse is the Fed's QE. There is so much new money in the system, but it's not moving around. Banks are hoarding money and not lending it out; thus, the more QE is used, the more the velocity drops, to the Fed's frustration. Why should the banks lend out this new money when they can send it back to the Fed and earn a small but guaranteed return, which will make their balance sheets look better?

I've shared with you many other charts and tables to show the predicament we are in, so for now I will show you only two more to highlight my main point: that the next crisis is just around the corner and will be much worse than the crisis in 2008.

Figure 10.4 needs little explanation. The real estate bust in 2008 had devastating effects on the housing market and economy. The housing market has dropped so much that new home sales volumes are at the same level they

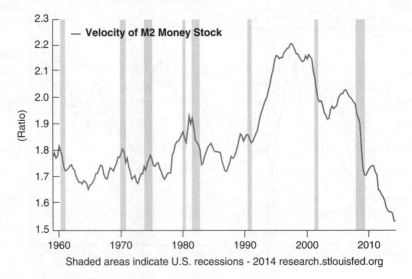

FIGURE 10.3 Velocity of M2 money from 1958 to June 2014
Source: Federal Reserve Bank of St. Louis

FIGURE 10.4 Sales of new single-family homes in the United States from 1980 to June 2014
Source: Federal Reserve Bank of St. Louis

were back in the 1980s. You wouldn't know this from reading or listening to the news. Instead you hear about how real estate prices are up 10% or even 20% in some markets from the bottom of 2010. A look at Figure 10.4 and you will see that the news is right, new home sales are up, but it's a far cry from new home sales in the earlier part of this century. It will take many more years, if not decades to reach the level it was back in 2007.

Another one of the Fed's unintended consequences, along with the prolonged effects of the global financial crisis, is the collapse in the labor force. As of July 2014, the unemployment rate in the United States stood at 6.2 percent.[1] Figure 10.5 shows that the percentage of those in the labor force in 2014 is the same as it was back in the 1970s. So, yes, the unemployment rate has dropped, but it is not because there are new jobs in the market. The drop in unemployment is due mainly to the decline in the number of people looking for work. Millions of people have simply given up looking for work, and if you're not looking for work, you're not unemployed. There are some severe structural problems in the economy, but it's not helping to have the Fed offer cheap money to banks and large companies. Companies, in particular, which the Fed assumed would love cheap money to enable them to hire more workers, instead decided to use this cheap money to buy back their shares. Stock buybacks by U.S. corporations are at a record level. These are a very risky proposition, since the market is at an all-time high and money is

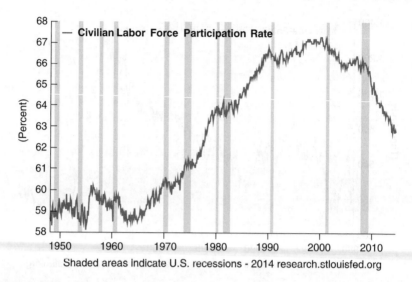

FIGURE 10.5   Labor force participation rate from 1948 to June 2014
Source: Federal Reserve Bank of St. Louis

still cheap. What happens when the market takes a break from rising? The shareholders are not going to be happy.

All of the solutions to addressing the problems in our financial system will be painful. As it stands today, none of our politicians, central bankers, or market regulators want to make any tough decisions, so the only way I see change coming is after the next crisis. When it happens—and it *will* happen—the severity of it will force change, much like the rapid expansion of the U.S. money supply forced President Nixon to abandon the Bretton Woods Agreement in 1971.

How then can we fix the system or build a better one? This is a complex question to answer, so I will address it in two parts. In the first part, I will highlight the main problems in our current system and suggest solutions from Islamic finance. In the second part, which appears in Chapter 11, I will discuss some of the other solutions being discussed in the market today.

The main problems in our system are debt, derivatives, money, and the lack of ethics in the field of finance. I will also spend a little time talking about the too-big-to-fail banks. Let's begin.

DEBT

Have you ever heard of debt falling? When we hear about debt, we tend to hear about rising debt or the level of debt growth, but to hear about debt falling is unusual. Look at all the types of debt—consumer, government, and corporate. For our financial system to survive, debt has to rise. Our money is built on debt and our economy is built on debt. We are not only hooked on debt but hooked on this notion of perpetual growth, without realizing that debt, economic growth, and all other things in life have their limits. You can see in Figure 10.1 how debt has ballooned since 1971, taking only a small pause during the global financial crisis in 2008. This pause in debt growth led the media to call this crisis the worst financial crisis since the Great Depression. Some are even calling it the Great Recession. The mere thought of declining debt causes chills down the spines of central bankers. In their book, debt can never fall because falling debt means financial crisis. So if debt must always be rising, it must also mean that a lot of this debt will never be repaid.

To shed some light on this, go back to the beginning of 2014, during the most heated debt ceiling debate in the United States. The ceiling was raised yet again in February 2014, this time to $17.2 trillion.[2] I don't know why there is even a debate on the topic, since the United States will always raise the debt ceiling. To not raise the debt ceiling would mean that the United States would default on its debt payments. To hear politicians say that the United States always pays its bills and cannot default is very misleading. If the country always pays its bills, then there would be no default if the debt ceiling were not raised. There would also be no need to raise the ceiling in the first place. Instead, let's call it what it is: a Ponzi scheme. The United States doesn't pay its debts, and this is why it constantly needs to borrow more money. It borrows more and more money that it never intends on repaying, and investors worldwide can't seem to get enough of U.S. debt. The fresh debt goes to pay off old debt, and the pile of debt keeps rising, which is music to central bankers' ears. This can go on as long as investors continue to buy U.S. debt. If and when they stop buying, then it's game over.

This cycle of an ever-increasing mountain of debt is at the core of our problems. Governments' and central bankers' inability to solve this problem is creating more instability in our system and making it even more fragile. On the surface it might seem that all is calm, thanks to the Fed and the European Central Bank, but under the surface the pressure is rising—it can be contained for only so long before blowing up.

What, then, is a solution to this problem? From an Islamic finance perspective, there is no debt. The only debt that exists is for charity. Financing is available for anyone or any entity that has assets with which to back the financing, hence the term *asset-based* or *asset-backed financing*. If governments want to borrow, they can't. Instead, they can get financing if they have assets to put up for sale or lease. Investors who give the government financing become actual owners of the assets being put up to back the financing.

Today, government bonds are backed by the government's promise to repay. What if it can't repay, like Argentina? In today's world, there are two options for the government if it cannot repay its debt: (1) default (i.e., don't pay) or (2) print money to pay the debt, causing inflation. The second option is the most attractive one for governments.

In Islamic finance, if there are no assets to back up the transaction, then there is no transaction. There is no promise to repay without assets being involved. Forget about the debt ceiling and completely drop it under this scenario. How much financing would the government seek if it had to put up assets every time?

The core of the problem—the truth few openly acknowledge—is that our economic system is carrying too much debt. A more robust system would be based on assets as opposed to our current system, which is based on promises. To change over to an asset-based or asset-backed system of finance would be detrimental to our economy. The best solution would be to transition to it slowly, over time. There would, however, be a big problem with more debt outstanding versus assets to back it with. Obviously, the world needs to grasp the reality of the situation and realize that a lot of debt already issued will never be repaid. There is no way else around it unless investors are willing to stand by and watch governments and central banks inflate it away. Either way, investors get little if anything back.

For the remaining debt that has a chance of being repaid, there are two options. The first option would be to redraw the agreements so that they are backed by assets, such as in a lease-to-own or operating lease situation as described in Islamic finance. Option two was already being discussed back in 2009. Nassim Taleb, the author of *The Black Swan,* came to the conclusion that there is too much debt in the system. Too much debt, according to his research, causes too much volatility and makes our financial system more fragile. He cites the dot-com bubble to show that the bust in 2000 did not lead to a severe economic slowdown as we saw in 2008 because it was primarily equity based. There was very little debt involved in financing Silicon Valley start-ups. The fragility in the system derives from the fact that debt has a nasty characteristic to it that we fail to properly value: You do not know if a loan is bad until the debtor stops repaying and eventually defaults. This is the hidden risk of debt, unlike equity investing, which has more transparent risk.[3]

Taleb's solution to this is to convert the debt into equity, which is in line with Islamic finance principles. The specific example he cites relates to home owners' holding underwater mortgages. Instead of waiting for them to default, banks should jump in and convert the loans into equity, similar to what I described in Chapter 8 with the diminishing partnership home financing. I fully agree with this solution and believe that it should be taken more seriously when discussing and debating what to do with all the debt in our system, instead of brushing it under the table. The alternative would be to default, which would hurt both sides. Equity, by its nature, creates a partnership whereby both sides have a vested interest in succeeding. With debt, there are always insurance and derivatives whereby banks and investors can bet on your failure and profit from it.

DERIVATIVES

Let's not forget what brought down the global financial system in 2008. It wasn't Jim, Bob, or Mike defaulting on his subprime mortgage payments in the United States; it was the default in derivatives that were based on these mortgages, which sent shock waves across the global market. The proof is in the bailouts. Instead of bailing out home owners, mortgage investors, and lenders, the Treasury ended up bailing out AIG, one of the largest issuers of credit default insurance at the time (i.e., derivatives) along with the big banks globally that invested in these mortgages as well as the default insurance. Prior to the crisis, governments and central banks had no idea how these instruments worked or how they were interrelated. The global financial crisis was a wake-up call for them, which they ended up blowing because, instead of dealing with the problem of the overgrown derivatives market that was right in front of them, they decided to give the big banks cheap money to keep it going, hoping that the problem would fix itself or go away. Instead, the derivatives market has continued to expand, growing 20 percent since the financial crisis, and is now in the $700 trillion range, according to the Bank for International Settlements.

No government or central bank has the firepower to fight a collapsing derivatives market, and, realistically, they are too afraid to deal with it because corporations and financial institutions are hooked on derivatives. Derivatives today generate a lot of profit for banks and other large corporations. To give up this gambling casino, which seems to be making them a lot of money, would be like shooting themselves in the foot. After all, they were given the go-ahead by the regulators to continue with business as usual. A good example of this situation is Berkshire Hathaway, headed by billionaire investor Warren Buffett. In 2003, he referred to derivatives as "weapons of mass destruction" because they are complex instruments few understand and pose a great risk to the financial system. Derivatives are similar to gamblers taking bets on a certain movement of an investment or financial product. This legalized Wall Street casino was "only" $85 trillion in size back then. Derivatives, as it turns out, are irresistible even to a company like Berkshire Hathaway, which loves to hate them. In the first half of 2014, the company reported profits of $391 million from derivatives trading (i.e., placing bets).

A derivative, put simply, is a contract between two parties whose value is determined by changes in the value of an underlying asset. Those assets could be bonds, equities, commodities or currencies. The majority of contracts are traded over the counter, where details about pricing, risk measurement and collateral, if any, are not available to the public.

—Mayra Rodríguez Valladares, faculty member, New York
Institute of Finance[4]

In other words, a derivative is a contract or a bet on the direction of a financial product. It does not have any intrinsic value. The largest segment of the derivatives market is based on interest rates, but there are virtually endless possibilities for what a derivative contract could be. You could create a derivative contract to bet on a growing number of home owners in Wichita, Kansas, defaulting on their mortgage payments. So if your bet comes true and more people lose their homes and are thrown out on the street in Wichita, you win!

New regulations such as Dodd-Frank in the United States and the European Market Infrastructure Regulation (EMIR) in the EU were supposed to fix some of the issues with derivatives, but they have yet to take effect. When they do, they will still fall short of addressing some of the biggest issues. Derivatives will still remain opaque when it comes to how banks sell them to clients, how and where they are recorded, and, most important, to what extent governments and taxpayers will be on the hook when it comes time for another bailout.

According to the Office of the Comptroller of the Currency, the four largest derivatives players in the United States are JPMorgan, Citibank, Bank of America, and Goldman Sachs. The size of JPMorgan's derivatives portfolio alone is about $70 trillion. Goldman Sachs, which has a derivatives portfolio of about $48 trillion, has included increased sales of derivatives to clients as part of its growth strategy.[5]

Little blowups in the derivatives market have been occurring since the most recent financial crisis. JPMorgan, for example, ran into trouble in 2012 when one of its traders, known as the London Whale, lost money trading for the bank's proprietary account. What was supposed to be trading to protect the bank against its investments blew up in the trader's face. The trader was said to be putting at risk only $67 million of the bank's money, but the eventual loss from unwinding all the trades ended up costing the bank over $6.2 billion. So how can one of the largest and smartest banks in the world lose more than 90 times its underlying investment? The answer is simple: Derivatives are too complex even for Wall Street's best and brightest. It took JPMorgan months to figure out exactly what happened.[6] If the bank itself couldn't figure out what went wrong, how can we expect regulators to know?

What's the solution to these issues? Again, the answer is simple: Derivatives, as they are today, do not belong in our financial system. What was invented as a way to protect investors from risk of loss ended up being a casino for banks and sophisticated investors to take bets, making the entire system more fragile and volatile than before derivatives existed. In the old days, the way investors would shelter themselves from loss was to diversify. It may not be as exciting as betting, but it's the prudent way to invest. There is no such thing as a riskless investment. If investors expect to make money in an investment, they should also be willing to take a loss and understand the risk associated with it.

TOO BIG TO FAIL

I've mentioned too-big-to-fail banks in previous chapters, but I feel that they deserve to be mentioned here again because they are also part of the problem in our financial system. The banks that have been labeled too big to fail by regulators have gone on to become too big to regulate and too big to jail, and are now too big to bail. The bailouts only created a moral hazard in our system and gave the banks a green light to do whatever they wanted in order to make money.

Once these banks get into trouble again, they will go back to the government and request another bailout. What's really happening here is blackmail. Big banks place high-stakes bets. If they win, they keep all the profits; if they lose, the taxpayers take the loss. Government's and regulators' fear of systemic financial failure as a result of a big bank failing has put them in this corner. The solution after the financial crisis called for breaking up the big banks so that none of them would be too big to fail, but politicians and regulators move at a snail's pace. It also helps that the big banks are among the top contributors to both political parties in the United States.

As soon as the banks got the "all clear" sign from regulators, they went off into more reckless behavior. HSBC, Citibank, and Standard Chartered were caught laundering money for terrorist groups and drug cartels. JPMorgan, Bank of America, and Goldman Sachs were caught lying and misleading investors about the mortgage bundles they were selling. U.S. and European banks were also caught rigging the global interest rate market known as LIBOR as well as rigging the foreign exchange market and the gold market. Since 2008, the banks have been extremely busy coming up with new, but illegal, ways to make money. The banks have paid billions of dollars in fines to settle these charges, yet not one banking executive has gone to jail. In HSBC's case, for example, the reason cited for refusing to file criminal charges for money laundering (a serious crime, I thought) against bank executives was out of fear that such charges would destabilize the banking system.[7] So there you have it: The big banks are, officially, too big to jail.

Today, unfortunately, the big banks have gone on to become too big to bail. Banks are money factories, literally. Contrary to common belief, central banks do not create money; they might help facilitate its creation by offering low interest rates, but, in the end, banks are the creators of money in our system. This gives them enormous power. In Figure 10.3 you saw how all the Fed's QE programs have failed to pump money into the economy because banks—not the central bank—control this function.

A first step in fixing this problem would be to bring back the Glass–Steagall Act, which separated commercial banks from investment banks. It worked well after the Great Depression until it was repealed in 1999. The next logical step would be to break up the big banks into small enough sizes that they are no longer too big to fail. The next time they get into trouble, we can let capitalism do its job and let them fail.

MONEY

There are two issues with money in our financial system. The first issue is treating money as a commodity and not as a medium of exchange. The second issue is the way money is created. Let's take a look at the first issue. According to the Bank for International Settlements (BIS), the total size of the global foreign currency trading market is $5.3 trillion per day, as of April 2013, up from $3.3 trillion in 2007.[8] Of this $5.3 trillion, roughly $2 trillion is spot trading. Much of the growth in currencies trading, however, has come from foreign exchange (FX) swaps, which represented $2.2 trillion of the $5.3 trillion in daily trading.

> An FX swap agreement is a contract in which one party borrows one currency from, and simultaneously lends another to, the second party. Each party uses the repayment obligation to its counterparty as collateral and the amount of repayment is fixed at the FX forward rate as of the start of the contract. Thus, FX swaps can be viewed as FX risk-free collateralised borrowing/lending . . . FX swaps have been employed to raise foreign currencies, both for financial institutions and their customers, including exporters and importers, as well as institutional investors who wish to hedge their positions. They are also *frequently used for speculative trading*, typically by combining two offsetting positions with different original maturities.[9]
>
> **—The Bank for International Settlements**

FX swaps are a type of derivative, which are commonly used for speculative purposes by hedge funds and other investors. Notice that the BIS considers FX swaps to be risk-free. If the last financial crisis taught us anything, it's that nothing is risk-free. It also shows us that the BIS and its central bank members still do not understand or properly value risk.

As I've explained earlier, derivatives that were intended to reduce volatility and risk in the market have had the opposite effect. Removing derivatives from our system would help stabilize it. From an Islamic finance perspective, we should also consider the definition of money compared with the conventional definition; money is not a commodity, nor is it an asset. On this basis, an FX swap would not exist, since money cannot be collateral. There is another issue with FX swaps from an Islamic perspective: You cannot lend something you do not own. Applying Islam's definition of money together with its financial principles would render the foreign exchange market a spot market only. This would eliminate the creation of derivatives off this market as well as remove speculation. Investors looking to profit from foreign currency movements should consider investing in assets in foreign countries.

On the second issue, let's consider how money is created. It is not created by government decree, nor is it created by the increase in a government's or central bank's precious metals holdings. In our new fiat system, money is created on the back of new debt issued. Most people would agree that the money supply (i.e., the amount of money coming into the system or leaving the system) is controlled by the central bank. This is only partially true. While the central bank may raise or lower interest rates as well as issue currency backed by government-issued debt, it is not the creator of a vast majority of debt or new money in the system. This role is controlled by the banks. When you get a new car loan from your bank, the money the bank gives you is new money it just created specifically for your loan. The same goes for your credit card. Every time you swipe your card for a purchase, that purchase was booked by your bank as a loan, and thus more new money was created. As long as the banks meet their reserve requirements as specified by the banking regulator, they are free to create as much money as they can.

The central bank's implied control over the money supply comes from its control over interest rates. As the theory goes, when the central bank offers high interest rates, banks would prefer giving it to the central bank and earning the high rate rather than lending it out with risk. High interest rates, therefore, absorb the excess lending capacity in the system, starving the local economy of access to credit. On the flipside, when the central bank offers low interest rates, banks are encouraged to keep as little money as possible at the central bank and instead lend it out as fast as they can to earn a return. The theory works well in normal times, but in abnormal times it doesn't. Take, for instance, what is happening today. The Fed, ECB, and Bank of Japan have been offering near-zero interest rates for years, yet these record low rates have failed to translate into new lending to the masses. Since the global financial crisis, banks have been cautious about lending to consumers. Instead, cheap money has flowed into riskier investments in search of a return, such as the stock market, emerging markets, and junk bonds, which would have otherwise ended up being parked at the central bank.

Central bankers' frustration at the lack of control they have over the money supply is clearly evident in how banks have treated their cheap money. A prudent financial system must have discipline and control over its money supply. Islamic finance has a solution to this issue: Remove its association with debt. By removing debt from money, two major changes will happen to the financial system. First, the rise or fall in the money supply will no longer be linked to the amount of debt in the system. Second, banks will no longer be in control of money creation. An entity authorized to issue money will be in control, which could be the central bank, a government entity, or another entity. One hopes that the issuing authority would have more discipline than the banks. From an Islamic finance perspective, the issuing authority would issue money based on the value of trade in the economy or based on the value of precious metals it holds. Islamic finance does not stipulate whether money should be backed by anything, such as gold, so long as it works as a medium of exchange. This in turn means that money would have no intrinsic value.

There are alternative solutions being discussed today for how to fix the financial system, all of which focus on how money is created and who should control it. I will discuss them in Chapter 11.

LACK OF ETHICS

Applying Islamic financial principles to our financial system also means applying ethics, which seem to have been tossed out a long time ago. In addition to all the illegal, criminal, and fraudulent activities in the banking sector, unethical behavior and activities are rampant in other parts of the system. For a financial system to be successful, it must have the trust of the people, companies, and governments it serves. It must also adhere to a strict code of ethics in order to be fair and just to all. Sadly, this is not the case today.

In previous chapters I have discussed some of the fraudulent, unethical, and in some cases illegal activities perpetrated by individuals and financial institutions. These activities have existed throughout the history of finance. There were, however, times when these activities were not as prevalent as they are today. Lax regulation, fear of prosecuting large firms, and overall opacity in the industry are factors that have led to a rise in these behaviors.

The finance industry has also suffered from an upside-down incentive model. Profits are seen as the ultimate incentive over all other social and ethical factors. One example of this is the predatory lending industry, which focuses on profits at the expense of the poor and disadvantaged. Subprime, as it is now called, is making a comeback today as financial institutions hunt for profits.

You don't need Islamic finance to tell you that these activities are unethical and should not be allowed. The reality is that the government and regulators have looked the other way, allowing fraudulent, illegal, and unethical activities to gain a foothold in the industry. In this chapter I have tried to cover the main problems in our financial system and suggest solutions using Islamic financial principles. In some cases, Islamic finance is not needed, as the problem and solution are obvious. Ethics transcends religions and is a common human value worldwide. By following a code of ethics, many of our problems would be solved. In other areas, we can look to Islamic finance to find solutions.

The biggest problem facing our financial system is debt. Islam's view on debt and alternatives to it offers a realistic solution to help build a better financial system for the future. To complement this solution, we must also remove the unnecessary risk and fragility in our system by getting rid of highly speculative and complex financial instruments. The derivatives market today can easily take down the entire financial system during a crisis.

My hope is that readers, thinkers, economists, policymakers, and regulators look beyond the bias and negative stereotypes of Islam and Islamic finance and consider what they have to offer the world of finance. The solutions an Islamic approach holds, I believe, will help us all have a better financial future.

SUMMARY

- Our economy is hooked on debt; without a constantly growing mountain of debt, our economy comes to a halt.
- The drop in the overall debt in our system during the global financial crisis nearly brought down the entire financial system.
- The Fed's quantitative easing policies have done little to help kick-start the economy, since we are now experiencing diminishing returns on debt. The more debt that is added to the system, the less effect it has.
- The key problems facing our financial system in addition to debt are the derivatives market, foreign currency market, too-big-to-fail banks, and other unethical activities.

- Islamic financial principles offer two solutions to our ever-increasing debt problem:
  1. Rewrite the debt agreements to be asset-based or asset-backed instead of being assetless.
  2. Convert the debt into equity, which will align both parties with the same incentive and goal.
- Government debt is backed only by its promise to repay and not by assets, which is a key flaw.
- We must come to the hard realization that a lot of outstanding debt will never be repaid.
- Derivatives are Wall Street's answer to bringing Las Vegas to New York, except that the derivatives market is much larger and more profitable.
- Banks, rather than the central bank, create the money in our system by issuing new loans.
- Illegal and unethical behavior is rampant among the too-big-to-fail banks. The solution is to bring back the Glass–Steagall Act and break them up into much smaller banks so that later on when they get into trouble, they can be allowed to fail.

CHAPTER 11

Evaluating Alternative Solutions

The global financial crisis of 2008 was supposed to be the trigger for governments and regulators to bring about change to the financial system. However, it's been more than six years since the collapse of Lehman Brothers and we have yet to see any real change. In the United States, politics and lobbying got in the way of any efforts for real change. In Europe, a sovereign debt crisis hit in 2010, which nearly brought down the entire European banking system. Reform plans were hastily put on hold so that the system could be propped up with yet more debt backed by European Central Bank (ECB) President Mario "Whatever It Takes" Draghi's promises. In Asia, both China and Japan preferred money-printing and ineffective stimulus plans over the more painful route of reform. As such, the financial system has become more dangerous and the problems even larger to solve.

The lack of real reform and real change to the financial system is the main reason we keep hearing politicians, economists, and central bankers talk about the economy still recovering. The world has not witnessed such a prolonged recovery since the Great Depression. If governments and central bankers were truly in control of the problem, then their money-printing and stimulus programs would have worked by now. The fact that they have not only means that they do not understand the problems, but also that they do not see the next crisis coming. The ECB, which has been unsuccessfully trying to fight off deflation, announced another harebrained stimulus plan in September 2014. The plan called for the ECB to buy bonds and asset-backed securities for the first time.[1] This is in addition to its negative interest program that began in June 2014, which charges banks 0 to −0.1 percent to hold their money at the ECB.[2] The launching of new stimulus plans six years after the crisis should be a clear indication of how ineffective the ECB has been at solving problems, yet financial markets react with cheers and stock rallies every time a new program is announced.

Central bankers, however, are not 100 percent at fault. In the panic days of 2008 and 2009, central banks were able to react more quickly than governments. Their goal was to act fast in order to calm markets while politicians drafted the necessary economic reforms to address the core problems. However, as markets calmed down, politicians took this as an indication that they could go back to business as usual and put off the painful reforms for another day. Passing tough economic reforms will not get them elected. If central banks had the power to fix our economic problems, then Zimbabwe would be the richest country in the world.

The inaction of governments, coupled with the bailouts for the big banks, help spark protest movements around the world, such as Occupy Wall Street. Other leading economists and think tanks, for their part, helped to push forward the discussion on solutions to the problems we face. Nassim Taleb, for example, has suggested converting debt into equity, as mentioned in Chapter 10. There are many ideas and proposals being discussed on what to do. Three, in my view, stand out the most, and I think they are relevant to discuss alongside my proposal of looking into Islamic financial principles. These three proposals are: (1) bringing back the gold standard, (2) implementing the Chicago Plan, and (3) dropping the U.S. dollar in favor of the IMF's special drawing rights (SDRs) as the world's reserve currency. Two proposals focus on controlling the money supply, while the third focuses on the money creators—the banks. All three, however, have a common goal: to bring discipline back into the financial system and limit the ability to create money at will.

THE GOLD STANDARD

Gold has been used as money for more than 5,000 years, yet a vast majority of modern economists believe that gold should not be part of the monetary system. Even throughout Islamic history, gold has been used as money more than a commodity. However, Islam does not specify what can constitute money; therefore, other forms of money can circulate in the system as well. Today, there are no countries on a gold standard. Switzerland was the last country to drop it in 2000. Before dropping the gold standard, the Swiss franc had to be backed by a 40 percent gold-reserve.[3]

The main feature of the gold standard is that governments fixed their currency exchange rates to gold and guaranteed their redemption or convertibility into gold at a set price. This restricted them from issuing an unlimited supply of money, since they could do so only if they acquired more gold. Silver and copper have also been used as money in history, but, in theory, money can be tied to other things. Gold, however, played this role very well because of its rarity, durability, divisibility, fungibility, and ease of identification. Other commodities—for example wheat, oil, or wood—would not serve this purpose well.

Modern economists and central bankers, such as former Federal Reserve chairman Ben Bernanke, do not like the gold standard because it restricts them from being able to increase the money supply as needed. The evidence Bernanke cited was that during the Great Depression, countries that left the gold standard earlier than other countries recovered sooner. The United Kingdom and Scandinavian countries, which left the gold standard in 1931, recovered much earlier than France and Belgium, which remained on the gold standard much longer.[4]

There are three main advantages of the gold standard and three main disadvantages. The first advantage is its long-term price stability. The gold standard makes it very difficult for governments to expand the money supply. Thus, it would be extremely rare to see high inflation under the gold standard. Hyperinflation would be impossible because the money supply can only grow at the rate at which the gold supply increases. A country could experience high inflation if it was involved in a war that destroyed a large part of the economy. It could also experience high inflation if new gold resources became available. This happened in the mid-1800s, during the California Gold Rush.

Second, the gold standard removes some types of financial repression. By "financial repression," I mean transferring wealth from creditors to debtors, particularly the governments that practice it. Governments in a fiat money system can reduce their debt burden by printing more money to pay their creditors, causing inflation. The creditors, in turn, lose out by being paid back in money that is worth less. This can be called a form of theft or a form of taxation; either way, a government that has the unrestricted ability to print money will do so 100 percent of the time. In 1966, former Federal Reserve chairman Alan Greenspan wrote: "Deficit spending is simply a scheme for the confiscation of wealth. Gold stands in the way of this insidious process. It stands as a protector of property rights. If one grasps this, one has no difficulty in understanding the statists' antagonism toward the gold standard."[5]

Third, it reduces uncertainty in international trade, since exchange rates are fixed. Any trade imbalances—such as where one country would have large gold reserves coming in from trade (a net exporter) while another country would have gold reserves leaving the country (a net importer)—would be offset by a balance-of-payment adjustment mechanism called the *price specie flow mechanism*.[6] The net importer would see a reduction in its money supply, causing deflation and making it more competitive. The net exporter would see an increase in its money supply, causing inflation and making them less competitive.

Its disadvantages are, first, short-run price volatility. Although the gold standard brings long-run price stability, it is historically associated with high short-run price volatility. This can lead to financial instability as lenders and borrowers become uncertain about the value of debt if the price of gold experiences rapid fluctuations.

Second, the unequal distribution of gold deposits makes the gold standard more advantageous for those countries that produce gold, such as China, Australia, the United States, South Africa, and Russia. Since the money supply would be determined by the rate of gold production, countries producing the most gold would have higher inflation.

Third, the gold standard acts as a limit on economic growth. A country cannot grow unless it has access to gold supplies. A growing economy would need to have access to gold, whereas a shortage of gold would hinder this growth. Some of the leading economists believe that economic recessions can be largely mitigated by increasing the money supply during economic downturns. The gold standard is often blamed for prolonging the Great Depression because, under the gold standard, central banks could not expand credit at a fast enough rate to offset deflation.

In today's financial world, however, these same economists do not see returning to the gold standard as being beneficial or practical. After all, requiring a currency to be 100 percent backed by gold would be challenging. The global money supply has grown exponentially since 1971. For a country to return to this would mean that it would have to remove a large portion of money circulating in the economy, leading to severe deflation, or buy up gold until its reserves reached 100 percent of the currency at the desired exchange rate. Not only would this be expensive, and most likely cost prohibitive, it would also push the price of gold up to a historic level.

However, there is a growing movement globally to see the return to sound money policies by using gold to back currencies. While a 100 percent backing would be an unrealistic goal, many of the proponents are pushing for a partial backing similar to the system Switzerland had in place prior to 2000. The irony is that some Swiss citizens and politicians have called for the return of the gold backing. In May 2014, Switzerland's lower house of parliament passed the Gold Initiative. The initiative called for the country's central bank to immediately stop any future sales of its gold reserves, return all gold reserves stored outside the country, and back the Swiss franc with 20 percent gold.[7] To become law, the initiative needed to pass a national referendum, which took place on November 30, 2014. The initiative failed to pass in the national vote.

The reasons, however, for the Swiss Gold Initiative were twofold. First, many Swiss do not trust their government to make sound money decisions, especially after pegging the Swiss franc exchange rate to the euro back in 2011, an unprecedented move in Swiss monetary history. Second, the Swiss have become skeptical of their gold holdings overseas. Approximately

70 percent of the Swiss National Bank's gold reserves are held in Switzerland, 20 percent at the Bank of England, and 10 percent at the Bank of Canada.[8] Their suspicion was heightened after Germany's fiasco with trying to return some of its gold in 2013. Germany's central bank, the Bundesbank, announced plans for returning 374 tons of gold it had stored at the Banque de France and Paris and 300 tons stored at the Federal Reserve in New York by 2020. After 18 months of trying to get some of its gold back, the Bundesbank was able to return only 37 tons—32 tons from Paris and only 5 tons from New York. The challenges of getting its gold back from the Fed have led many to speculate on whether the Fed has the gold.[9] The gold could have been lent out, leased, or sold, but the world will never know since the Fed is not transparent in its holdings. There is a good chance, however, that the Fed doesn't have this gold, which would be devastating to the trust built into the financial system. It may have sold gold it doesn't own. The New York Fed is the top storage facility for central bank gold worldwide. Trust is everything to central banks, and losing trust cannot be good for the financial system.

The Swiss and German experiences are clear indications that trust is beginning to fade. There are other signs of cracks in this system. China has made no secret of its intention of having its currency, the yuan, become a reserve currency. What is not very well known, however, are its plans of backing the yuan with some gold to give it the credibility it needs.[10] There are also a growing number of states in the United States seeking to make gold and silver legal tender as well as to be able to issue their own currencies. There are currently 16 states with such initiatives, including Colorado, Indiana, Georgia, Minnesota, Virginia, and Washington. Support for these movements is coming from the growing mistrust of central banks and governments in handling money.[11] Another reason for the rise in the number of movements and initiatives around the world calling for a return to the gold standard, or at least to make gold legal tender, is to put some control over the money supply in the hands of the masses and not central bankers.

Though a return to a 100 percent gold backing is highly unlikely, there is a good reason for having a currency backed at least partially by gold. Such a move would bring credibility to the currency. It would also bring some discipline back to the money creation system by having the central bank buy more gold to hold as a reserve if it wants to expand the money supply. This added discipline would be the greatest benefit of a return to the gold standard. China, incidentally, has bigger plans for its currency. It, too, sees partial gold backing as a key element in bringing credibility to its currency, which it desperately wants if it is to challenge the U.S. dollar as a global reserve currency.

THE CHICAGO PLAN

The Chicago Plan[12] targets the creators of money in the financial system. The plan calls for the elimination of fractional reserve lending by requiring banks to put up 100 percent reserves for their deposits, effectively killing their money creation abilities.

The initial plan was drafted in 1926 by a Nobel Prize winner in chemistry, Frederick Soddy, but it didn't get very far except for a little interest from Professor Frank Knight at the University of Chicago. Knight immediately picked up the idea and revised it by 1933 before submitting it in a memorandum to U.S. President Franklin Roosevelt. University of Chicago economist Henry Simons joined Knight's efforts and revised the plan yet again. He also teamed up with Yale economist Irving Fisher, who supported the plan. Roosevelt seriously considered the plan as a way for the United States to get out of the Great Depression.

The plan, which became known as the Chicago Plan, was sidelined during World War II. It has been kept there for much of the past decades except for the occasional discussion and/or revision by other interested economists. It wasn't until the global financial crisis that the plan found new following and support. The plan's champions today are two economists working for the International Monetary Fund (IMF): Jaromir Benes and Michael Kumhof. In August 2012, Benes and Kumhof published an IMF working paper titled "The Chicago Plan Revisited," which has sparked renewed discussion and debate on the plan in light of the financial fiasco the world faced during the most recent crisis.

Supporters see four key advantages in implementing the plan:

1. The elimination of the credit boom-and-bust cycles by preventing banks from creating money and credit.
2. The elimination of bank runs by requiring banks to have 100 percent reserve backing for deposits.
3. Allowing the government to issue money at zero interest and debt-free to reduce the burden on government finances.
4. The dramatic reduction of debt in the economy.

In this scenario, banks would act much like they did in the early days of banking, operating as financial intermediaries. There would be no need for deposit insurance, since deposits would be fully available for anyone to take out at any time. For banks to issue new credit, they would need to go to the Treasury and borrow. The government would have the sole responsibility for issuing money and credit in the economy. This, supporters believe, would ensure better control over the money supply and better discipline. The IMF economists in their study of implementing this plan today highlight the fact that not only would debt be drastically reduced, but also long-term economic growth would increase to 10 percent, with low inflation.

Banks would still play a major role in the economy as financial intermediaries, but their function as issuers of credit and speculators would be gone. Private institutions, such as private equity firms and venture capitalists, on the other hand, would be free to invest and offer credit as their shareholders saw fit. The profits as well as the risk of loss would be on them and not the public or the government.

The government, in this scenario, would play the biggest role—not only as the sole issuer of money but also in the transition phase as the buyer of all outstanding government debt. Since the new money issued by the government would be debt-free, the old money, which was issued on the back of debt, would need to be taken out of the system. This would be done through the Treasury. The Treasury would cancel all debt against Treasury credit in a debt buyback. The banks, in turn, would be able to use this credit to issue loans and offer other forms of credit.

Opponents of the plan say that it would cause a lot of damage to the economy and create a deflationary spiral as debt is canceled out. They also believe that making credit harder to get would stifle economic growth instead of promoting it. In addition, the rise of alternative institutions to offer credit would create another hazard: the reemergence of shadow banks, which could compete with the government in issuing "money."

The main criticism, however, concerns giving governments the authority to issue money, given their track record at debasing the currency over time. Though I like some of the aspects of this plan, I feel that there is one important element that has not been taken into consideration. First of all, I like the fact that this plan calls for limiting the issuance of debt in favor of equity. I also believe that money issued on the back of equity rather than debt is based on sound economic policy. However, I don't see how the supporters of this plan envision handling the trillions of dollars in derivatives. After all, the largest portion of the derivatives market is based on interest rates from debt instruments. For this reason, I have doubts that this plan will work as intended.

SPECIAL DRAWING RIGHT (SDR)

In the world of fiat currencies, countries whose currencies are considered to be global reserve currencies face a particular challenge. These countries must be willing to provide the world with an extra supply of their currencies to meet world demand, as they are held as foreign exchange reserves. This demand often conflicts with a country's national monetary policy, causing trade deficits and current account deficits. The U.S. dollar, which is the leading global reserve currency, is a perfect example of the dilemma. This economic conflict of interest is known as the Triffin dilemma, named for American-Belgian economist Robert Triffin, who first identified it back in 1960.[13]

The realization that the U.S. dollar cannot be the world's reserve currency forever has prompted some of the leading economists and countries to look for solutions. Jared Bernstein, a former economic advisor to President Barack Obama, recently said, "The privilege of having the world's reserve currency is one America can no longer afford."[14] Brazil, Russia, India, China, and South Africa, known as the BRICS nations, are working on one solution. In July 2014, BRICS leaders agreed to set up a transnational bank to rival the IMF and World Bank and enable them to transact with each other without using the euro or U.S. dollar as the base currency.[15]

However, the IMF, with support from other member countries, has another solution: the SDR. The special drawing right (SDR) is an international reserve asset. It's considered to be an asset solely by virtue of the fact that it is based on a basket of fiat currencies. It was created by the IMF in 1969 to supplement the existing official reserves of member countries. The SDR is like a currency but is currently used only at the IMF. Member countries are allocated SDRs based on a proportion to their quota share at the IMF. SDRs can be used as reserves, since they can be exchanged for other currencies at the SDR exchange rate. The value of the SDR is based on the exchange rates of the U.S. dollar, the euro, the yen, and the pound sterling.[16]

When the IMF issues SDRs, it increases the global money supply. There is no limit to the amount of SDRs it can issue so long as member states agree to it. It creates SDRs out of nothing except for the commitment of its members. Some critics say that SDRs are not real money, since they cannot be used or traded by individuals or corporations, and they see the ability to create an unlimited amount of SDRs as inflationary. Supporters say that SDRs could help maintain price stability and would be deflationary.

SDRs were designed to offer liquidity to the global economy in times of crisis. In fact, they were used during the global financial crisis for this purpose. At the time, the Federal Reserve, the ECB, and the Bank of Japan were facing limits to the amount of liquidity they could offer. The IMF stepped in to fill the gap, as its planners envisioned. Some economists and business figures believe that the IMF has more sinister plans for the SDR. The most outspoken figure on this topic is James Rickards, economist, investment banker, and author of *Currency Wars*, a best-selling book on the topic. Rickards discusses the IMF plans to make the SDR the world's currency. The reason for doing this, he says, is to centralize and control the issuance of global money. In doing so, the IMF would remove any transparency or democratic process from money, as it would no longer be in the hands of elected officials but, rather, in the hands of technocrats or "imminent experts."

Since the most recent financial crisis, however, the IMF has made its intentions clear. It does indeed plan on replacing the dollar as a global reserve currency. In a 2011 paper titled "Enhancing International Monetary Stability—a Role for the SDR?," the IMF lays out its plans for creating such a global currency, including the creation of an SDR bond market.[17] Prominent figures, including George Soros and former U.S. Treasury official Ted Truman, have come out in favor of using the SDR to combat financial crises. International organizations such as the United Nations have also come out in favor of the IMF's SDR.[18]

It's impossible to tell which one of these solutions will prevail, if any. None of them are perfect, and further discussion and debate are needed before jumping into a new system. Calls for the return to the gold standard have been the loudest, mainly because gold has the longest history of being used as money. It also has a history of enforcing discipline among governments and central banks. One of the drawbacks of returning to the gold standard is the supply of gold. The global money supply has grown exponentially over the past 43 years, making a return to a 100 percent gold reserve system impossible. What has been suggested, however, is more along the lines of the Swiss Gold Initiative, which calls for the currency to be 20 percent backed by gold. Such a system is possible, but on a global level it would still be seen as challenging, given the limited gold supplies.

The Chicago Plan offers an alternative solution by addressing the source of money creation in the economy. The biggest issue with this plan is swapping the mountains of debt already in the system with credits, allowing the banks to use them to lend again. On top of this, there hasn't been much thought given to the handling of derivatives if such a plan were implemented. I fear that this alone is enough to revisit this plan yet again with derivatives in mind before predicting a positive outcome.

The IMF's SDR is the most interesting of the three because I see this as the most likely solution to be chosen by world leaders and central bankers—the simple reason being that it imposes little change on the current system and allows for the continuation of the fiat system for a while longer. This time, however, instead of relying on the U.S. dollar as the world's reserve currency, the United States' Triffin dilemma would be lifted and the SDR would become the world currency. If the world goes the route of the SDR, rest assured that it will only be a temporary solution, as the main problems will still be out there—namely, too much debt and too many derivatives.

I believe that the solution that stands the best chance of building a new financial system will be based on sound financial principles. It is also my belief that Islamic finance has a lot to offer the global economy and the new financial system. Islamic finance has clear solutions for dealing with the two biggest issues in our system: debt and speculation (derivatives). It offers alternative tools to debt in financial transactions and has an answer to all forms of speculation—avoid them at all costs. Two elements not explicitly mentioned in the solutions we've discussed here are ethics and equality. These two elements need to play a leading role in our financial system for it to benefit everyone and not just a select few. So far, Islamic finance is the only solution offering ethics and equality a central role in its system.

SUMMARY

- Solutions to the problems in our financial system have been known for a long time, yet they have always been tabled for another day.
- The global financial crisis triggered renewed debate and discussion on implementing real solutions, but, thanks to the quick action by central banks, markets were calmed and politicians again saw a chance to hold off on real change.
- Many fail to realize that politicians and central bankers do not understand the problems, nor do they know how to fix them. If they did, the world would not be witnessing yet more money printing and stimulus programs six years after the crisis began.
- There are many solutions being discussed by some of the leading economists and thinkers, but three stand out the most: the gold standard, the Chicago Plan, and the IMF's SDR.
- The gold standard has been garnering a lot of attention because it is understood better than the other solutions being proposed. A 100 percent gold reserve backing, however, would be nearly impossible today. Instead, a 20 percent backing along the lines of the Swiss Gold Initiative is a more likely scenario.
- The Chicago Plan calls for the elimination of fractional reserve lending and replacing all government debt with Treasury credit. The lack of clarity on how derivatives would be handled increases the doubt that this plan would be able to succeed.
- Proponents of the SDR would like to see it become the global reserve currency. Plans are already in the works at the IMF to prepare for such a scenario. Since this is the easiest plan for politicians and central bankers to implement, I believe it will be tried first during the next crisis. The SDR, however, is not a long-lasting solution, as it fails to address the key problems of too much debt and derivatives.

Conclusion

If history has taught us anything about money and financial systems, it is that they never last forever. Every currency in history has died a tragic death either through war or through mismanagement. Every financial system in the world has had a beginning and an ending. Our current financial system will inevitably go the same way as previous financial systems, making way for something new. Since a financial system can last decades or even centuries, we tend to be overconfident about its ability to survive change, and we tend to overlook the mismanagement.

Our current economic model is built on the need for constant growth with unlimited access to resources. We are naïve to believe that this is possible. Our resources have limits, and growth has limits. Every living thing in nature has limits to its growth; otherwise, trees would be reaching the ends of the atmosphere along with humans, animals, and every other living creature. We have become so used to endless growth that we have brushed aside the reality of finance and economics.

We are living in interesting and unusual times—interesting because we are on the verge of entering into a new financial system; unusual because never before in history has the world carried so much debt on its shoulders. I believe we have reached the limits of where our current financial system can take us. Actually, I think we have outlived it by several years. The current financial system, based on debt and fiat money, will surely end—and end tragically, I'm afraid—but the good news is that the problems with the current system will finally be addressed and a new and better system will emerge.

Debt is at the heart of the problem—so much so that the global economy can no longer grow without an increasing amount of new debt. We are at the point where we are seeing diminishing returns from debt; more debt is needed for less and less economic growth. Debt, however, is not the problem itself, but a symptom. Recklessness and lack of discipline are the problem. The unstoppable growth in debt is a clear indication that policymakers and central bankers have lost all hope of containing the real problem. The economic theories that helped shape our current system need to be revisited.

The current debate on money and finance are all attempting to address the ills of the current system, but none of them offer the perfect solution, leaving the door wide open to propose new theories and offer new solutions. One such solution would be to look at the principles of Islamic finance as offering an ethical and equitable alternative to help solve the problems that have plagued modern finance. At the heart of this is the way Islamic finance handles debt—or, more precisely, the way it doesn't handle debt.

It's encouraging to see some of the proposals by leading economists and thinkers already leaning toward this route by replacing debt with equity and looking at bringing back social and ethical values to finance, which have been lost over the years. My hope is that those leading the discussions and debates give Islamic finance a chance to show modern finance what it has to offer.

Notes

Chapter 1: A Brief History of Financial Systems and the Birth of Money

1. Glyn Davies, *A History of Money from Ancient Times to the Present Day*, 3rd ed. (Cardiff: University of Wales Press, 2002).
2. Allan Chester Johnson, Paul Robinson Coleman-Norton, Frank Card Bourne, and Clyde Pharr, *Ancient Roman Statutes: A Translation with Introduction, Commentary, Glossary, and Index*, reprint (Clark, NJ: The Lawbook Exchange Ltd., 2003).
3. David Kinley, *Money: A Study of the Theory of the Medium of Exchange* (Phoenix, AZ: Simon Publications), 2003.
4. David Graeber, *Debt: The First 5,000 Years* (New York: Melville House, 2011).
5. Ibid.
6. J. Dyneley Prince, "Review: The Code of Hammurabi," *The American Journal of Theology*, vol. 8, no. 3 (July 1904), pp. 601–609.
7. http://www.commonlaw.com/Hammurabi.html.
8. http://biblehub.com/genesis/17-13.htm.
9. F. W. Madden and F. W. Fairholt, *History of Jewish Coinage, and of Money in the Old and New Testament* (1864).
10. http://www.jewishvirtuallibrary.org/jsource/History/weightsandmeasures.html.
11. Graeber, *Debt*.
12. J. Williams, J. Cribb, and E. Errington, *Money: A History* (London: British Museum Press, 1997).
13. http://rg.ancients.info/lion/article.html.
14. M. Moïssey Postan and H. J. Habakkuk, *The Cambridge Economic History of Europe: Trade and industry in the Middle Ages* (Cambridge, UK: Cambridge University Press, 1987).
15. http://www.pierre-marteau.com/editions/1701-25-mint-reports/report-1717-09 -25.html.
16. A. M. Andreades, *History of the Bank of England* (Abingdon, UK: Frank Cass & Co., Ltd), 1966.
17. http://pubs.usgs.gov/of/2002/of02-303/OFR_02-303.pdf.
18. Daniel Headrick, *Technology: A World History* (New York: Oxford University Press, 2009).
19. Marco Polo, *The Travels of Marco Polo, a Venetian, in the Thirteenth Century: Being a Description, by that Early Traveller, of Remarkable Places and Things, in the Eastern Parts of the World* (1818).

20. Davies, *A History of Money.*
21. http://www.britannica.com/EBchecked/topic/613719/Umayyad-dynasty.
22. Mohd Nazri Bin Chik, "Sukuk: Shariah Guidelines for Islamic Bonds," http://www.bankislam.com.my/en/Documents/cinfo/Sukuk_ShariahGuidelines.pdf, posted July 2, 2013.
23. Nathif J. Adam and Abdulkader Thomas, *Islamic Bonds: Your Guide to Issuing, Structuring and Investing in Sukuk* (London: Euromoney Books, 2004), p. 42.
24. Davies, *A History of Money.*
25. Ibid.
26. http://encyclopedia-of-money.blogspot.com/2011/10/seizure-of-mint-england.html.
27. http://www.banking-history.co.uk/history.html.
28. http://research.stlouisfed.org/publications/review/81/05/Classical_May1981.pdf.
29. Ibid.
30. Youssef Cassis, *Capitals of Capital: A History of International Financial Centres, 1780–2005* (Cambridge, UK: Cambridge University Press, 2006).
31. http://www.law.cornell.edu/constitution/articlei.
32. http://www.richmondfed.org/banking/federal_reserve_membership/.
33. http://www.federalreserve.gov/aboutthefed/section7.htm.
34. http://www.firstworldwar.com/.
35. Michael Clodfelter, *Warfare and Armed Conflicts: A Statistical Reference to Casualty and Other Figures, 1500–2000,* 2nd ed. (Jefferson, NC: McFarland, 2002).
36. Niall Ferguson, *The Pity of War* (New York: Basic Books, 1998).
37. Sally Marks, "The Myths of Reparations," *Central European History,* vol. 11, no. 3 (September 1978).
38. Ferguson, *The Pity of War.*
39. Craig K. Elwell, *Brief History of the Gold Standard in the United States,* Congressional Research Service Report for Congress, June 23, 2011.
40. Robert M. Dunn, Jr. and John H. Mutti, *International Economics,* 6th ed. (New York: Routledge, 2004).
41. Robert J. Carbaugh, *International Economics,* 10th ed. (Mason, OH: Thomson Southwestern, 2005).
42. Marc Flandreau, Carl-Ludwig Holtfrerich, and Harold James, *International Financial History in the Twentieth Century: System and Anarchy* (Cambridge, UK: Cambridge University Press, 2003).
43. Henry Thompson, *International Economics: Global Markets and Competition,* 2nd ed. (Singapore: World Scientific, 2006).
44. Barry J. Eichengreen, *Golden Fetters: The Gold Standard and the Great Depression, 1919–1939* (New York: Oxford University Press, 1995).
45. https://www.bis.org/.
46. http://secondworldwar.co.uk/index.php/fatalities.
47. Alexander DeConde, Richard Dean Burns, and Louise Bilebof Ketz, *Encyclopedia of American Foreign Policy,* vol. 1 (New York: Scribner, 2002), p. 95.
48. Carbaugh, International Economics, 10th ed.

49. Maurice D. Levi, *International Finance,* 4th ed. (New York: Routledge, 2005).
50. http://www.imf.org/external/about/history.htm.
51. http://www.worldbank.org/en/about/history.
52. Adrian Buckley, *Multinational Finance* (Harlow, UK: Pearson Education Limited, 2004).
53. Peter Rosenstreich, *Forex Revolution: An Insider's Guide to the Real World of Foreign Exchange Trading* (Upper Saddle River, NJ: Financial Times–Prentice Hall, 2005).
54. Ibid.
55. Barry Eichengreen, *Exorbitant Privilege: The Rise and Fall of the Dollar and the Future of the International Monetary System* (Oxford, UK: Oxford University Press, 2011).
56. Fabrizio Saccomanni, *Managing International Financial Instability: National Tamers versus Global Tigers* (Cheltenham, UK: Edward Elgar Publishing, 2010).
57. http://www.imf.org/external/np/exr/facts/sdr.HTM.

Chapter 2: Past Financial Crises and Their Causes

1. C. Kindleberger and R. Aliber, *Manias, Panics and Crashes: A History of Financial Crises,* 6th ed. (London: Palgrave Macmillan, 2011).
2. "The Slump That Shaped Modern Finance," *The Economist,* http://www.economist.com/news/essays/21600451-finance-not-merely-prone-crises-it-shaped-them-five-historical-crises-show-how-aspects-today-s-fina.
3. http://hnn.us/article/61931.
4. http://butnowyouknow.net/those-who-fail-to-learn-from-history/history-of-economic-downturns-in-the-us/.
5. Chrystia Freeland, *Sale of the Century: Russia's Wild Ride from Communism to Capitalism* (New York: Crown, 2000).
6. http://www.ipu.org/wmn-e/suffrage.htm#Note3.
7. http://online.wsj.com/mdc/public/page/2_3047-djia_alltime.html.
8. http://www.livinghistoryfarm.org/farminginthe30s/money_08.html.
9. http://www.livinghistoryfarm.org/farminginthe30s/farminginthe1930s.html.
10. Robert J. Carbaugh, *International Economics,* 10th ed. (Mason, OH: Thomson Southwestern, 2005).
11. J. Blum, R. Cameron, and T. G. Barnes, *The European World: A History,* 2nd ed. (Boston: Little, Brown, 1970), p. 885.
12. http://www.hyperhistory.com/online_n2/connections_n2/great_depression.html.
13. David Hammes and Douglas Wills, "Black Gold: The End of Bretton Woods and the Oil-Price Shocks of the 1970s," *The Independent Review,* vol. IX, no. 4 (Spring 2005).
14. Daniel Yergin, *The Prize: The Epic Quest for Oil, Money, and Power* (New York: Simon & Schuster, 2008).
15. Margret Reid, *The Secondary Banking Crisis, 1973–75: Its Causes and Course,* 2nd ed. (London: Macmillan, 1982).
16. E. Philip Davis, "Comparing Bear Markets—1973 and 2000," *National Institute Economic Review,* January 2003.

17. William L. Silber, *Volcker: The Triumph of Persistence* (London: Bloomsbury Press, 2012).
18. Jocelyn Sims and Jessie Romero, "Latin American Debt Crisis of the 1980s," Federal Reserve Bank of Chicago and Federal Reserve Bank of Richmond, http://www.federalreservehistory.org/Events/DetailView/46.
19. Institute of Latin American Studies, *The Debt Crisis in Latin America*, p. 69.
20. Michael Pento, *The Coming Bond Market Collapse: How to Survive the Demise of the U.S. Debt Market* (Hoboken, NJ: Wiley, 2013).
21. Gregory Ruggiero, "Latin American Debt Crisis: What Where Its Causes, and Is It Over?" Independent Study, Professor Pantos, March 15, 1999, http://www.angelfire.com/nj/GregoryRuggiero/latinamericancrisis.html.
22. Manuel Pastor, Jr., "Latin America, the Debt Crisis, and the International Monetary Fund," JSTOR, http://www.jstor.org/discover/10.2307/2633823?uid=3739256&uid=2&uid=4&sid=21103938613507, retrieved May 22, 2012.
23. Sims and Romero, "Latin American Debt Crisis of the 1980s."
24. Richard Bookstaber, *A Demon of Our Own Design* (Hoboken, NJ: Wiley, 2007), pp. 7–32.
25. G. Bock, R. Byrnes, and F. Ungeheuer, "Wall Street's October Massacre," *Time*, October 26, 1987.
26. http://www.thefinanceguy.co.uk/market-crashes-part-iv-1987-black-monday-global-market-crash/.
27. "Black Monday Ten Years After," Motley Fool, October 17, 1997, http://www.fool.com/Features/1997/sp971017CrashAnniversary1987Timeline.htm.
28. Ibid.
29. Bert Ely, "Savings and Loan Crisis," *The Concise Encyclopedia of Economics*, 2nd ed., http://www.econlib.org/library/Enc/SavingsandLoanCrisis.html.
30. Kenneth J. Robinson, "Savings and Loan Crisis 1980–1989," Federal Reserve Bank of Dallas, http://www.federalreservehistory.org/Events/DetailView/42, November 22, 2013.
31. Brett Messing and Steven Sugarman, *The Forewarned Investor: Don't Get Fooled Again by Corporate Fraud* (Pompton Plains, NJ: Career Press, 2006).
32. Robinson, "Savings and Loan Crisis 1980–1989," http://www.federalreservehistory.org/Events/DetailView/42.
33. Ibid.
34. Japan Real Estate Institute, "Index of Urban Land Price by Use," 2004.
35. Doug French, "Illusion of the Age of Keynes," *Mises Daily Index*, January 25, 2010.
36. Yalman Onaran, "Kill the Zombie Banks!," Salon Media Group, http://www.salon.com/2011/11/25/kill_the_zombie_banks/, November 25, 2011.
37. T. Husain, *Kuwaiti Oil Fires: Regional Environmental Perspectives* (Oxford, UK: BPC Wheatons Ltd., 1995).
38. Joseph A. Whitt, "The Mexican Peso Crisis," *Economic Review*, Federal Reserve Bank of Atlanta, January/February 1996, https://www.frbatlanta.org/filelegacydocs/J_whi811.pdf.
39. Keith Bradsher, "House Votes to Request Clinton Data on Mexico," *New York Times*, March 2, 1994.

40. Alan Greenspan, *The Age of Turbulence: Adventures in a New World* (New York: Penguin, 2007).
41. Janet Yellen, "The Asian Financial Crisis Ten Years Later: Assessing the Past and Looking to the Future," Speech to the Asia Society of Southern California. February 6, 2007.
42. http://www.adb.org/sites/default/files/KI/2003/rt29.pdf.
43. Naris Laplamwanit, "A Good Look at the Thai Financial Crisis in 1997–98," Columbia University, Fall 1999, http://www.columbia.edu/cu/thai/html /financial97_98.html.
44. David Liebhold, "Thailand's Scapegoat? Battling Extradition over Charges of Embezzlement, a Financier Says He's the Fall Guy for the 1997 Financial Crash," Time.com, December 27, 1999.
45. Yellen, "The Asian Financial Crisis Ten Years Later."
46. http://www.henciclopedia.org.uy/autores/Khor/Malaysia.htm.
47. "Malaysia," *World Fact Book*, Central Intelligence Agency (CIA), https://www .cia.gov/library/publications/the-world-factbook/.
48. http://www.adb.org/sites/default/files/KI/2001/rt11_ki2001.xls.
49. Joseph Stiglitz, "The Ruin of Russia," *The Guardian* (London), April 9, 2003.
50. David M. Kotz, "Russia's Financial Crisis: The Failure of Neoliberalism?," University of Massachusetts, 1998.
51. The Bank of Sweden Prize in Economic Sciences 1997, Robert C. Merton and Myron S. Scholes pictures. Myron S. Scholes with location named as "Long Term Capital Management, Greenwich, CT, USA," where the prize was received.
52. Greenspan, *The Age of Turbulence*.
53. K. Burton and S. Kishan, "Meriwether Said to Shut JWM Hedge Fund After Losses," Bloomberg, July 8, 2009, http://www.bloomberg.com/apps/news %3Fpid%3Dnewsarchive%26sid%3DaU2YYpahTt0w.
54. http://www.federalreserve.gov/monetarypolicy/openmarket.htm.
55. http://articles.latimes.com/2006/jul/16/business/fi-overheat16.

Chapter 3: The Global Financial Crisis of 2008

1. Massimo Calabresi, "Congress and the Bailout Plan: Business as Usual," *Time*, September 23, 2008.
2. Andrew Sorkin, Diana Henriques, Edmund Andrews, and Joe Nocera, "As Credit Crisis Spiraled, Alarm Led to Action," *New York Times*, October 1, 2008.
3. http://www.foxnews.com/story/2008/09/23/fbi-investigating-potential-fraud-by -fannie-mae-freddie-mac-lehman-aig/.
4. Ari Levy and Elizabeth Hester, "JPMorgan Buys WaMu Deposits; Regulators Seize Thrift (Update1)," Bloomberg, September 26, 2008.
5. http://quotes.wsj.com/DJIA/index-historical-prices.
6. Jeanne Sahadi, "Bailout Is Law: President Bush Signs Historic $700 Billion Plan Aimed at Stemming Credit Crisis," CNNMoney.com, October 4, 2008.
7. http://www.usatoday.com/story/money/business/2013/09/08/chronology-2008 -financial-crisis-lehman/2779515/.

8. http://www.forbes.com/2010/07/02/return-liar-loans-personal-finance-no-doc .html.

9. Ibid.

10. Frank J. Fabozzi and Franco Modigliani, "Mortgage and Mortgage-Backed Securities Markets" (Cambridge, MA: Harvard Business School Press, 1992).

11. A. J. Levitin, and S. M. Wachter, "Explaining the Housing Bubble," http:// papers.ssrn.com/sol3/papers.cfm?abstract_id=1669401, April 12, 2012.

12. Ibid.

13. Charles Duhigg, "Loan-Agency Woes Swell from a Trickle to a Torrent," *New York Times,* July 11, 2008.

14. http://blogs.marketwatch.com/capitolreport/2013/05/29/fannie-and-freddie-had -a-bad-wednesday-but-not-their-worst/.

15. Vinod Kothari, *Securitization: The Financial Instrument of the Future* (Hoboken, NJ: Wiley, 2006).

16. "The Financial Crisis Enquiry Report," Financial Crisis Enquiry Commission, http://www.gpo.gov/fdsys/pkg/GPO-FCIC/pdf/GPO-FCIC.pdf.

17. Matthew Philips, "How Credit Default Swaps Became a Timebomb," *Newsweek,* September 26, 2008.

18. Michael Simkovic, "Leveraged Buyout Bankruptcies, the Problem of Hindsight Bias, and the Credit Default Swap Solution," *Columbia Business Law Review,* vol. 2011, no. 1 (2011), p. 118.

19. James Rickards, *Currency Wars: The Making of the Next Global Crisis* (New York: Penguin, 2012).

20. Ari Weinberg, "Shaking Steady Freddie," *Forbes,* December 11, 2003.

21. http://www.cbo.gov/publication/10339.

22. http://www.nbcnews.com/id/12373488/.

23. http://legalnewsline.com/issues/class-action/236380-report-both-sides-in-fannie -mae-suit-move-for-summary-judgment.

24. http://www.marketwatch.com/story/sec-charges-6-ex-fannie-freddie-execs-with -fraud-2011-12-16.

25. Glenn Simpson and James Hagerty, "Countrywide Friends Got Good Loans," *Wall Street Journal,* June 7, 2008.

26. http://money.cnn.com/2010/10/15/news/companies/mozilo_SEC/index.htm?hpt =T2.

27. http://www.bloomberg.com/news/2010-04-16/goldman-used-abacus-to-shuffle -debt-risk-like-beads.html.

28. The Financial Crisis Enquiry Report.

29. Tracy Alloway, "Goldman's Uneasy Subprime Short," *FT Alphaville,* December 10, 2010.

30. Leslie Wayne, "Goldman Pays to End State Inquiry into Loans," DealBook, *New York Times,* May 11, 2009.

31. "Goldman Settles with S.E.C. for $550 Million," *New York Times,* July 15, 2010.

32. Ibid.

33. http://money.cnn.com/news/specials/storysupplement/bankbailout/.

34. http://www.fdic.gov/bank/individual/failed/banklist.html.

35. http://money.cnn.com/2008/03/28/magazines/fortune/boyd_bear.fortune/.

36. The Financial Crisis Enquiry Report.
37. Geoff Chaplin, *Credit Derivatives: Trading, Investing, and Risk Management* (Hoboken, NJ: Wiley, 2010).
38. Chad Bray, "HSBC to Appeal $2.46 Billion Judgment," *New York Times,* October 18, 2013.
39. http://www.boston.com/business/articles/2009/03/03/hsbc_ends_us_subprime _lending/.
40. Gavin Finch and Howard Mustoe, "HSBC Sells U.S. Consumer, Homeowner Debt for $3.2 Billion," Bloomberg, March 6, 2013.
41. Hyun Song Shin, "Reflections on Modern Bank Runs: A Case Study of Northern Rock," Princeton University, August 2008.
42. http://news.bbc.co.uk/2/hi/uk_news/politics/7258492.stm.

Chapter 4: Solutions Create More Problems

1. "Troubled Hypo Takes More Help from German Govt," Reuters, February 11, 2009.
2. James Felkerson, "$29,000,000,000,000: A Detailed Look at the Fed's Bailout by Funding Facility and Recipient," Working Paper No. 698, Levy Economics Institute, December 2011.
3. Robin Harding, "Quantitative Easing Explained," *Financial Times,* November 3, 2010.
4. Mayur Sontakke, "Must-Know: How the Fed May Deal with Its Bloated Balance Sheet," Market Realist, May 29, 2014.
5. Annalyn Censky, "QE2: Fed Pulls the Trigger," CNNmoney.com, November 3, 2010.
6. http://www.federalreserve.gov/monetarypolicy/maturityextensionprogram.htm.
7. Sontakke, Mayur. "Must-Know: How the Fed May Deal with Its Bloated Balance Sheet."
8. http://www.federalreserve.gov/newsevents/press/monetary/20121024a.htm.
9. http://www.cnbc.com/id/101279385.
10. Gary Duncan, "European Central Bank Opts for Quantitative Easing to Lift the Eurozone," *The Times,* http://www.thetimes.co.uk/tto/business/economics /article2150407.ece, May 8, 2009.
11. Sarah Arnott, "Downward Revision for Third-Quarter Growth," *The Independent,* December 23, 2010.
12. http://www.bankofengland.co.uk/publications/Pages/news/2012/066.aspx.
13. Glen Allen, "Quantitative Easing—A Lesson Learned from Japan," Oye! Business, November 3, 2010.
14. http://www.bbc.co.uk/news/business-15472839.
15. Heather Stewart, "Japan Aims to Jump-Start Economy with $1.4tn of Quantitative Easing," *The Guardian,* April 4, 2013.
16. Ambrose Evans-Pritchard, "China Explores Bond Buying in First Hint of QE," *The Telegraph,* June 1, 2014.
17. http://www.bis.org/publ/otc_hy0811.pdf.
18. http://www.statista.com/statistics/268750/global-gross-domestic-product-gdp/.
19. http://www.bis.org/publ/otc_hy1405.pdf.

20. David Lieb, "State Governments May Be Expanding Wealth Gap," Huffington Post, June 5, 2014, http://www.huffingtonpost.com/2014/06/05/state-governments-wealth-gap_n_5451155.html.

Chapter 5: The Next Financial Crisis and the New Financial System

1. http://www.reuters.com/article/2013/12/24/emerging-debt-issuance-idUSL6N0K21WW20131224.
2. http://www.usatoday.com/story/money/markets/2014/05/18/junk-bond-investors-warning-signs/9150199/.
3. http://www.reuters.com/article/2013/04/03/us-usa-qe3-subprimeauto-special-report-idUSBRE9320ES20130403.
4. http://fortune.com/2014/08/20/auto-loan-delinquencies-rise-as-subprime-lending-gains-steam/.
5. http://www.ibtimes.com/us-student-debt-reaches-11-trillion-surpasses-credit-card-debt-auto-loans-1583980.
6. http://www.foxbusiness.com/economy-policy/2014/06/03/next-big-bailout-student-loans/.
7. "JPMorgan Doubles CEO Jamie Dimon's Salary Despite Billions in Fines," *The Guardian,* January 24, 2014.
8. Dominic Rushe, "HSBC Money-Laundering Investigation Letters Spark Questions over Rushed Fine," *The Guardian,* May 30, 2013.
9. "Too Big to Jail: Two Big British Banks Reach Controversial Settlements," *The Economist,* December 13, 2012.
10. http://www.economist.com/node/21558281.
11. Liam Vaughan, Gavin Finch, and Bob Ivry, "Secret Currency Traders' Club Devised Biggest Market's Rates," Bloomberg, December 19, 2013.
12. Steve Slater and Huw Jones, "Barclays Slapped with $44 Million Fine over Gold Price Fix," Reuters, May 23, 2014.
13. Bruno Waterfield, "Eurozone Paves Way for Third Greek Bail-out," *The Telegraph,* February 3, 2014.
14. Michael Aniero, "Treasury Yields Rise, Now Yield More Than Spanish Bonds," *Barron's,* June 9, 2014.
15. http://www.bloomberg.com/infographics/2013-12-20/blackstones-big-bet-on-rental-homes.html.

Chapter 6: Overview and History of Islamic Finance

1. John Glover, "Debt Exceeds $100 Trillion as Governments Binge," Bloomberg. March 10, 2014.
2. Alsadek H. Gait and Andrew C. Worthington, "A Primer on Islamic Finance: Definitions, Sources, Principles and Methods," University of Wollongong, School of Accounting and Finance Working Paper Series No. 07/05, 2007.
3. *Merriam-Webster Dictionary,* http://www.merriam-webster.com/dictionary/interest.

4. *Oxford English Dictionary*, http://www.oxforddictionaries.com/definition /english/usury.
5. Interview with Sh. Mohamed Ali Elgari, a prominent Shariah scholar based in Jeddah, Saudi Arabia, April 2010.
6. Abdul Gafoor, A.L.M., "Interest-Free Commercial Banking, Islamic Banking," 1995.
7. Bernardo Vizcaino, "IDB Aims to Triple Size of Infrastructure Fund to $2 bln," Reuters, June 27, 2014.
8. "Bill Gates Partners with Jeddah Bank for $2.5bn Fund," *Arabian Business*, June 30, 2014.
9. www.difc.ae.
10. Liam Hardy, "The Evolution of Participation Banking in Turkey," *Al-Nakhla*, Online Journal of Southwest Asia and Islamic Civilization, Winter 2012, The Fletcher School, Tufts University, http://fletcher.tufts.edu/~/media/Fletcher /Microsites/al%20Nakhlah/archives/Winter2012/Hardy_Final.pdf.
11. http://www.tabunghaji.gov.my/en/web/guest/profil-korporat.
12. www.bnm.com.my.
13. Ibid.
14. Chien Mi Wong, "Hong Kong Debuts Landmark $1b Sukuk," *FinanceAsia*, September 11, 2014.
15. Catherine Moye, "The Muslim Mortgage Trap: Islamic Law Can Add a Fortune to the Cost of Buying a House," *The Telegraph*, November 30, 2002.
16. www.ahliunited.com.
17. Shane Croucher, "Help to Buy: Islamic Mortgages Now Offered Under Scheme," *International Business Times*, February 11, 2014.
18. Elaine Moore and Thomas Hale, "UK Sukuk Bond Sale Attracts £2bn in Orders," *Financial Times*, June 25, 2014.
19. Alexander Stimpfle, "Islamic Finance Made in Germany: The 2004 Sukuk Issue by the State of Saxony-Anhalt," GRIN Verlag, August 3, 2011.
20. Mirna Sleiman and Bernardo Vizcaino, "Gulf Investors Plan First Euro Zone Islamic Bank in Luxembourg," Reuters, November 26, 2013.
21. Tarek Fatah, "Sharia Banking Goes Bankrupt," Huffington Post, October 17, 2011.
22. www.amanafunds.com.
23. www.lariba.com.
24. http://www.libertyaircraft.com/airplane-company/2-history.php.
25. Kuwait Finance House.
26. www.arcapita.com.

Chapter 7: The Key Principles of Islamic Finance

1. "Intrade Shuts amid Investigation," March 11, 2013, BBC News, http://www.bbc .com/news/business-21743455.
2. "Functions of Money—The Economic Lowdown Podcast Series," vol. 1, episode 9, Federal Reserve Bank of St. Louis, http://www.stlouisfed.org/education _resources/economic-lowdown-podcast-series/functions-of-money/.

Chapter 8: Islamic Financial Instruments as Alternatives

1. Bob Howard, "HSBC Imposes Restrictions on Large Cash Withdrawals," BBC News, January 2014.
2. http://www.kuwait.nbk.com/personal/accounts/savings_en_gb.aspx.
3. Kuwait Finance House Annual Report, 2013.
4. Kuwait Finance House Annual Report, 2005 and 2013.
5. National Bank of Kuwait Annual Report and Financial Statements, 2013.
6. Factors Chain International, http://www.fci.nl/news/detail/?id=502.
7. http://www.themalaysianinsider.com/malaysia/article/mas-issues-rm2.5b-perpetual-sukuk-risky-financing-for-working-capital.
8. http://blog.thomsonreuters.com/index.php/will-airline-sukuk-take-flight/.
9. http://www.nasdaqdubai.com/press/ge-capital-lists-recently-completed-500-million-sukuk-on-nasdaq-dubai.
10. http://www.arabianmoney.net/islamic-finance/2009/10/14/1bn-abu-dhabi-islamic-bond-healthy-for-capital-markets/.
11. http://www.bloomberg.com/news/2014-03-09/global-debt-exceeds-100-trillion-as-governments-binge-bis-says.html.
12. Elffie Chew, "Japan Lacking Sukuk Rules Spurs Malaysia Debuts: Islamic Finance," Bloomberg, June 9, 2014.
13. "The New Kings of Capitalism, Survey on the Private Equity Industry," *The Economist*, November 25, 2004.
14. Anise C. Wallace, "Nabisco Refinance Plan Set," *New York Times*, July 16, 1990.
15. Islamic Development Bank Annual Report, 2013.
16. Global Sukuk Report 1H 2014, KFH Research Ltd., July 2014.
17. Ben Edwards, "U.K. Becomes First Western Government to Sell Islamic Bonds," *Wall Street Journal*, June 25, 2014.
18. Global Sukuk Report 1H 2014, KFH Research Ltd., July 2014.
19. Bernardo Vizcaino, "Luxembourg Approves Bill Paving Way for Sukuk This Year," Reuters, July 10, 2014.
20. Bernardo Vizcaino, "Luxembourg's Debut Sukuk Sees Strong Demand from Government Accounts," Reuters, October 1, 2014.
21. Chien Mi Wong, "Hong Kong Debuts Landmark $1b Sukuk," *FinanceAsia*, September 11, 2014.
22. Elaine Moore and Robin Wigglesworth, "South Africa Joins Sukuk Bond Rush," *Financial Times*, September 17, 2014.

Chapter 9: Criticisms, Shortcomings, and Misconceptions of Islamic Finance

1. http://reformdrugpolicy.com/wp-content/uploads/2011/09/AfghanTaliban Opium.pdf.
2. "Taleban in Texas for Talks on Gas Pipeline," BBC News, December 4, 1997, http://news.bbc.co.uk/2/hi/world/west_asia/37021.stm.

3. http://www.washingtoninstitute.org/policy-analysis/view/the-terrorist-funding
   -disconnect-with-qatar-and-kuwait.
4. Richard Lacayo, "Iran-Contra: The Cover-Up Begins to Crack," *Time*, June 24,
   2001.
5. Angelos Kanas, "Pure Contagion Effects in International Banking: The Case of
   BCCI's Failure," *Journal of Applied Economics*, May 1, 2005.
6. Stephanie Clifford, "The Cost for Arab Bank Is a Complex Calculation," *New
   York Times*, September 23, 2014.
7. http://www.iiabank.com.jo/en/OurProfile/Ourhistory.aspx.
8. Hong Leong Islamic Bank.
9. "Non-Muslims Flock to 'Safe Haven' Sharia Bank Protected from the Crunch
   by Non-Gambling Rule," *Daily Mail*, October 6, 2008, http://www.dailymail
   .co.uk/news/article-1070430/Non-Muslims-flock-safe-haven-Sharia-bank
   -protected-crunch-non-gambling-rule.html.
10. http://www.morningstar.com.
11. Nick Goodway, "Struggling Islamic Bank of Britain Is Bailed Out with £20m by
    Qatar," *London Evening Standard*, July 27, 2010.
12. Camilla Hall, "The Investment Dar: Creditors Stand By for 'Problem Child' Pay-
    ment," *Financial Times*, April 24, 2013.
13. Asa Fitch, "Gulf Finance House to Raise $500 Million," *The National*, Novem-
    ber 17, 2010.
14. Paul McNamara, "UM Financial's Omar Kalair Wanted by Police," *The Islamic
    Globe*, February 19, 2014.
15. Alby Gallun, "Condo Developers Charged with Defrauding Muslims, Banks,"
    Crain's Chicago Business, November 17, 2010.
16. Peter Eavis, and Michael Corkey, "Bank of America's $16 Billion Mortgage Set-
    tlement Less Painful Than It Looks," DealBook, *New York Times*, August 21,
    2014.
17. Vasileios Pappasa, Marwan Izzeldina, and Ana-Maria Fuertesb, "Failure Risk
    in Islamic and Conventional Banks," Lancaster University Management School,
    UK and Cass Business School, City University London, UK. June 29, 2012.
18. http://www.bis.org/publ/otc_hy1405.pdf.

Chapter 10: Preventing Future Crises—Real-World Solutions from Islamic Finance

1. Federal Reserve Bank of St. Louis, Economic Research.
2. Jeanne Sahadi, "Where's the Debt Ceiling Now?," CNNMoney, February 12,
   2014.
3. Nassim Nicholas Taleb and Mark Spitznagel, "Time to Tackle the Real Evil: Too
   Much Debt," *Financial Times*, July 13, 2009.
4. Mayra Rodriguez Valladares, "Derivatives Markets Growing Again, with Few
   New Protections," DealBook, *New York Times*, May 13, 2014.
5. Michael J. Moore, "Three Bankers Bolster Blankfein as Goldman Trading Sinks,"
   Bloomberg Business Week, May 5, 2014.

6. Gretchen Morgenson, "JPMorgan's Follies, for All to See," *New York Times,* March 16, 2013.
7. Matt Taibbi, "Gangster Bankers: Too Big to Jail, How HSBC Hooked Up with Drug Traffickers and Terrorists. And Got Away with It," *Rolling Stone,* February 14, 2013.
8. http://www.bis.org/publ/rpfx13fx.pdf.
9. http://www.bis.org/publ/qtrpdf/r_qt0803z.htm.

Chapter 11: Evaluating Alternative Solutions

1. Katy Barnato, and Katrina Bishop, "Draghi: ECB to Purchase Asset-Backed Securities," CNBC, September 4, 2014.
2. "ECB Imposes Negative Interest Rate," *BBC News,* June 5, 2014.
3. Barry Eichengreen, Jaime Reis, and Jorge Braga de Macedo, *Currency Convertibility: The Gold Standard and Beyond,* Taylor & Francis, May 16, 1996.
4. Ben Bernanke, "Remarks by Governor Ben S. Bernanke: Money, Gold and the Great Depression," H. Parker Willis Lecture in Economic Policy, Washington and Lee University, Lexington, Virginia, March 2, 2004.
5. Alan Greenspan, "Gold and Economic Freedom," http://www.constitution.org/mon/greenspan_gold.htm (originally published in the *Objectivist* newsletter, 1966).
6. "Advantages of the Gold Standard," *The Gold Standard: Perspectives in the Austrian School,* The Ludwig von Mises Institute, http://mises.org/books/goldstandard.pdf.
7. Catherine Bosley, "Swiss Parliament Recommends Rejection of Initiative on SNB Gold," Bloomberg News, May 5, 2014.
8. Ibid.
9. Mark O'Byrne, "Germany Still Wants Its Gold Back—Repatriation Campaign Continues," MaxKeiser.com, June 24, 2014, http://www.maxkeiser.com/2014/06/germany-still-wants-gold-back-repatriation-campaign-continues/.
10. Marina Maksimova, "China Reportedly Planning to Back the Yuan with Gold," Russia BTH Asia Pacific, July 17, 2013.
11. Blake Ellis, "States Seek Currencies Made of Silver and Gold," CNN Money, February 3, 2012.
12. Jaromir Benes and Michael Kumhof, "The Chicago Plan Revisited," IMF Working Paper WP/12/202, Research Department, International Monetary Fund, August 2012.
13. "Money Matters: An IMF Exhibit—The Importance of Global Cooperation—System in Crisis (1959–1971)," International Monetary Fund, http://www.imf.org/external/np/exr/center/mm/eng/mm_sc_03.htm.
14. Jared Bernstein, "Dethrone 'King Dollar,'" Op-Ed, *New York Times,* August 27, 2014.

15. Silvio Izquierdo, "BRICS Nations to Form Bank to Rival World Bank, IMF," Associated Press, July 16, 2014, http://www.huffingtonpost.com/2014/07/16 /brics-nations-bank_n_5591436.html.
16. International Monetary Fund, http://www.imf.org/external/about/sdr.htm.
17. James Rickards, *Currency Wars: The Making of the Next Global Crisis* (New York: Penguin Group, 2012).
18. http://www.brettonwoodsproject.org/2009/04/art-564135/.

Index

Page numbers followed by *f* or *t* refer to figures and tables, respectively.